PELICAN BOOKS

Bricks of Shame

Winner of the Oddfellows Social Concern Book Award

Vivien Stern is Director of the National Association for the Care and Resettlement of Offenders (NACRO). Before she went to NACRO in 1977, she worked in education and subsequently race relations. Running NACRO brings her into direct contact with the problems faced by discharged prisoners: the organization aims to relieve these by providing hostels, work and training schemes, and education centres. NACRO is also interested in the wider aspects of crime and over the last few years has developed a major programme of neighbourhood crime-prevention schemes. Through its practical experience, NACRO has been able to present evidence on the penal system and its effects to many official inquiries and Select Committees.

Vivien Stern is a one-time member of a Home Office committee (the Prior Committee) which recommended an entirely new system for hearing disciplinary cases against prisoners in prison. In the course of that inquiry she visited many prisons in England and Wales and some in Canada and West Germany. This is her first book. She is also the author of *Imprisoned By Our Prisons: A Programme of Reform*, published in 1989.

VIVIEN STERN

Bricks of Shame

Britain's Prisons

PENGUIN BOOKS

PENGUIN BOOKS

Published by the Penguin Group
27 Wrights Lane, London w8 5tz, England
Viking Penguin Inc., 40 West 23rd Street, New York, New York 10010, USA
Penguin Books Australia Ltd, Ringwood, Victoria, Australia
Penguin Books Canada Ltd, 2801 John Street, Markham, Ontario, Canada l3r 1b4
Penguin Books (NZ) Ltd, 182–190 Wairau Road, Auckland 10, New Zealand

Penguin Books Ltd, Registered Offices: Harmondsworth, Middlesex, England

First published 1987
Second edition 1989
10 9 8 7 6 5 4 3 2 1

Made and printed in Great Britain by
Richard Clay Ltd, Bungay, Suffolk
Filmset in 10 on 12 pt. Photina

. . . every prison that men build
Is built with bricks of shame,
And bound with bars lest Christ should see
How men their brothers maim.

Oscar Wilde

The Ballad of Reading Gaol

Contents

List of Tables

Acknowledgements

This book could not have been written without the support and cooperation of many people. First of all I must thank the Council of NACRO and in particular the Chairman, Tony Christopher, who has trustingly supported me in this as in every other new venture. I must thank my colleagues at NACRO, who had to take on extra work while the book was being written, as did Tony White of NCVO.

A number of people have given specific and detailed help. From NACRO, in particular I would like to thank Paul Cavadino, on whom I, in common with many others in the penal system, depend for our information; Jill Matthews, who thought up the book's title; and Mervyn Barrett, Carol Gaça, Judy Tavanyar, Elizabeth Barnard, Barbara McCauley, Karen McDonald, Helen Jones and Carol Riddington.

People with wide experience of the penal system have given considerable help. Thanks are due to Andrew Ashworth, Penelope Brook, Silvia Casale, Professor Stephen Cretney, Ian Dunbar, Arthur de Frisching, Navnit Dholakia, David Evans, David Faulkner and John Staples. I am very grateful to Rod Morgan for all his advice and encouragement. Professor Sean McConville of the University of Illinois at Chicago and Norman Bishop, recently retired from the Swedish prison administration, supplied useful information. Particular thanks must go to Dr Hans Tulkens, former head of the Dutch prison administration.

There would have been no book without Dilys Thompson, who worked the word processor night and day. Above all I must thank Clare Gregory who showed outstanding dedication, patience, stamina, ingenuity and loyalty.

For the second edition I must also thank Stella Fry for her support and hard work, and express my appreciation of the efforts made by many prison service officials to give help and advice.

Finally I am grateful to Frederick Stern, Renate Mills and Ian Martin.

I   An Affront to a Civilized Society

The prison problem

> If any reader unfamiliar with the prison system finds it diffi-
> cult to picture the squalor in which many inmates of local
> prisons are expected to spend their sentence, let him imagine
> finding himself obliged to stay in a hotel so overbooked that
> he has to share his room with two complete strangers. The
> room itself is so cramped that . . . if he wants to walk up and
> down, the other occupants must first lie on their beds . . .
> the hotel management insists that guests remain in their
> rooms for all but an hour or so a day and must take their
> meals there . . . the atmosphere rapidly becomes fetid, especi-
> ally since neither the reader nor his room-mates have been
> able to take a bath for some days . . . there is no lavatory
> either, and the reader and his companions are faced with
> the prospect of relying . . . upon chamber-pots . . . if the
> reader does not conclude that such an experience lasting
> several days would be degrading and brutalizing he is being
> less than honest with himself.[1]

The year 1986 marked the beginning of a new phase in the
history of Britain's prison service. In the spring prisons
suddenly burst into the headlines. For two weeks the public
was reminded of the long-running crisis in the prisons, a crisis
that had been going on for at least twenty years. In an un-
usually public act, the prison governors, through their trade
union, wrote to the Prime Minister expressing their worries
about the state of the prisons. She replied, reminding them
that her government had been pouring money into the prison

service with a rise of nearly 400 per cent in capital spending on prisons since the Conservatives came to power in 1979.[2] The cliffhanging negotiations between the Home Office and the Prison Officers Association culminated in the eventful night of 30 April when prison officers imposed an overtime ban and prisoners in eighteen prisons caused damage costing £4.5 million and rendered one prison, Northeye in Bexhill, completely uninhabitable. Thus were brought to a head in one night two long-running and unresolved symptoms of the prison problem, the deep-seated dissatisfaction of prison officers and the permanently simmering resentment of prisoners about the way they are treated. The trauma was so great that in the same week even the hawkish *Daily Mail* published an article calling for fewer people to be sent to prison and for better prison conditions.[3]

Since 1986 the drama has repeated itself many times on a smaller scale, not replicating the mass flare-up of April 1986 but causing cumulatively as much damage. Reporting trouble at prisons in Scotland, England and Wales has become part of the broadcaster's routine: October 1986, Edinburgh and Risley Remand Centre; January 1987, Barlinnie, Glasgow; September 1987, Peterhead; March 1988, Bedford; May 1988, Perth and Rollestone army camp; June 1988, Haverigg in Cumbria and Hindley Youth Custody Centre; July 1988, Lindholme in South Yorkshire and Longriggend Remand Centre in Scotland; August 1988, Haverigg and Lindholme again.

This is how prisons impinge on public consciousness, in bursts of mayhem, scandal or outrage. The day-to-day deadening routines, the slowly worsening conditions, the assaults on human dignity and the erosion of prison staffs' wish to do a better, more humane job do not make headlines.

Prison must be one of the least known aspects of British life. The number of people who have ever been in a prison or visited one is small. Apart from the prisoners themselves and their families, probation officers, members of official prison committees, some clergy and a few welfare workers, the general public has no personal experience of prisons. Very few of the thousands of people who drive every day down Parkhurst Road in North London past Holloway prison have the remotest idea what is going on behind the high red-brick wall only a few yards from the main road, or spare a thought for the 470 or so women locked up there. Scarcely any among the crowds hurrying towards the shopping centre in the middle of Oxford are aware as they pass the old castle, first built in 1071, that it is a prison, still in use, and housing about twice as many prisoners as it has room for.

Perhaps only those who visit prisons, as relatives, lawyers or probation officers, are aware from necessity of the complexity of the system, of the vast administrative machine that is needed to allocate, classify, feed and clothe 50,000 prisoners: allocate places so that at the end of each day every prisoner has a bed to lie on, even if it is only a camp bed put up in a disused prison workshop; classify prisoners so that they all get a number and are put in the level of security they are deemed to need; feed, clothe, bathe and search an ever-changing population, unpredictable in numbers and location; and get to court on time the more than one in five who are there pre-trial and may have to be escorted to any court in the country.

The mystery that shrouds even the most mundane parts of the operation of the prison system is not easy to explain. It is probably a product of two factors. One is the public's wish not to know, not to have even to think about people who it is felt have, by their own actions, put themselves beyond the reach of legitimate concern. There is an urge to be able to forget them, and reassurance comes from knowing they have been 'put away' for a long time. In the words of HRH The Princess Anne, Patron of the Prison Service Annual Award Scheme: 'I fear that when offenders are put in prison, then most people forget about them – or perhaps more accurately would like to forget about them.'[4] The other factor is the obsession with secrecy that is deeply embedded in the culture of the prison administration, an obsession that has in recent years been tempered by attempts to lift the veil, but which still represents the prevailing instinct. In 1983 a prison doctor got into trouble with his employers, the Home Office, for writing to *The Times*, in his capacity as chairman of his professional association, about the low hygiene standards in prisons and the health hazards these caused.[5] He commented, 'I had to accept the rebuke that I should watch what I did in future.'[6]

Those who have only the newspapers and television to inform them about life in prison could be forgiven for carrying away a confused picture. On the one hand are depicted Porridge-type characters, living in a holiday camp atmosphere and exchanging jokes with prison officers. On the other hand are the television pictures (often the same one) of young men locked up for twenty-three hours a day with two others in cells built in Victorian times for one, sharing a plastic bucket for a lavatory. Famous people going to prison always make the newspapers. The months spent by champion jockey Lester Piggott in Highpoint prison for tax evasion were squeezed for anything of the remotest interest. Sex, drugs, Lester Piggott's state of mind, whether smoked salmon was being smuggled in, have all featured. Questions about the regime of the prison, the rationale of putting people there at all, did not. So it is hard for the casual observer of our prisons to know from the selected segments of information which are available what the prison problem really is. Is it simply poor conditions – practices such as slopping out, which is required whenever there are no lavatories in cells and prisoners are locked up for hours on end? It was a discussion of slopping out which provoked the Conservative MP Michael Shersby to tell the head of the Home Office during a meeting of the Public Accounts Committee:

> I put it to you that people in this country do not regard it as part of the penalty of being confined to prison that men and women have to occupy cells where they are obliged to perform their bodily functions in this way ... I find it very difficult to criticize conditions in other countries, where admittedly all kinds of inhuman practices take place, when this sort of thing still goes on in British prisons. I am ashamed of it ...[7]

If poor conditions are the problem, will the massive new investment in prison buildings cure the problem?

It is reasonably well known that we lock up more people, relatively, than many similar countries. In England and Wales, in 1986 we had 93 prisoners for every 100,000 people in the population. This is much less than the United States, which at more than 300 prisoners for every 100,000 inhabitants has one of the highest prison populations in the world, and less than Turkey, which had 102. But it is much more than Japan, which had half the England and Wales figure (46) and, nearer home, much more than the Netherlands (34) or Belgium (62). Why is this? Is it related to a high crime rate or does our use of imprisonment have an impetus of its own? Does it protect people from crime or is the Archbishop of Canterbury right to say: 'In many cases it can be argued that prison is a short-term economy, which brings with it no longer-term solutions. Instead it leads to the perpetuation of a criminal "class"...'[8]

Numbers are certainly the starting-point of any debate on prisons. Put simply, demand for places continually outstrips the supply of them. The facts about numbers are clear. There is officially room in the prisons for around 44,000. There are more than 50,000 prisoners to cram in. Prison over-crowding has a prominent place in the analysis of the prison problem. It sometimes has such a prominent place that it obscures other deep-seated questions. In 1985 the Prison Officers Association published a document which said:

... the Prison Service is in a parlous state ... *Prison industries* are at a minimum. *Bathing* for inmates cannot be guaranteed on a weekly basis. *Clothing change* for inmates cannot be guaranteed weekly. *Exercise* has become an *ad hoc* provision. Sleeping *arrangements* in cellular accommodation cannot be guaranteed in some institutions.[9]

What can a prison officer's job be like in such circumstances? How, over the years, have prison officers reached a point of such discontent that they were able to secure overwhelming support for industrial action in April 1986 and impose an overtime ban?

The lot of prison administrators in 1989 is not a happy one. Difficulties crowd in from all directions. On one side are the courts sending more and more people to prison and creating the volatile and upwardly surging prison population which races far ahead of any building programme designed to contain it. Then there is the Treasury, concerned at evidence about waste of resources in the prison system, enforcing cash limits and urging budgetary controls. On the other side are the prison officers, deeply disillusioned by years of poor industrial relations and working with no clear indication as to what society expects of them. The prison administrators can never forget the small number of long-term prisoners – some highly dangerous, some seriously mentally disturbed – a minefield with serious political consequences if anything goes wrong. Then from outside come the MPs and penal reform groups, constantly reminding them that our prison system is unnecessarily restrictive and lags far behind that of some other countries in simple humanity.

As the civil servants of the Prison Department grapple with their task they cannot be encouraged by the thought that so many before them have tried and failed. The prison system is outstanding in the persistence of its problems and their iron-clad resistance to solution. In 1966 Lord Mountbatten said: 'It should be more widely known than it is that there are still thousands of prisoners sleeping three in a cell designed in the nineteenth century for one man.'[10] More than twenty years later things are no better. In these very same cells, built over a hundred years ago for one person 5,000 prisoners are living three to a cell and nearly 14,000 are living two to a cell. In 1952, when a parliamentary committee looked at prisons, they were concerned about the lack of suitable work for prisoners to do all day and the short working hours.[11] Prisoners were spending up to $13\frac{1}{2}$ hours a day in their cells, they said.[12] They would not be impressed with the position today where many prisoners in local prisons spend more than twenty hours a day in their cells, nearly one in three of all prisoners has no work at all, and the number of hours worked has fallen, as the population has risen, from 17.6 million in 1976 to 8.5 million in 1986.

Prison officers' dissatisfaction with their jobs and wish to do more worthwhile work goes back to 1963 when a resolution went through their annual union conference calling for involvement in rehabilitation and aftercare. A Working Party to discuss these possibilities was set up and discussed them until 1981 with no noticeable result. The problems of running the prison system on a high use of overtime were raised in 1952 when the Estimates Committee said high overtime was no way to run a system.[13] Overtime for prison officers was officially abolished in 1987, 35 years later.

The difficulties arising from the need for prison staff to escort prisoners to and from court were first identified by a committee that sat in 1895, the Gladstone Committee.[14] In 1983 the Chief Inspector of Prisons identified the long-standing nature of the problem and the many times it had been addressed. Yet, he said, 'so far nothing has resulted',[15] a phrase which could stand as a fitting epitaph to all-too-many reports on prisons and their recommendations. In 1986 escorting prisoners to court was 'scrutinized' by an efficiency team from the Home Office and the Lord Chancellor's Department. In 1988 a government Green Paper came out setting out the options for privatizing all or part of the system for remand prisoners, including escorts. Perhaps by 1995, a century after the Gladstone Report, the problem will have been solved.

The problems have been a long time in the making. The high use of prison by the courts, over which the prison service has no control, keeps those who run the service in a perpetual state of crisis. They have always managed – so far – to cope with crisis – either, since the early eighties, by filling up the police cells at such places as Lambeth police garage in London, in 1985 by the hurried purchase of an old RAF station in South Yorkshire, now Lindholme prison, in 1987 by an increase in remission for short-term prisoners so that 3,000 people were released earlier than they would otherwise have been, and in 1988 by opening two army camps staffed by military personnel. But they pay a high price for coping. All their resources and all their energy go into day-to-day survival. The deep-seated and long-standing problems continue rumbling beneath the surface like a volcano. Occasionally they erupt.

It remains to be seen whether the events of 1986 constituted such a shock to the prison service psyche that the formidable array of interlocking problems will at last be grasped. The alternative is to face the twenty-first century with too many prisoners, often locked in overcrowded cells with no sanitation, and disgruntled and aggrieved staff who do not know what society expects of them.

The problems have taken a long time to grow. They will not be solved easily. But an attempt must be made. This book tries to show the way. It will not please everybody. Many prisoners will say it fails completely to convey the sheer degradation of prison and the harm it does to people. Some who have devoted all their working lives to trying to make the system better will feel that their efforts are not properly appreciated. Those who believe it is in society's interests to treat prisoners with cruelty because of the harm they have inflicted on others will not be at all satisfied. For those though who feel that for too long we have condemned 29,000 staff and 50,000 prisoners to disgusting conditions of work and life, giving them no clear idea what prison is for and no support from society to carry out a proper task, it is to be hoped that this book will provide a brief history of how we got to where we are today, what the obstacles are to reform, and how they can and must be overcome.

2   People in Prison

Whom do we lock up?

> Anyway, when they gave us our bedding and took us
> through to the wing, the first thing I associated it with was
> that 'Porridge', that TV series. I didn't know what to expect.
> It was antiquated, as if it was out of the Victorian times or
> out of the movies. The movies was the only thing I had to go
> by. I expected homosexuality, junkies, god knows what . . . I
> was put in a cell with another guy . . . he was a good chap.
> He'd done two or three prison sentences before, he was
> about four or five years older than me, but he had travelled
> a lot as well so we had a little bit in common. And he was
> quite a clean person, had some self-respect. It's important, I
> believe, to keep some sort of self-respect; like when I saw
> that you had to piss in a bucket I was digusted.
>
> A prisoner, in prison for the first time, talking to James
> Campbell, author of *Gate Fever*.[1]

Few people who go to prison* for the first time will know
what to expect. Many will be surprised at the complexity of the
great prison machine, and confused by the prison language
and culture that old hands know so well. Prisons house many
different types of people and fill a range of different functions.
The starting-point for looking at the prison system is the people
in it, who they are and what they are there for.

Locking up people in prisons has a long history. Since 1361

---

* 'Prison' and 'prisoner' will be used throughout to refer to all prison service
establishments including young offender institutions and remand centres
and all those sent to them, including young offenders.

magistrates have been able to send all sorts of people to prison: drunkards, beggars, vagrants, poachers. The prisons were the responsibility of local magistrates and were called bridewells, or Houses of Correction. They were mainly for minor offenders. Until the last century the serious offenders, who were tried by judges in the courts, were either hanged or transported. In the eighteenth century hanging was available for a range of offences, for example, murder, maliciously cutting any hop-binds growing on poles in any plantation of hops, rape, riotous assembly, pick-pocketing to an amount of twelve pence and over, destroying the heads of fish-ponds and being in the company of gypsies, destroying turnpikes, desertion from the army or trying to remove parts of Westminster Bridge. As time went by however, hanging began to seem somewhat disproportionate for many of these offences. Transportation also became more problematic as fewer places were prepared to receive transported felons. America refused to take any more after the 1776 War of Independence. In 1787 transportation to Australia and Van Diemen's Land – now Tasmania – started but came under more and more criticism. Transportation formally ended in 1867. The main criticisms of it that were made at the time have a familiar ring. It was argued that it did not really work. It was not unpleasant enough; in fact some people actually welcomed it. It did not therefore deter crime. Also it was expensive. Prison would be much better. As was said in 1779:

... if many Offenders, convicted of Crimes for which Transportation hath been usually inflicted, were ordered to solitary Imprisonment, accompanied by well-regulated Labour, and Religious Instruction, it might be the means, under Providence, not only of deterring others from the Commission of the like Crimes, but also of reforming the Individuals, and inuring them to Habits of Industry.[2]

Transportation was gradually replaced by imprisonment, first on the hulks. Those brought up on Charles Dickens's *Great Expectations* will have a picture of the hulks and their occupants. The child, Pip, the hero of *Great Expectations*, out on the Essex marshes, bumps into 'A fearful man, all in coarse grey, with a great iron on his leg.'[3] Back home, he discovers that out on the river there are prison-ships, called hulks, for those who murder, and rob and forge and 'do all sorts of bad'.[4] Eventually Pip sees one of the prison-ships.

By light of the torches, we saw the black Hulk lying a little way from the mud of the shore, like a wicked Noah's ark. Cribbed and barred and moored by massive rusty chains, the prison-ship seemed in my young eyes to be ironed like the prisoners.[5]

The hulks were not really very satisfactory. They were too small and the discipline and management were very lax. In the nineteenth century big convict prisons began to be built, some of which (such as Pentonville, opened in 1842) are still in use today. In 1877 direct central control of prisons was established and the various prisons, that is the 113 local prisons run by local authorities as well as the big convict penitentiaries that had recently been built, all came under the control of a prison commission responsible to the Home Secretary. The Prison Commission laid the foundations of the prison system we have today.

The modern prison system serves many functions, and contains all sorts and conditions of men – and a few women. Prison is predominantly a male matter and of the population in England and Wales under 4 per cent is female.[6] In Scotland the percentage of women is also around 4 per cent but in Northern Ireland it is much lower at 1.7 per cent.[7] These low percentages are general throughout Europe. No Council of Europe country has more than 6 per cent of its prison population composed of women.[8]

There is a sizeable proportion of black people in prison. In 1981 the Home Office said that.

the proportion of the prison population from the ethnic minorities has been growing especially among the young. For example, in Ashford Remand Centre the black population is now about 50 per cent and in young offender establishments like Rochester, Blantyre House and Dover, it is about 30 per cent.[9]

Figures available for the first time in 1986 showed that the proportion of black people in prison generally was about twice their proportion in the comparable age groups in the popula-

tion at large.[10] In 1985 about 8 per cent of male prisoners and
12 per cent of female prisoners were of 'West Indian or African
origin' and about 2.5 per cent were of 'Indian sub-continent
origin'.[11] Since then the proportions have risen. In 1987, for
men of 'West Indian or African origin' they reached 9 per cent
and for women 17 per cent. The prison population contains
people from many countries and a variety of religions, including Moslems, Jews, Sikhs, Christians, Hindus, Buddhists, Mor-
mons, Greek Orthodox, Pentecostalists, Spiritualists, Christian
Scientists, Jehovah's Witnesses and Ethiopian Orthodox.

The age range is fourteen–seventy, but not only is prison
predominantly a man's place – it is also a young man's place.
Over a quarter of those serving sentences are aged under
twenty-one, and the prison population has been getting
younger. In 1955 19 per cent were aged under twenty-
one.[12]

What else do we know about the prison population? The
answer is, not a great deal. Even basic information like how
many prisoners are married, how many were unemployed on
coming to prison, and what medical or psychiatric problems
they have is recorded for each individual prisoner but is not
collated and made available. Research by Roger Shaw into the
personal circumstances of adult prisoners in Leicester prison
led him to the conclusion that 100,000 children in any one
year may have a father who goes to prison.[13]

The scanty information we do have gives a picture of a
population suffering from many disadvantages. A study carried
out in 1972 of sentenced men in prisons in the South-East
found that about a third were homeless, and these were the
men most likely to be minor offenders, to have been convicted
before, to have no family and friends and to be rated as mentally
disordered. The last jobs of three quarters of the prisoners had
been manual work (compared with 62 per cent of men in the
country as a whole). Those described as having stable work
histories numbered 35 per cent. The rest were described as
unstable. Other studies have found that men serving sentences
of up to eighteen months were isolated, lonely, homeless, had
poor work records outside, had a drink problem and were often
mentally disordered.[14] The Home Office told the Education

Select Committee that around 15 per cent of prisoners were illiterate.[15]

Perhaps the most striking feature of the prison population to an outsider is the high level of mental disorder. Any visitor to the average large city prison must be shaken to see the number of prisoners clearly mentally disturbed. Few subjects have been debated more earnestly than the plight of mentally disordered people in prison. On few subjects can there be so much agreement – they should not be there. Yet the situation continues, barely improving from one year's end to the next. The facts are clear. On any one day there are in prison between two and three hundred prisoners who suffer from mental illness to the point where they could be detained in hospital for treatment under the Mental Health Act. Many hundreds more are clearly disturbed and need psychiatric help. Giving evidence to a House of Commons committee at the end of 1985, the British Medical Association estimated that borderline mentally abnormal prisoners 'may constitute between 20 per cent and 30 per cent of the sentenced population and they are people who are rejected wherever they present'.[16] The Home Office, giving evidence to the same committee, said of mentally abnormal prisoners who are not detainable under the Mental Health Act: 'These are characteristically trivial offenders, disturbed rather than mad . . . it may be that prison is not the most desirable environment for such individuals, but in fact, it is frequently the only asylum available . . .'[17]

Dr Richard Smith, in his book *Prison Health Care*, reviewed all the studies of prisoners' health and concluded: 'many prisoners are anxious and depressed, many of them have abnormal personalities, and more of them are mentally subnormal than in an equivalent group in the community.'[18]

Every now and then, often enough for it to be described as a regular occurrence, a judge comments on the lack of facilities. For example, on 19 March 1988, the *Guardian* told us:

An Old Bailey judge criticized a health authority yesterday for leaving a mentally handicapped man in prison for eight months after failing to find him a place in a psychiatric hospital . . . Judge Thomas Pigot said he could not accept such a disgraceful state of affairs could exist in a civilized society . . . The judge spoke out during the case of Gary

Tuer, aged 25, who was convicted of sex offences last July. He has a mental age of seven . . .

When in prison such a prisoner will go to the prison hospital. Conditions in prison hospitals are not all they might be. A prison doctor said of his own prison hospital:

The writer's prison hospital operates on a ratio of one hospital officer to approximately eight patients. The usually accepted ratio in regional secure units for nursing the mentally disturbed is more than two nurses per patient. Clearly, the prison ratio permits little more than custodial duties and does not even constitute 'humane containment' for the mentally ill in prison. Many prison hospitals have no occupational therapy for their patients and no programme of rehabilitation.[19]

The conditions in which mentally ill women, mostly untried and on remand, have been held at Holloway prison have been a cause of particular concern. The psychiatric unit at Holloway, called C1 wing, which houses around forty prisoners, has been widely condemned. Nick Davies, Home Affairs correspondent of the *Observer*, who did so much to publicize the conditions in C1 wing, was invited into the wing by Holloway's governor. He wrote:

The noise is the first clue to what is happening inside: from the first moans of the morning it can sometimes go on all day in a miserable cacophony of foul abuse and pitiful wails and screams, occasionally broken by the crashing of someone destroying all the cardboard furniture in her cell.[20]

Many incidents of self-mutilation were reported, including one of a woman who gouged out her eye. The Howard League for Penal Reform, in the course of preparing a report on women in the penal system, visited Holloway's C1 unit. They say:

we were shown a cell still in a state of total chaos created the day before by a woman who had barricaded the cell, wrenched the basin from the wall, smashed it with her hands and feet and slashed herself with the jagged edges of the broken basin. The blood was still on the floor.[21]

In December 1984 the Government set up a committee to

look into a number of matters relating to Holloway prison. The Committee, in its report, quoted a former visiting psychiatrist as saying of C1 wing: 'C1 is generally badly designed and badly situated. It is overcrowded, architecturally claustrophobic and is situated on the lower ground floor thus giving it the "feel" of a dungeon.'[22]

The Committee agreed that the building was impossible and recommended a new purpose-built unit. It agreed that many of the criticisms of the unit were justified and deplored 'the fact that inmates spend so much time locked up and inactive, without means of diversion or occupation'.[23] It also highlighted the major problem of the incompatibility of combining a hospital which cares for people and tries to treat them, and a prison which disciplines them and punishes them when they break the rules. Promises were made to improve the existing conditions and eventually to build a better place than C1 wing for such women, but still within the prison setting. Despite the promises however, the pace of improvements to C1 was so slow that it gave rise to criticism in Parliament. At the end of 1985, Lady Ewart Biggs raised the question in the House of Lords, drawing attention to six cases of self-mutilation, two major fires and many floodings in November alone.[24] The suicide by hanging of a 44 year old prisoner in December 1985 prompted further criticism, especially when the responsible Minister at the time, Lord Glenarthur, revealed that so far changes had actually amounted to an assessment of 'the condition of the fabric in some detail before planning the changes that can be made'.[25]

Work actually began in February 1986. A senior medical officer was appointed with management responsibility. Staff went on a special training course. In August 1986 a new day room next to the wing was provided, and prisoners were allowed out of their cells for much of the time. Nevertheless the big question is unanswered. Is prison the right place for such severely disturbed women, whose need is for treatment?

Not only women suffer in this way. On 1 August 1980 a man from Dudley in the West Midlands, Barry Prosser, was sent on remand to Winson Green prison in Birmingham, charged with damaging a lock valued at £1.62. On 12 August he was moved to the hospital wing and put in a special cell, called a strip cell. On 15 August he went back to court. The magistrates convicted him of damaging the lock but sent him back to Winson Green for medical reports to see if he should go to a secure mental hospital. On 19 August he was dead. That afternoon a post-mortem was held which, according to the Home Office Minister at the time, Patrick Mayhew, 'revealed the full and horrifying extent of Mr Prosser's injuries. The pathologist's report was that Mr Prosser had extensive bruising all over his body. His stomach, his oesophagus and one of his lungs had been ruptured, and the pathologist thought that the cause of death was a blow, probably by a heavy weight.'[26]

The police investigated and in December 1980, a senior hospital officer at Winson Green prison, Melvyn Jackson, was charged with Barry Prosser's murder. A stipendiary magistrate decided there was not enough evidence to proceed. In April 1981 an inquest was held. The inquest jury returned a verdict that Barry Prosser had been unlawfully killed. Following the inquest the Director of Public Prosecutions decided to charge Melvyn Jackson and two others with Barry Prosser's murder. In September the case came up and a different magistrate decided the evidence was insufficient to go ahead. The Director of Public Prosecutions then took the unusual step of seeking and being granted a voluntary bill of indictment against the three officers so the case could bypass the magistrates and go direct to the Crown Court for trial. A three-week trial took place in March 1982. The jury found all three officers not guilty. A petition containing 4,624 signatures calling for a public inquiry into the death was presented to the House of Commons by Mrs Prosser's MP. Mrs Prosser and her family kept up a vigil outside the prison every Saturday for a considerable time.

There was no public inquiry. The Chief Inspector of Prisons inspected Birmingham prison from 16 to 20 November 1981. On publication of the Report the Home Secretary made a statement. The Chief Inspector had identified some shortcomings in the hospital and medical services at Winson Green, but 'the Inspectorate has concluded that the hospital at Birmingham provides a high standard of care for its patients. I welcome this conclusion and hope that it will not be overshadowed by the

Table 1 Average number and percentage of untried and convicted unsentenced prisoners

Year	Average number of untried and convicted unsentenced prisoners	Percentage of average prison population
1977	5,281	13
1978	5,631	13
1979	6,132	15
1980*	6,438	15
1981	7,030	16
1982	7,432	17
1983	7,960	18
1984	8,741	20
1985	9,742	21
1986	10,082	21
1987	11,162	23

* from 1980 includes prisoners in police cells, all of whom are assumed to be on remand
Source: Prison Statistics, England and Wales 1987 and The Prison Population in 1987, *Home Office Statistical Bulletin*

concern about Mr Prosser's death.'[27] Mrs Prosser eventually received compensation from the Home Office. Melvyn Jackson left the prison service.

Barry Prosser was in prison so that medical reports could be written about him. What are the other reasons for people to get sent to prison in the first place? Every year, on 30 June, a snapshot is taken of the prison population, showing how it is made up, the length of sentences being served and what offences have brought people into prison. It also shows the numbers of people not there to serve a sentence, that is, the remand prisoners. The pre-trial function, holding people until their case comes up, and holding those who have been tried but not yet sentenced, continues to provide much work and many problems for the prison service. There are more and more of these prisoners as shown in Table 1 above.

The number of people kept in custody before their trial went down in the mid-seventies following action by the Home Office, first through a circular on Bail Procedures and then the 1976 Bail Act, which reduced the numbers held in prison before trial. Since 1980 however, the numbers of untried and unsentenced prisoners on any one day have been going steadily upwards. The length of time people wait before their trial is the key factor, and this has steadily increased. In 1977 men spent twenty-nine days and women twenty-two days in custody, before their trial. In 1987 the figures had nearly doubled to fifty-six days for men and forty-five for women. In Northern Ireland the position is very different. In 1986/7 the number of prisoners waiting for their trial fell by 11 per cent. Untried prisoners make up only 13 per cent of the Northern Ireland prison population.[28]

On 30 June 1987 there were 10,669 men and women in prison untried or unsentenced. There were nearly 300 civil prisoners, that is, people who have not made their maintenance payments, are in contempt of court, or are held under the Immigration Act. The other four fifths of the prison population there on that date were serving a sentence imposed by a court.

A substantial minority of young and older alike was serving what are considered in England and Wales to be short sentences. 40 per cent had been sentenced to eighteen months or less. A range of activities – burglary, theft, criminal damage, arson, driving under the influence of drink – accounted for over 20,000. Just over 12,000 were there for offences involving violence, 2,300 for sexual offences and 3,500 for drug-related offences.

The 30 June 1987 snapshot gives one picture of the prison population. A look at the flows in and out in the course of a year – receptions and discharges in prison language – gives quite another. Just over 86,000 people actually came into custody under sentence during 1987. Over 52,000 of these were serving sentences of eighteen months or less and about 16,000 three months or less. Nearly 19,000 people went to prison in 1987 for not paying a fine for periods that can range from two to 345 days.[29]

At the other end of the scale there are the long-sentence prisoners. On 30 June 1988 about 4,100 people were serving more than ten years. Some of these are life-sentence prisoners – a steadily growing proportion of the population. Over 2,300 on any one day are serving life sentences, that is about 5 per cent of the prison population in England and Wales. In Northern *does this make a dif. in priz. disc*

Ireland the picture is very different – there over a quarter of the sentenced prison population is serving a life sentence.[30]

So the prison system does much more than carry out the sentence of a court to deprive someone of liberty. It holds the untried, the unsentenced, the civil prisoners. It acts as a social service, a hospital, a place where reports are written, an educational establishment for people under school-leaving age, a nursery for mothers and their young babies, and a drug-re-habilitation facility (in 1987–8 2,600 prisoners were dependent on drugs when they were received into custody).[31] It contains prisoners whom many other prisoners would like to injure because of the nature of their offences, and prisoners who want to injure or kill themselves. Between April 1987 and March 1988 a thousand prisoners injured themselves intentionally and 310 attempted suicide. Another thirty-seven succeeded.[32]

The way the prison service organizes itself reflects to some extent the many different jobs it has to do. It has to cope with sentenced prisoners, convicted of a range of crimes from the most trivial to the unspeakably heinous. It holds unsentenced prisoners, who have to be brought to court, and ideally be kept separate from sentenced prisoners. It has men and women who have to be held separately. It has young offenders, who should not be housed with adult offenders.

In dealing with sentenced prisoners the main sifting process is categorization. Sentenced prisoners are categorized according to how much of a security risk they are into security categories A, B, C and D. A is the highest and prisoners in Category A are those for whom escape would be highly dangerous to the public or the police or the security of the State. At the other end of the scale Category D is used for prisoners who are unlikely to escape, and if they do the public will not be endangered. Normally Category D prisoners are held in open prisons, that is, prisons where there is little physical security to keep the prisoners in. All prisoners in open prisons are Category D. If they abscond (the Prison Department word for escaping from an open prison) they are recategorized up again to Category C or even B.

Women are kept separately from men so this means a separate part of the organization. Although the population of women is increasing much faster than the population of men – an increase of 25 per cent between 1977 and 1987 compared with 16 per cent for men – the numbers involved are very much smaller. Thus women in prison tend to be the neglected area of penal policy, barely mentioned in official reports. A Home Office research report notes 'virtually all the published accounts of research on adult prisons and prisoners in England and Wales since 1970 relate to males'.[33] The House of Commons Expenditure Committee under its chairman of the time, Janet Fookes, MP, started an inquiry into women in the penal system but it was interrupted by the 1979 General Election and dropped.

In the women's prison system eight establishments are provided for sentenced women as well as a top-security separate wing in Durham men's prison and three remand centres which take women. Babies also have their place in prison. Three of the women's prisons, Holloway, Styal and Askham Grange, have mother and baby units which can cater for thirty-nine mothers with their babies at any one time. Babies can stay in Holloway and Styal until they are nine months old and in Askham Grange up to eighteen months old. After reaching those arbitrary ages they have to be separated from their mothers and placed elsewhere, usually in care or with relatives.

Women prisoners are in many respects the poor relations – not only in the relative neglect of their problems. They also pay the price of their small numbers and the consequent small number of prisons they can go to by being placed frequently hundreds of miles from their homes. For instance women in Holloway or Durham can come from almost anywhere in England and Wales or from Northern Ireland.

Organizing prisoners awaiting trial or sentence is focused around getting the right prisoner to the right court on the right day, so location is very important. Such prisoners are kept in remand centres such as Pucklechurch or Risley (nicknamed Grisly Risley) or in local prisons like Birmingham, Leeds or Wormwood Scrubs. There is little time for anything else, so those prisoners not going to court spend sometimes as many as twenty-three hours of the day locked in their cells.

These organizational factors produce one of the major scandals of the prison system: the holding, often for long periods, of nearly 11,000 remand and unsentenced prisoners – people not convicted of any offence or not sentenced to prison – in the worst conditions the prison system has to offer. The privileges granted to remand prisoners – that they are allowed to wear their own clothes, have more frequent though shorter visits and letters, a greater variety of articles sent in by relatives and friends, and are not obliged to work – in no way compensate for the overcrowding they are subjected to.

The position of remand prisoners has aroused particular parliamentary concern. In 1981 the House of Commons Home Affairs Committee declared that:

Cell sharing, long periods locked up, and, for the majority, all the considerable disadvantages of the old Victorian prisons ... would be intolerable enough when inflicted on persons found guilty of an offence, but for the many persons still awaiting trial, and innocent before the law, these experiences are completely insupportable.[34]

Seven years later, nothing has improved for remand prisoners. The Chief Inspector inspected Risley Remand Centre in 1988 and was obviously shocked by what he found. He concluded:

Male inmates remanded to Risley enter an institution which is profoundly depressing. Apart from the times when they are being processed either to or from court or to see relatives or legal advisors, they are for most of the time forgotten people.[35]

Remand prisoners not in remand centres are no better off. They are cheek by jowl in the overcrowded local prisons with a variety of prisoners: those serving short sentences, civil prisoners, young people awaiting allocation. Local prisons, or locals as they are known, are the gateway to the system, the warehouse for those serving short sentences whom there is no time to place elsewhere, the 'sin bins' for disruptive prisoners from long-term prisons, as well as the overflow when other parts of the system are full. Out of the locals, some prisoners are transferred to training prisons – the usually less crowded, more recently built part of the system, often in a rural area –

where there are more facilities. Prisoners who are deemed to need high security, and are invariably serving long sentences, usually go to the top-security prisons, described as dispersal prisons, where the level of security is the most oppressive but the physical conditions are some of the best the prison system has to offer.

Young men under twenty-one are destined for a different part of the system yet again, the young offender system. Run by a different group of officials in the Home Office and with its own rules and regulations, the young offender system contains young offender institutions, the former youth custody centres and detention centres, with every appearance of prison except the name.

So, spending time in prison can mean many different experiences – being locked up with two other young men in a smelly cell for most of the day, waiting seven weeks to go to court for trial and then being released and given a community service order, bringing up a newborn baby in the mother and baby unit of Holloway, coping with mental illness in a prison hospital, working in the greenhouses of an open prison and sharing a dormitory with the most middle-class elements of the prison population, learning how to survive the bullying and intimidation in a dormitory in a young offender institution, or settling down for a long spell in an electronically controlled, not overcrowded, top-security prison on the Isle of Wight.

This is what we use prison for. We now go on to consider this usage. Is it too much or too little? In our use of prison how do we compare with other countries?

3   Too Many Prisoners

The use of imprisonment by the courts

> The appellant pleaded guilty to forging a banknote and utter-
> ing it, and asked for two other offences to be considered. She
> was sentenced to nine months' imprisonment.

> LORD JUSTICE SHAW: The circumstances were that the appli-
> cant went to a tobacconist's shop and asked for a packet of
> cigarettes and presented in payment what appeared to be a
> carefully folded £5 note. When the woman in the shop
> unfolded it, she saw it appeared to be made up of a series of
> strips stuck together with Sellotape and so she called the
> police. On inquiry it turned out that she had managed, by
> cutting up six £5 notes into a series of strips and sticking
> them together again, to produce seven notes . . . this Court
> has decided, in mercy, it will reduce the sentence, quite
> properly imposed at the Crown Court in Manchester – no
> one can criticize the sentence at all, but in the particular
> circumstances, having regard to the family difficulties
> which have arisen – to concurrent sentences on each count
> of such length as will enable her to be released from prison to-
> morrow.[1]

Do we have too many prisoners? We certainly have more
prisoners than we have room for – 6,100 more in June 1988 –
and this has been the case for many years. More than thirty years
ago, in 1952, a parliamentary report remarked on the 'undesirable overcrowding in local prisons in England and Wales'.[2]

Lord Mountbatten, who was called in by the Home Secretary
in 1966 to inquire into prison escapes, wrote in his report:

Table 2   Prison overcrowding since 1966

Year	Average daily population	Certified normal accommodation	Percentage occupied
1966	33,086	31,274	106
1968	32,461	32,474	100
1970	39,028	32,992	118
1972	38,328	36,236	106
1974	36,867	35,342	104
1976	41,443	36,675	113
1978	41,796	37,735	111
1980	42,109	38,930	108
1982	43,707	38,570	113
1984–5	43,618	39,400	111
1986–7	47,134	41,647	113

Source: Home Office Statistics

Ever since the last War the prisons have been grossly over-crowded. Even the remarkable achievement of increasing the number of establishments since 1945 from 39 to 106 has not kept pace with the enormous growth in the prison population. In the last year alone it has gone up by well over 2,000 for which six additional establishments of 350 inmates each would be required.[3]

It was very different before the war. In 1928 the prisons were only just over half full, with 11,000 prisoners for over 20,000 cells. In 1938 the number of prisoners was still around 11,000 but many prisons had been closed, reducing the number of places by nearly 5,000, as they were not needed.

The facts of overcrowding are simple. The number of prison places rises. The number of prisoners rises erratically but inexorably. As Table 2 shows, in the last twenty years the catching-up process has only worked once, in 1968 – and that was a very shortlived alignment between population and accommodation. Even then, with the best-ever match between people and places to put them, the Prison Department was under heavy pressure. Prisons were still overcrowded. In December 1968 5,058 prisoners were living three to a cell built for one, and 1,804 were housed two to a cell. By 1970 the gap between people and accommodation was the biggest ever.

In June 1988 the population was 49,578, in accommodation

Table 3   Highest-ever prison population

Date	Prison population	Certified normal accommodation	Percentage occupied	Number in police cells
Nov. 1979	43,036	38,494*	112	–
March 1980	44,626	38,930*	115	–
July 1981	45,500	38,789*	117	–
March 1985	46,046	39,311	117	–
June 1985	47,503	39,804	119	100
July 1985	48,099	40,283	119	100
Feb. 1987	48,465	41,505	117	315
March 1987	49,082	41,650	118	390
May 1987	49,255	41,688	118	360
June 1987	50,265	41,994	120	590
July 1987	50,354	42,005	120	753

* Figures for end of December of that year
Source: Home Office Statistics

for 44,179 and the percentage occupation was 112 per cent. In addition 724 prisoners were outside prison, in cells in police stations and under courts.

A common point of reference for the discussion of numbers is a speech made by Roy Jenkins in 1975 when he was Home Secretary:

The prison population now stands at over 40,500. It has never been higher. If it should rise to, say 42,000, conditions in the system would approach the intolerable and drastic action to relieve the position would be inescapable. We are perilously close to that position now. We must not just sit back and wait for it to happen. If we can prevent it, we must do so.[*]

We could not prevent it, it seems. In October 1976 the 'intolerable' figure was reached. Since then accommodation and population have gone up and headlines signalling the highest-ever prison population have been a recurring feature, as Table 3 shows.

These figures would suggest that each prison has to struggle to find room for an extra twelve–twenty prisoners for every hundred it is built to cater for. This does not sound very difficult and may prompt the question, 'why is such a fuss made about overcrowding?' In fact, overcrowding is much more complicated than the bare figures would suggest. Table 4 shows one

Table 4 Most overcrowded prisons

Prison	Population	Certified normal accommodation	Percentage occupied
Leeds	1,367	642	213
Leicester	425	204	208
Bedford	319	155	206
Birmingham	1,109	575	193
Oxford	245	127	193
Manchester	1,784	970	184
Lincoln	640	359	178
Shrewsbury	299	174	172
Hull	615	369	167
Dorchester	224	139	161
Reading	287	178	161

Figures for June 1988
Source: Home Office Statistics

aspect of the management of overcrowding – the way it is concentrated in certain prisons.

In fact overcrowding is concentrated in the local prisons, which cater for those on remand, for short-sentence prisoners, and for many other prisoners awaiting allocation or transfer, or needing a new placement. Although their places in the table may vary, Oxford, Birmingham, Leeds, Bedford, Leicester, Manchester and Lincoln have long lived with overcrowding and it is getting no better. A decade ago these same seven prisons were at the top of the overcrowding league table.

There are two reasons why overcrowding is not just a matter of finding room for an extra thirteen prisoners for every hundred, why overcrowding is concentrated. First, prison accommodation is very inflexible. We saw in the last chapter how many different types of institution there are – remand centres, local prisons, training prisons, women's prisons, Category C prisons, open prisons, dispersal prisons, young offender institutions – and all have their appropriate clientele. Remand centres are for prisoners awaiting trial or sentence. Young offender institutions cater only for offenders aged under twenty-one. A Category C prison will not take prisoners in the higher security categories A and B. A women's prison cannot take men. Remand prisoners are supposed to be kept separate from convicted prisoners and young men under twenty-one from adults, though this is an aspiration more honoured in the breach than the observance. A recommendation made by the Chief Inspector after inspecting Brockhill Remand Centre was that remand and convicted inmates should be kept separate in accordance with standing instructions.[5] Flexibility is not totally ruled out. Establishments for young people, formerly divided into detention centres, where those sentenced to four months or less, were sent, and youth custody centres for those serving longer sentences, were amalgamated in October 1988 and became young offender institutions. New Hall and Send detention centres, formerly the homes of the notorious short, sharp shock experiments have become respectively a women's prison and a training prison for men. An open prison, Ashwell, became a closed prison in 1987 and Foston Hall, a closed prison, became an open one in the same year. Cookham Wood in Kent was built as a young offenders' remand centre but then used for women prisoners. In women's prisons, adults and young offenders mix, which increases flexibility.

But these are minor flexibilities in a basically inflexible system. Having empty places in young offender institutions is no use at all to a harassed prison official desperately looking for empty cells for convicted men designated security Category B.

Some inflexibility in an institutional system is inevitable. The second explanation for the concentration of overcrowding is not inevitable – but a result of a clear policy choice about what prisons should aim to do. The policy is put very clearly, with more confidence than would be expressed in later years, in the Prison Department Report for 1966:

During the period since 1945 the local prisons have been increasingly overcrowded but the training prisons and borstals have been preserved from the effects of overcrowding so that progress with the treatment and training of offenders should continue.[6]

The Chief Inspector makes the same point fifteen years later, in 1981. He says:

Overcrowding is almost entirely restricted to local prisons. This is not a matter of coincidence but rather a result of a deliberate Prison

Table 5   How overcrowding is concentrated

Part of the system	Population	Certified normal accommodation	Percentage occupied
Local prisons for men	17,256	11,237	154
Remand centres and prisons for men	4,155	3,388	123
Prisons for women	1,639	1,550	106
Closed prisons for men (except dispersals)	13,272	13,122	101
Open prisons for men	3,130	3,312	95
Youth custody centres for men	6,621	7,091	93
Dispersal prisons	2,707	2,968	91
Youth custody centres for women	137	299	46

Figures for June 1988
Source: Home Office Statistics

Department policy to optimize the regime in training prisons and make best use of the facilities available there.[7]

Table 5 shows how the policy of concentrating overcrowding in the local prisons for men and protecting the other part of the system, that is, the training prisons, has been carried out with almost total accuracy. The men's open prisons contain almost exactly the right numbers. The closed prisons have only 1 per cent overcrowding whereas the locals have over 50 per cent.

Prison overcrowding is not, of course, a feature only of the system in England and Wales. In the United States and Canada it is widespread. In the United States the courts have intervened in thirty-four states to reduce the numbers because the overcrowded conditions contravene the Constitution. In Canada, in the province of Ontario, the prison officers' union joined with prisoners in 1983 to bring a suit against the Attorney-General of Ontario, alleging violations of the Canadian Charter because of overcrowding in the Toronto jail and the Metropolitan Toronto West detention centre. Following a change of government in Ontario the case was settled out of court.[8]

In Holland there are also pressures on the prisons. Since

overcrowding is not allowed – prisoners may not share cells – around 250 prisoners at any one time have to stay in police cells longer than the four days the law permits. Some suspects whom the prosecutors wish to keep in custody have to be sent home. There is a big building programme in hand to increase the number of prison places from around 4,700 to over 7,000 by 1990. On the other hand, between February 1983 and February 1987 the prison population went down in Austria, West Germany, Italy, Norway, Sweden and Turkey – while it went up in England and Wales by 8 per cent.

Nearer home the comparison is interesting. In Northern Ireland for instance, in 1986/7, 'the total prison population ... which peaked at just over 3,000 late in 1977, continued to decline, contrary to the trend in Great Britain and many other Western countries'.[9] Also in Northern Ireland – a position that must make prison administrators in England and Wales green with envy – prison capacity is 2,388 and the average population is under 2,000.

The problems of space are also less acute in Scotland. In 1986 the average daily population of 5,588 was the highest ever. There was accommodation for 5,337 prisoners so overcrowding was not a major issue.

The overcrowding in prisons in England and Wales has provoked widespread condemnation. A Prison Department report of 1966 set out the implications of overcrowding in words that later commentators have not bettered. The Report speaks of 'the human need for sufficient living space to provide both privacy and shared activities',[10] the pressures to get the housing, feeding, clothing, bathing and provision of work and recreation to the prisoners, the sheer difficulty of exercising a thousand prisoners which may 'tend to be accompanied by constant exhortations to hurry, with the result that some [prisoners] are defiant and others are made anxious'.[11] The Report also notes the degree of tolerance required to share a cell with two others, the consequent ill-temper in prisoners that may lead to violence, the shortage of sluices and water points to cope with the basic human requirements.

David Waplington, a prison governor from Leeds prison, high in the overcrowding league table, set out, in a letter to the

Prison Service Journal in 1986, his perceptions of what over-crowding means for prisoners, not just the physical indignities but also:

> being kitted out with ill-fitting inadequate and shoddy clothes because there's never enough to go round and never enough right sizes. The disgraceful indignity of noisy, cramped and inadequate family visits ... a situation where prisoners are treated as less than individuals – like passive objects on an assembly line or cattle going to market; ... we are forced to discourage individuality because we haven't time to listen and explain ... Prison rules are broken every day in these situations ... how can the Medical Officer fulfil his requirement to see every reception in an establishment which has been receiving an average of 140 prisoners on weekdays ... two minutes per examination per prisoner ...[12]

Few could read these accounts without feeling that something should be done. But what? Here paths diverge. Some would argue that the answer is obvious – we need more prisons. Others would say it's obvious – we need fewer prisoners.

Do we have too many prisoners? We can perhaps begin to make progress towards an answer if we look at how we compare in our use of imprisonment with other, broadly similar, countries. Figures are regularly published by the Council of Europe showing comparative imprisonment rates. Home Office ministers used to be briefed to argue that the figures were not comparable. However, after a search for the specifics of the incomparability proved fruitless, the argument was quietly dropped. The figures now feature regularly in Home Office speeches where they are cited with great confidence.[13]

The UK has been near the top of the Council of Europe tables for some time and, as the years go by, has been steadily approaching first place. In 1984, for instance, the UK was fourth from the top, behind Austria, West Germany and Turkey. In September 1987 it was third, behind Austria and Turkey, but as Table 6 shows, the gap is closing fast.

We have seen that in our system prison plays a major role, more so than in many other countries of western Europe. We now go on to consider how this comes about.

How do people end up in prison? The simple answer is that,

Table 6   Prison population of member states of the Council of Europe on
1 September 1985, 1986 and 1987

Country	Detention rate per 100,000 of population		
	1 September 1985	1 September 1986	1 September 1987
Austria	109.0	102.5	97.5
Belgium	62.5	62.2	67.4
Denmark	63.0	65.0	62.0
France	71.6	84.0	88.9
West Germany	92.0	87.9	84.9
Greece	35.8	38.8	40.9
Ireland	55.6	52.4	55.0
Italy	76.5	76.3	60.8
Netherlands	34.0	34.0	37.0
Norway	44.9	48.5	46.0
Portugal	93.0	82.0	84.0
Spain	57.5	64.6	70.2
Sweden	49.0	49.0	51.0
Switzerland	63.5	66.6	–
Turkey	139.0	102.3	99.4
UK	96.5	95.3	95.8
England, and Wales	–	93.3	94.1
Scotland	–	108.9	105.9
N. Ireland	–	116.0	119.1

Source: Council of Europe

with the exception of some civil prisoners, they are sent there,
either by magistrates or by a judge. Some are sent there on
remand; others are sent there to serve a sentence. Some end up
there because the court imposes a fine on them which ultimately they cannot or will not pay.

The people held on remand are those who have not been
given bail, about 14 per cent of all those coming before the
courts on a criminal charge. The Bail Act of 1976 requires the
courts to give defendants bail whenever they can. They can
only refuse bail when they believe that it would have serious
consequences, either that defendants will abscond and not turn
up for the trial, or they will commit more offences while on
bail, or they will put the frighteners on witnesses or interfere
with the course of justice or (because the case is notorious for
some reason) they will be in danger themselves. Every eight
days a person remanded in custody must be brought back to

court. The court can then remand for another eight days, but defendants have a choice and need only appear themselves at every fourth hearing so long as they agree and their legal representative is there.

The most surprising feature of the remand system is the large number of people kept in custody before their trial who do not get a prison sentence when their case eventually comes to court. After an average time spent in custody of over eight weeks for men and over six weeks for women, six out of ten men and four out of ten women subsequently get a prison sentence. In 1986 over 2,000 men and 136 women kept in prison till their trial were found not guilty or charges were dropped. Nearly 17,000 men and 1,400 women kept in custody before their case came to court were not sentenced to prison at their trial.

The question is often asked, why did the remanding court think they were serious enough offenders to keep in prison before the trial and the sentencing court feel that prison was not merited and that a community service order or a probation order would do as a punishment for the offence? One explanation sometimes given is that the courts decide a taste of prison for a remand prisoner is a sufficient punishment alongside a non-custodial penalty. Another explanation is that they are kept in prison so that reports can be written about them. Early in 1986 considerable comment was aroused by the case of a seventeen-year-old woman who was remanded to prison by Dover magistrates and sent to Holloway so that social inquiry reports could be written for allegedly stealing a pint of milk. Since 'spiky-haired Katherine' lived in a squat where a probation officer could not be expected to track her down to write a report about her, prison seemed to be a place where everyone would be sure of finding her. She was released after thirteen days when her solicitor took the case before a High Court judge. When the case came back before the magistrates Katherine was granted a conditional discharge, one of the mildest penalties available to the court.

To complete the picture of how bail is granted it needs to be said that the chance of being bailed will be better in some magistrates courts than others. A report published by the

Prison Reform Trust, *The Bail Lottery*,[14] shows great variations between one court and another. For example, in 1984 your chance of getting bail in Dorset was 64 per cent, whereas in Bedfordshire it was 97 per cent. Even in neighbouring areas there were great differences. For instance, in Uxbridge in West London, 71 per cent of people were given bail. In Harrow the figure was 96 per cent. A similar picture of variations between one court and another also emerges from the consideration of how courts pass prison sentences.

In 1987 over 74,000 sentences of immediate custody were passed. Of these, 26,100 were passed by magistrates courts. Magistrates also sent 19,000 people to prison for not paying their fines. The higher court, the Crown Court, sent 48,100. Since magistrates' powers are limited to a sentence of six months' imprisonment (with a twelve months' maximum for more than one offence) the sentences they pass are shorter. In 1987 the average length of sentence given to men aged twenty-one or over was just under three months, whereas in the Crown Court it was over 19 months. Currently, sentences are getting longer. In 1983 the average was 10.9 months. In 1987 it was 15.1 months. The increase of 126 days in the average sentence length with full remission of one half is the equivalent of a year's imprisonment for 7,088 adult men. With one third remission (the amount given to prisoners serving more than a year) it means an increase of 9,450 adult men, enough people to fill eleven prisons the size of Wormwood Scrubs.

A lot of information is available on the proportionate use of prison and other penalties, usually expressed in percentage terms, that is, out of every hundred people sentenced by the courts for indictable offences how many were sent to prison, how many were fined, discharged or were given other penalties. These figures show that between the early 1950s and 1974 the proportionate use of custody by courts in England and Wales fell. Since 1974 this trend has been reversed and the proportionate use of custody has been going up and up. Table 7 shows this process.

One question prompted by these figures might be, since there seems to be more crime and crime seems to be more serious, is

Table 7   Proportionate use of custody

Year	Percentage of those aged seventeen and over sentenced for indictable offences receiving immediate custodial sentences	
	Males	Females
1977	17	3
1979	18	4
1981	18	4
1983	19*	5*
1985	21*	6*
1987	21*	7*

*including partly suspended sentences
Source: Criminal Statistics, England and Wales, 1987

it not right that the proportionate use of prison should be rising? The courts cannot be expected to put armed robbers on probation. This would account for sentences getting longer and for the prison population getting bigger.

There is indeed a grain of truth in this argument. The proportion of all notifiable offences, i.e. the more serious offences that involve sex or violence, has gone up over the years, from 4.8 per cent to 5 per cent. The proportion of those received into prison whose offences involved sex or violence has also increased over the past five years, by about 7 per cent. But the major impact on the size of the prison population has come from a more punitive attitude to offences generally, violent, non-violent, very serious and less serious. For example, in 1982 the courts found it quite reasonable to send to prison 14 per cent of those convicted of violence against the person. Five years later they sent 20 per cent. For sex offences the percentage rose from 22 to 37 per cent. For the non-violent property offence of burglary the proportion also rose from 30 to 35 per cent, for drug offences from 10 to 21 per cent and for indictable motoring offences from 12 to 15 per cent.

There is another argument. Surely the difference between 1982 and 1987 is that offenders have got worse. Their offences are more serious and they commit many more of them. It is admittedly difficult to measure objectively the seriousness of one burglary compared with another, but there is one objective measure – number of previous convictions. Presumably those sent to prison in 1982 had fewer previous convictions, better past records, than the criminals of 1987. The figures suggest a startling continuity. In 1982 87 per cent of adult men sent to prison on whom information was available had three or more previous convictions. In 1987 the figure was 84 per cent. In 1982 70 per cent of seventeen–twenty-year-old men had three or more previous convictions. Five years later the figure was 69 per cent.

This trend is in spite of more than a decade of official policy that prisons should be a last resort and alternatives used whenever possible. If we go back to 1975 the then Home Secretary, Roy Jenkins, said:

I think all recent Home Secretaries would concur in seeking a substantial reduction in the prison population as the central objective in a policy designed to create tolerable conditions in our prison system and to deal with offenders in the community to the maximum possible extent.[15]

Merlyn Rees, Home Secretary from 1976 to 1979, in the Foreword to a Home Office document, *A Review of Criminal Justice Policy 1976*, wrote:

A major preoccupation must continue to be to reduce the prison population and thus relieve the pressure on prison staff. In this context the general thrust towards shorter prison sentences and the less frequent use of custodial disposals seems right.[16]

William Whitelaw, now Viscount Whitelaw, who took over as Home Secretary in 1979, was more outspoken than his predecessors. The outcome of his outspokenness is dealt with in more detail in Chapter 8. It is only necessary here to refer to one of many speeches he made on these lines, the one he gave to the Conservative Central Council in Bournemouth on 21 March 1980 when he said:

It is no use continuing to over-burden the staff who have to run the system . . . with petty offenders who can be dealt with just as well in other ways . . . We must ensure that prison is reserved for those whom we really need to contain in custody and the sentences are no longer than necessary to achieve this objective . . . we shall need, and in this the courts have their part to play, to see that the prisons are not allowed to remain cluttered up with trivial and inadequate offenders who are no real threat to anyone, except possibly themselves.

Why has this official policy, supported at the highest level, failed to make any substantial impact? Why have we not managed to substitute non-custodial sanctions for prison? What are the 'other ways' that William Whitelaw suggested would do 'just as well' for petty offenders?

There are four main 'alternatives to custody': fines, probation orders, community service orders, and suspended sentences – all of them, of course, backed up by the threat of prison, the ultimate sanction if the fine is not paid, the community service not performed. The fine is the most used sanction of the court – 40 per cent of all those over seventeen found guilty of indictable offences were fined in 1987. The fine has many advantages as a penal sanction. It costs nothing (unless the person fined does not pay); in fact it brings in revenue to the system, nearly £160m in 1986–7. The social damage and disruption caused by the fine should not be as great as custody – and it is clearly punitive. Its great disadvantage, of course, is that it presupposes some money to pay it with. The courts are therefore reluctant to fine convicted people who have no money, such as the unemployed living on income support or single parents bringing up children on their own, even though a very small fine can be a substantial punishment for someone in such circumstances. This is probably why the proportionate use of the fine has been dropping, from 56 per cent of all those over seventeen found guilty of indictable offences in 1977 to 40 per cent ten years later.

Probation orders and community service orders are both run by the probation service. Probation orders involve convicted people, with their consent, in programmes ranging from seeing a probation officer regularly to discuss progress and problems, to committing themselves to attend certain schemes, such as day centres where up to sixty days' attendance can be compulsory, live in hostels, or accept help for problems such as mental illness, drink or drugs.

Community service orders are the latest in the pantheon of

alternatives and the fastest growing, as Table 8 (p. 40) shows. Community service orders were introduced by the Criminal Justice Act 1972 and after an experimental start in six areas were gradually introduced throughout the country in 1975 and 1976. They were one of the ideas put forward by the Advisory Council on the Penal System in its report *Non-Custodial and Semi-Custodial Penalties*, published in 1970. Community service orders combine many elements which make an 'alternative to custody' marketable to courts and public. They involve deprivation for the people given the order, who have to give up free time at evenings or weekends to undertake activities not of their own choosing. They have to spend this time doing something constructive, for example decorating and maintaining buildings used by charities or churches, helping in schools or clubs for the handicapped, or making toys for deprived children. They are cheap – a community service order cost on average £450 in 1985–6.[17] They are quite successful, by simple and obvious measures. In 1987 three-quarters of all community service orders were satisfactorily completed.

Another alternative to sending people to prison immediately is to suspend the sentence so that, provided they keep out of trouble for the length of time that the sentence is suspended, they will have all the stigma of a prison sentence on their record but will not actually have to have served one. In 1987 29,000 suspended sentences were handed out by the courts. A quarter of these were subsequently activated, and 7,400 people had to serve their suspended sentence as well as whatever new sentence was given.

So there *are* alternatives. In fact, not only do we have one of the highest prison populations in Europe – we also have more alternatives than most other West European countries. Unfortunately the experience of the last ten years would suggest that creating 'alternatives to prison' has not made the inroads into the prison population that those promoting the official policy would have liked.

In 1984 a debate took place about a possible 'new' alternative to prison, that is weekend or part-time prison. The debate engendered by the idea is worth looking at in greater detail because it illustrates very well what has happened to earlier enthusiasms for 'alternatives'.

Throughout the seventies many official committees and commentators pursued the chimera of creating new alternatives to prison. The logic behind this pursuit went something like this. Prison is the basis of the whole system of penal sanctions. Reducing the use of prison will therefore only be acceptable if something new is devised to put in its place that is unpleasant and gives everyone the feeling that an experience almost like prison has been inflicted on the convicted person, but without its costs and consequences. A sub-committee of the Advisory Council on the Penal System chaired by Baroness Wootton was set up specially to consider such possibilities. In its report, published in 1970, it advocated setting up community service orders, and also suggested weekend imprisonment because 'continuous custody has several extremely undesirable by-products'. So the sub-committee tried to think up 'a form of custody that would enable offenders who have jobs to keep them, make it possible for them to maintain contact with their families, and minimize the prisoner's need to rely on his fellow inmates for companionship'.[18]

In 1978 another official committee, the Expenditure Committee of the House of Commons, recommended that some experiments in weekend prison be set up as a possible new alternative to prison.[19] In its Annual Report for June 1981 the Magistrates Association recommended consideration of an entirely new measure – day imprisonment, which would be a 'genuine' alternative to total custody.[20] In 1983 the Parliamentary All-Party Penal Affairs Group recommended that both day detention and weekend prison should be considered by the Home Office.

Yet when a Green Paper was put out in 1984 asking for comments on a proposal to establish day or weekend prison, the overwhelming response from the organizations consulted was negative and even one of its main proponents, the Magistrates Association, was less than fervent in its support for the Green Paper proposals.

Two main arguments against the idea of part-time prison emerged from the response. One was that it would undoubtedly be very expensive. The other was that it would have the contrary effect to that intended. The object was to reduce the prison population by allowing some people to serve their prison sentences part-time. The outcome would be to increase it.

In arguing this, the organizations opposed to the idea presented evidence that suspended sentences, originally devised for just the same reasons – to act as an alternative to custody – had in fact increased it. Courts have had the power to suspend sentences of imprisonment since 1968. The suspended sentence was introduced in the hope that it would reduce the use of imprisonment. Yet as early as 1970 doubts were being expressed. The Prison Department Report for 1970 says:

> About 60 per cent of those receiving suspended sentences will not on present trends be convicted during the operational period of the suspended sentence. On the other hand the courts may impose a suspended sentence on an offender who would before 1967 have been fined or put on probation. If such an offender commits a further offence and the suspended sentence takes effect, probably accompanied by a second sentence of imprisonment, the net effect is to increase the prison population. The best estimate that can be made at present is that the positive and negative effects of suspended sentences on the size of the prison population about cancel each other out.[21]

The Advisory Council on the Penal System came to a similar conclusion. They felt that the evidence was 'not very encouraging'. If, they said, 'the main object of the suspended sentence was to reduce the prison population, there are considerable doubts as to whether it has achieved this effect. It may even have *increased* the size of the prison population.'[22]

Similar doubts apply to the use of community service orders. While the figures suggest that community service has stopped some people going to prison, it is likely that much of its use is for people who were formerly given probation orders, and for unemployed people who cannot afford to pay fines.

Using this evidence, it was argued that one could expect no more successful outcome from a new 'alternative' such as part-time prison. Something more drastic than new 'alternatives' would be needed if the courts' use of prison was to be reduced.

The Home Office bowed to the overwhelming weight of the arguments and the proposal for part-time prison has been

Table 8 Proportionate use (percentages) of various sentences or orders for those aged seventeen or over sentenced for indictable offences

Year	Fine	Community service	Probation	Immediate custody
1977	56	3	7	14
1979	54	4	7	15
1981	49	7	8	16
1983	46	8	9	17
1985	42	8	10	19
1987	40	9	10	19

Source: Based on Criminal Statistics, England and Wales, 1987

quietly dropped. The Criminal Justice White Paper published in March 1986 noted that 'the Government has decided not to pursue the proposal'.[23] The reasons given were that existing sentencing powers were sufficient without anything new, there was little agreement on the form of a new sentence, and many of those consulted had expressed the fear that a new measure would not be an alternative to custody but an alternative to other non-custodial penalties.

The aspiration has not died however. In 1988, faced with exploding prison populations and simmering prisons, the Home Office tried again. In July a Green Paper, *Punishment, Custody and the Community*, appeared, full of admirable sentiments.

Imprisonment reduces offending only by restricting the opportunities for a limited period. Imprisonment is likely to add to the difficulty which offenders find in living a normal and law-abiding life. Over-crowded local prisons are emphatically not schools of citizenship.[24]

The Green Paper identified the problem as lack of confidence on the part of the courts and the public in existing community sanctions. Ways of creating such confidence were proposed, including the creation of a new 'package' sentence, with various elements to it: compensation to the victim, day activities, even house arrest. Unfortunately though, the Green Paper carefully skirts around the question of how any new order will be used instead of prison, rather than be seized upon joyfully by the courts as the toughened-up version of existing probation and community service orders that they have long been arguing for.

Table 8 shows how likely this is to happen. The 'alternatives' have made no inroads into the use of custody between 1977 and 1987. It also shows how penalties substitute for each other while custody continues on its upward path – the use of fines has dropped and fines have been replaced by community service, perhaps a direct result of increased unemployment, which means people have no money to pay fines with. Otherwise the proportions remain much the same.

Why has it been so difficult for a Home Office policy, stated frequently and sincerely by one Home Secretary after another, that the use of prison should be reduced and non-custodial penalties used whenever possible, to take hold in the Magistrates Courts and the Crown Court? Why are sentencers so resistant to hearing the messages of the policymakers?

First, the whole idea of sentencers being influenced by Home Secretaries is highly contentious.

Andrew Ashworth, of Worcester College, Oxford, and editor of the *Criminal Law Review*, writes of the great 'taboo' that inhibits discussion of sentencing policy. He says:

In the late 1970s a succession of official committees considered ways of furthering various elements of penal policy described in the last chapter; each of them considered the potentiality of changes in sentencing practice, and each of them clearly felt inhibited from recommending changes by 'the principle of judicial independence'.[25]

The taboo comes out quite clearly in the almost apologetic Foreword by the Home Secretary to the latest edition of the sentencing handbook for magistrates and judges. The Foreword says that the first edition of the handbook came out in 1964 following the recommendation of an official committee. 'The Committee,' the Home Secretary says, 'considered it entirely proper for the Executive to supply basic factual material of this kind.' He goes on: 'My predecessor's intention to produce a new and updated version met with a favourable response from representatives of circuit judges and magistrates.'[26]

So there is the taboo. Secondly, sentencing is carried out in a very individual way which makes it very resistant to persuasion from the policy-makers. Variations in sentencing between one part of the country and another, between one court and another in the same county, are very great. The statistics show that in 1986 South Tameside sent 23 per cent of all their adult male offenders convicted of an indictable offence to custody, whilst Rotherham magistrates sentenced 8 per cent. Newcastle sent 9 per cent whilst Sunderland, next door, sent three times as many. Liverpool sent 12 per cent, Manchester sent half as many again, 19 per cent. Home Office studies also show great variations. Obviously some of these differences are accounted for by differences in the seriousness of the crimes for which offenders are convicted. Violence and house burglary are likely to be dealt with more severely than riding a bicycle without lights or stealing a bar of chocolate from a shop. The Home Office research therefore compared how courts dealt with similar cases. They found that one court in their sample sent 7 per cent of burglars to prison whereas another sent 47 per cent. One court fined 19 per cent of burglars and another fined 62 per cent. Fewer than one in two hundred first offenders at one court were sent to prison. At another that fate befell more than one in ten. At one court 48 per cent of first offenders guilty of shoplifting were fined compared with 86 per cent at another.[27]

It is no wonder that with such arrangements, the intentions of the policy-makers, even if they were accepted as legitimate, are thwarted. There is no mechanism for translating them into practice. The nearly 28,000 magistrates are not servants of government to be issued with the latest rulebook. They build up their own sentencing culture in their particular court. Some think community service should be an alternative to prison and work hard to try and make it so. Other Benches think it should be used when it is appropriate in severity and would do the defendant good. Some think young people taking and driving away other people's motor cars should automatically be sent away and locked up for a while. Others, when faced with a juvenile joyrider, think of the banger-racing project down the road which channels young people's enthusiasm for cars into constructive directions.

Undoubtedly all those who pass sentences on offenders use prison as a 'last resort' – it is just that for some the 'last resort' comes more readily than for others. But what is in sentencers' minds when they pass a prison sentence? What do they feel it will achieve? And are they right? Chapter 4 looks at what prison is for.

4   A Good and Useful Life

What is prison for?

PRISONS

ENGLAND AND WALES

The Prison Rules 1964 as amended by the Prison (Amendment) Rules of 1968, 1971, 1972, 1974, 1976, 1981, 1982, 1983

Part I

PRISONERS

General

Purpose of Prison Training and Treatment

1   The purpose of the training and treatment of convicted prisoners shall be to encourage and assist them to lead a good and useful life.[1]

I do not think you necessarily make a man better by taking away his liberty and making him share one cell with two equally undesirable characters. It is a perfectly possible view that you do reform because it is such a horrible experience for him, but it is not a view I happen to share.

The Lord Chancellor, Lord Hailsham, 1981.[2]

We saw in Chapter 2, 'People in Prison', what a variety of purposes prison serves, providing at one end of the scale a top-security, all-electronic, high-technology escape-proof Alcatraz for professional criminals, terrorists and spies – and, at the other, a warm if rather spartan refuge for homeless, rootless alcoholics where at least they get regular meals and medical care, with many gradations between these extremes. In Chapter 3 we looked at the use of prison by the courts. In this chapter we ask the question, what is prison for? Does it do good? Does it work? Here we come up against the central and one of the most deeply felt debates of the prison system – what can and should prisons do with and for those in their charge?

Such a discussion must start from the consensus that prison is not intended to be cruel, harmful, degrading or unjust. The punishment is being taken away from the community and losing freedom. The days when prisoners were sentenced to hard labour and had to work a treadmill are over and done with. Even at the 1983 Conservative Party Conference the then Home Secretary, Leon Brittan, in the midst of announcing a range of new tough measures, felt it right to assert, 'Whatever we think of the people we send to prison, we send them there *as* a punishment and not *for* punishment.'[3]

How is this translated into a rationale for those who work in the prison system? Officially Prison Rule 1 – 'to encourage and assist them to live a good and useful life' – still sets the tone. After all, the Prison Rules of 1964, outdated as they are, still constitute the statutory basis of the prison system. Prison Rule 1 enshrines the view (going back to the Gladstone Report of 1895) that prison should aim to reform prisoners, to send them out, if not cured of the disease of crime, at least less likely to suffer from bouts of it than when they entered. The Gladstone Report put it like this:

. . . prison discipline and treatment should be more effectually designed to maintain, stimulate or awaken the higher susceptibilities of prisoners, to develop their moral instincts, to train them in orderly and industrial habits, and whenever possible to turn them out of prison better men and women, both physically and morally, than when they came in.[4]

For its time the Gladstone Committee was being quite progressive. The Report was an attempt to reform a bleakly punitive system. The Old Holloway prison, built in 1852, had above

the gate the encouraging sentiment: MAY GOD PRESERVE
THE CITY OF LONDON AND MAKE THIS PLACE A
TERROR TO EVIL-DOERS.

Throwing prisoners into an entirely dark cell had only been
discontinued in 1884.[5] In many prisons in 1895 prisoners still
worked alone in their cells and were not allowed to mix with
other prisoners for fear of moral contamination or uprisings. In
the convict prisons male prisoners were not allowed to speak
to each other, except for purposes connected with labour, for
the whole of their sentence. Women prisoners were allowed to
talk under supervision for an hour a day. The Committee discovered that no harm had come from allowing women this
privilege and recommended that: 'the privilege of talking might
be given after a certain period as a reward for good conduct on
certain days for a limited time and under reasonable supervision to all long-sentence prisoners . . .'[6] They recommended
this because imposing silence on a prisoner for say fifteen or
twenty years seemed to them 'unnatural'.

The Gladstone Report's approach to imprisonment gradually
permeated official thinking and passed into the rhetoric of the
prison authorities. The view that crime was some sort of disease
that 'treatment' (note the use of the medical term 'treatment'
in Prison Rule 1) could cure was certainly widely held and
with a great deal of enthusiasm in the fifties and sixties. Its
high point was perhaps 1959 when a White Paper, *Penal Practice in a Changing Society*, asserted:

The constructive function of our prisons is to prevent the largest
numbers of those committed to their care from offending again. Since
the report of the Gladstone Committee in 1895 it has been accepted
that this end will not be reached by a regime designed simply to deter
through fear. The object should be, in the words of that Committee, to
send the prisoners out 'better men and women, physically and
morally, than when they came in'.[7]

A decade later these high hopes were becoming dimmer. A
1969 White Paper, *People in Prison*, reflected a belief in treatment but with a less optimistic tone. The overriding purpose of
the prison system was to be 'the protection of society'.[8] The
White Paper says that the service has two aims. First, to hold

those committed to it in conditions 'currently acceptable to society'. Secondly, in dealing with prisoners there is an obligation on the service to do all that may be possible within the currency of the sentence 'to encourage and assist them to lead a good and useful life'.[9] The report is still enthusiastic about different types of prison to suit different types of prisoner and has a section on 'rehabilitation', which can be described as reformation, re-education, treatment, or training. In the meantime the belief in treatment had gone so far that nearly all women in prison were deemed to be sick and in need of treatment. In 1968 the Home Secretary announced the redevelopment of Holloway prison, saying, 'Most women and girls in custody require some form of medical, psychiatric or remedial treatment.'[10] Holloway would therefore be rebuilt basically as a hospital with only a small area devoted to 'normal custodial facilities'. Even at that time, as criminologist Alison Morris points out, 'the evidence for this claim was not strong'.[11]

This view, called variously 'the treatment model' or 'rehabilitation', is now thoroughly out of fashion. The arguments against it, in principle and practice, are many. First, it is meaningless to regard everyone who commits criminal offences as sick and in need of treatment. Some are indeed sick, and should be receiving treatment in hospital, not punishment in prison, but most are not. Breaking the law is a very common activity throughout society, indulged in by all classes, all ages (though with a leaning towards the young), the employed and unemployed, male and female, the powerful and the powerless. Three out of ten men born in 1953 had a criminal conviction (excluding most motoring offences) by the time they reached the age of twenty-eight.[12] There is no reason to think that those born in 1963 are any different, nor that those born in 1973 will behave very differently. The estimate made by the criminologist D. P. Farrington, that over four out of ten men will get a conviction some time in their lives, seems reasonable – and, taking account of crimes not reported and perpetrators not caught, one could assume that the number who put themselves in a position to be convicted is higher still. Such an assumption is borne out by a survey carried out by National Opinion Polls for London Weekend Television. Nearly nine out of ten men interviewed under the age of thirty-five admitted to committing a criminal offence in their teenage years.

So in principle there is something very wrong with the idea that those who get sent to prison are sick and in need of treatment. In practice, the idea suffers from a large dose of unreality. Take, typically, a young man from a relatively impoverished urban background, with poor education, few job prospects, and a disrupted and unsupporting home. Put him for six months in a cell with three others from similar backgrounds, sometimes for twenty-three hours a day, sometimes with the odd few hours in a workshop doing monotonous tasks or in an education class once a week. And then send him back whence he came, still impoverished, with job prospects a little worse than before because of the stigma of a recent prison sentence. Any connection with 'rehabilitation' or 'treatment' must be of the remotest. Even in the more favoured establishments, where prisoners live in single cells with integral sanitation and have a range of activities to engage in after working hours, realism suggests that more modest aims might be appropriate. It is good to know that even at the time of the Gladstone Committee's optimism that locking people up and subjecting them to inhumanity could make them better human beings if done in the right way, there were sceptics. Sir Godfrey Lushington, head of the Home Office at the time, expressed the essential contradiction at the heart of imprisonment, how can you train people for freedom by putting them in captivity? He told the Committee:

I regard as unfavourable to reformation the status of a prisoner throughout his whole career; the crushing of self-respect, the starving of all moral instinct he may possess, the absence of all opportunity to do or receive a kindness, the continual association with none but criminals . . . I believe the true mode of reforming a man or restoring him to society is exactly in the opposite direction of all these; but, of course, this is a mere idea. It is quite impracticable in a prison. In fact the unfavourable features I have mentioned are inseparable from prison life.[13]

In the face of such contradictions and the disillusion of the seventies and eighties, even to formulate an agreed list of more modest aims has proved difficult and contentious. The debate has crystallized around a set of slogans or catchphrases, all of which have become so loaded that just to mention them can provoke unreasoned rage in their opponents. These catchphrases are 'the justice model', 'humane containment' (or as it is described by its detractors 'warehousing') or 'positive custody'.

The essence of the 'justice model' is that the penal system exists to deliver justice – not to cure people or help people. It argues that the 'treatment' model allowed injustice to creep in – for example by making decisions about how long people stayed locked up, not on the basis of what their crime deserved but in order to allow the 'treatment' to work. The theory behind borstal training, for instance, was that the institutions should decide when during a two-year period a borstal inmate should be released; this to depend on how well she or he was doing at the borstal training.

The 'justice model', in its most humane version, lays stress on a prisoner's right to be well-treated, kept in hygienic conditions, and given the freedom to accept or reject the education, training and counselling opportunities available. It also calls for much more clarity about prisoners' rights and machinery through which such rights can be maintained.

'Humane containment' as a phrase assumed prominence in the debate that surrounded the work of the May Committee, which, in 1979, produced the first major official report on the prison system since the Gladstone Report in 1895. The Committee considered evidence from two academics who have specialized in studies of the prison system, Roy King and Rod Morgan. They advocated a system of secure and humane containment based on three principles: minimum use of custody, minimum use of security and the 'normalization' of the prison. The May Committee did not like the sound of this, noting, inexplicably, that 'humane containment' suffers from 'the fatal defect that it is a means without an end' and that 'it can only result in making prisons into human warehouses – for inmates and staff. It is not therefore a fit rule for hopeful life or responsible management.'[14] They went on: 'Prison staff cannot be asked to operate in a moral vacuum and the absence of real objectives can in the end lead only to the routine brutalization of all the participants.'[15] The Committee advocated a new concept, 'positive custody', which though worthy was defined in the Report in terms as vague and unrealizable as the Prison Rule 1 it sought to replace.

By 1983 realism and clarity had advanced somewhat. Faced with massive overcrowding, poor conditions, deteriorating opportunities for work and education, and low staff morale, the Prisons Board – the management group for the prison service – developed a new definition of the service's task, which, though not precise, moved nearer to a basis for action which could be measured. The new definition, recognizing the economic climate of 1983, starts off: 'To use with maximum efficiency the resources of manpower, money, buildings and plant made available to it by Parliament in order to fulfil the following functions: . . .'[16]

The four functions are not over-ambitious (infinitely less ambitious than King and Morgan's humane containment) and may be summarized as follows:

1   To keep untried and unsentenced prisoners in custody until it is time to bring them to court and then get them to the right court on time.
2   To keep sentenced prisoners in custody for as long as they are meant to be in custody.
3   To provide 'as full a life as is consistent with the facts of custody', particularly concentrating on basics such as medical care, food, baths and clean clothes, work, education and exercise.
4   To help prisoners keep in touch with the community and prepare them for their return to it (if possible).

It may seem a sad decline from the high ideals of changing human beings and sending them back out into the world crime-free to aspirations of giving prisoners a regular bath and ensuring they get their visits from their families. However, since we are still a long way from realizing even these modest ambitions for a good proportion of our prisoners, it at least has the advantage of being both measurable and achievable.

The discussion so far has focused on how the prison service responds to changing views of the right way to deal with convicted criminals and how it turns the messages from the com-

Table 9   Percentages of offenders discharged in 1984 reconvicted within two years: by type of custody and sex

Type of custody	Males	Females
Adult prisoners	47	31
Young offenders		
Detention centres	62	–
Youth custody aged 15–16 on sentence	80	43
Youth custody aged 17–20 on sentence	66	42
Young prisoners	59	45
Total for young offenders	65	42
Total for all offenders	55	34

Source: Prison Statistics, England and Wales, 1987

mentators and politicians into a task that constitutes a satisfying and worthwhile job for 29,000 staff. There is also, of course, the wider question, what part does prison play in the control and prevention of crime? Or, as the Home Office rather coyly expresses it in its handbook, *The Sentence of the Court*: 'The sanctions available to the courts are designed at least partly as punishments, but it is natural to ask to what extent they also serve to prevent crime.'[17] Another way of formulating this question is, does prison work? This usually means, does it stop those who are sent there committing crimes again? Facts and figures in answer to this are straightforward. No, it is not very successful.

Table 9 shows that the majority of people leaving prison are not so chastened by their ordeal that they refrain from committing more crime. The young especially seem to pay it little heed (note the rate of 80 per cent for the fifteen–sixteen-year-olds). Even the average male adult seems to be prepared to risk it again in many cases. Of those leaving prison in 1984, three out of ten were back inside by 1986.

An interesting case study of the effectiveness of locking people up is provided by the 'short, sharp shock' experiment for young men. The idea that doing something quite nasty to aggressive and disorderly young men from the working classes will stop them in their tracks and turn them into peaceful and law-abiding citizens has a long and inglorious history.[18] It has come to the aid of many a politician faced with a clamour from supporters about how there has been a failure to clamp down on youthful law-breaking and it came to the aid of William Whitelaw at the Conservative Party Conference in 1979. He promised new 'glasshouse'-type centres for young 'thugs and hooligans' that would 'wipe the smiles off their faces'. He said:

> These centres will be no holiday camps. I hope that those who attend will not ever want to go back. From 6.45 a.m. to lights out at 9.30 p.m. life will be conducted at a brisk tempo. Much greater emphasis will be put on hard and constructive activities, on discipline and on tidiness, on self-respect and respect for those in authority. We will formally introduce drill, parades and inspections. Offenders will have to earn their limited privileges by good behaviour.[19]

An experiment was to be set up, at one senior detention centre, New Hall in Yorkshire (for seventeen–twenty-one-year-olds), and one junior, Send in Surrey (for fourteen–seventeen-year-olds). The aim was to be: 'To assess whether young offenders can be effectively deterred from committing further offences by spending a period of weeks in a detention centre with a more rigorous and demanding regime.'[20]

The experiment started on 21 April 1980 and was evaluated by the Prison Department's own young offender psychology unit. The evaluation was overseen by a committee which included two outside academics. The researchers looked at two main questions, were the regimes more rigorous and demanding, and were young offenders deterred by them?

A number of interesting facts emerged from the evaluation report, which was published in July 1984. Personality tests on the young offenders in the centres showed that they 'contained a disproportionate number of temperamentally difficult and unhappy individuals'.[21] About 10 per cent were illiterate. Of those who had left school, nearly half were unemployed when they were sent to the detention centres. The changes that were made meant that the increased physical education was at the expense of daytime education classes. At the senior detention centres increased physical education was at the expense of time given to work. A workshop at Send and a training course in building skills at New Hall were closed.

So, the response to illiterate, unemployed youths was to cut the education and the training course and substitute more physical education. It was rumoured at the time that the physical education department of the prison service was most reluctant to take part in the new regimes because they said it detracted from their professionalism. It appears from the report that the young men enjoyed the physical education. What they liked least was the dirty, boring work. By comparison the drill was popular 'and aspects of physical education positively attractive'.[22]

The main finding was that the experiment 'had no discernible effect on the rate at which trainees were reconvicted'.[23] Unfortunately Mr Whitelaw's hope that those who attended would never want to go back was not fulfilled. The rate at which the young men in the experimental centres committed further offences was the same as for those in non-experimental centres.

No one with any knowledge of penal matters could have been surprised at these findings. Nor was anyone with experience of the importance of politics in penal matters surprised to hear that the reaction to the report proving the experiment had failed was to extend it to the rest of the detention centre system. Leon Brittan, then Home Secretary, announced the extension on 24 July 1984, saying: 'In incorporating much of the experimental regime on a permanent basis it will provide a penalty to which courts can turn with confidence when dealing with an offender for whom a short period in custody is necessary.'[24] But there was to be one change. The aspect they had enjoyed, the drill, was to be dropped, and replaced with hard work. The end of the story is well known. Detention centres as such were abolished in October 1988.

The evaluation of the new detention centre regimes is just another addition to a shelf full of volumes establishing that prison does not do a lot of good in terms of persuading people to give up a life of crime. On the other hand, does it do harm? Does a spell in prison make it more difficult for people to resist the temptations of crime and lead a law-abiding life?

It is generally agreed that it does. Common sense suggests that those who are spending all their time, day in day out, with people all characterized by having broken the law will devote some part of that time to talking about what they all have in common, that is, breaking the law. They will probably discuss their successes and failures and dream about doing it more successfully and getting away with it next time. As a nineteenth-century prison inspector put it:

It is painful to reflect that the remedy provided by law for the correction of the offender, should only tend to render him more criminal. Of many children whom we have seen in prison, we hesitate not to affirm, that absolute impunity would have been far less mischievous than the effects of their confinement ... The detail of exploits, the most successful modes of committing depredations, the disposal of plunder, the narrative of escapes, the phraseology of thieves; these subjects are in the highest degree alluring to the young offender, and are eagerly discussed.[25]

Going to prison also has practical implications which make it difficult for people coming out to keep any good resolutions they may have made about going straight. It is even harder to get a job than it would be without a prison record. Speaking at a conference on unemployment and offenders in 1985, the Controller of Group Resources at the Legal and General Insurance Company said: 'I would say that with the majority of employers the situation is – if they know that the applicant is an ex-offender they won't touch them with a barge-pole. If they don't know they are an ex-offender and find out later, then they are almost certain to sack them.'[26]

A home has often been lost and it is very difficult for an unemployed person – much less an ex-prisoner – to find somewhere decent to live. Those who went to prison without much self-confidence or ability to make decisions for themselves will probably find it even harder to manage without the mind-deadening regimentation of a prison.

If, pursuing a good resolution to go straight, they give up all their old friends, going straight can present the quite unattractive option of a boring, lonely existence in a hostel or rented room, eking out the week on income support.

Maybe not much has changed since James Greenwood, a nineteenth-century journalist and novelist, wrote of a prisoner in the 1860s:

He comes out of prison, determined to reform. But where is he to go? What is he to do? How is he to live? Whatever may have been done for him in prison, is of little or no avail, if as soon as he leaves the gaol he must go into the world branded with crime . . . Frequently the newly discharged prisoner passes through a round of riot and drunkenness immediately on his release from a long incarceration, as any other man would do in similar circumstances . . . The discharged prisoner leaves gaol with good resolves, but the moment he enters the world, there rises before him the dark and spectral danger of being hunted down by the police, and being recognized and insulted, of being shunned and despised by his fellow workmen, of being everywhere contemned and forsaken.[27]

There is another way though in which prison can be said to work. It works, even if not for those sent to it, if its existence deters all those who do not end up sent to it. Deterrence is a very complex question. According to criminologist Keith Bottomley it is 'one of the most difficult aspects of penal policy on which to reach firm conclusions'.[28] Overall, it would seem that the fact that there is prison may deter some people on some occasions from committing some offences (although we do not know whom, when and which) but the amount of prison, that is, three months or twelve months or two years, seems not to affect the amount it deters.

To return to the evaluation report of the detention centre experiment, the researchers looked at the effect of introducing the new 'tougher' experiments on crime rates in the area round the courts where defendants were eligible to go to the new centres. They found that it had no effect on crime rates overall; it did not affect trends in crime among young people generally, nor in the areas where use of the pilot centres was available to the courts.

Research suggests that having tough penalties can deter but usually for offences that are at the bottom of the scale of seriousness, for example, illegal parking, and often only for a short time, perhaps while people weigh up the likelihood of being caught. Different people and groups are likely to react very differently to penal measures designed to deter crime. Many serious crimes are committed in such emotional circumstances that it is highly unlikely that thoughts of the consequences, for example, 'How many years in prison will I get for doing this?', enter into the calculation much at all.

Evidence also suggests that in general people have only a vague idea of what sentences the courts give for what offences – so the level of sentences handed out to particular individuals does not have a wider effect. Even when a particularly heavy sentence is handed out, and intended as a deterrent, and is therefore highly publicized, it seems not to have the desired effect. Researchers from the Home Office followed up the case of a youth given a twenty-year sentence for his part in a violent attack and robbery of a man in Birmingham. The sentence received wide publicity in Birmingham and nationally – and was intended to be 'a deterrent sentence', that is, to show others what would happen to them if they committed similar crimes, and thus stop them. The researchers studied the rate of robberies reported in Birmingham for several months before and after the trial and found that the figures were quite unaffected by the trial and the much-publicized sentence.[29]

What does seem to influence people more than the severity of punishment they might get is whether they are likely to get caught – and the consequences of being caught: that is, publicity, being in the newspapers, everyone knowing about it. The offender caught in crime for the first time is more likely to ask 'Will it be in the papers?' than 'Will they send me to prison?'[30] As the American academic Philip Cook puts it, 'An arrest for shoplifting, followed by a dismissal of charges, may be of little consequence for an unemployed teenager, but may ruin the life of a college professor.'[31]

Philip Cook also summarizes very well the difficulty of working out how to deter people from committing crime by adjusting the punishments available: 'the quest for a single set of universally applicable estimates of deterrence effects is hopeless . . .'[32] There seems therefore to be no reason to justify specific prison sentences or their length in terms of deterring the public at large from committing further crimes.

Another way of answering the question, does it work? might be to calculate how much crime it reduces by putting out of circulation those who would otherwise be committing crime. This is also a difficult question and researchers have come up with widely differing answers – but it is reasonable to conclude that the overall amount of imprisonment has no great effect on crime rates. The crimes reported to the police are only a proportion of those committed – the percentage of offenders who get caught for committing those crimes is only a percentage of those who commit crime – and the percentage of those sent to prison is only a percentage of those who are caught. Prison therefore is a very haphazard, selective and limited way of reducing crime. Its effectiveness in containing serious or dangerous offenders and thus ensuring they do not continue to commit crime is very great. But these are a small proportion of the prison population. Its effectiveness in reducing the amount of middle-range crimes against property, especially those committed by the non-professional criminal, is probably slight. Two Home Office researchers, Stephen Brody and Roger Tarling, studied what is called 'the incapacitation effects of imprisonment' and concluded that sending fewer people to prison would have a negligible effect on the recorded crime rate. They calculated that if actual prison sentences were reduced by six months, the time prisoners spend in prison would be reduced by 40 per cent and the number of convictions would increase by 1.6 per cent.[33]

This general discussion is perhaps best summed up in the way done by the Home Office itself in the handbook for courts, *The Sentence of the Court*:

The research evidence . . . suggests that within the realistic range of choice, imposing particular sentences, or particularly severe sentences, has a very limited effect on crime levels.[34]

Longer periods of custody do not produce better results than shorter ones.[35]

The probability of arrest and conviction is likely to deter potential offenders, whereas the perceived severity of the ensuing penalties has little effect.[36]

No realistic increase in prison terms would make a substantial impact on crime rates simply by virtue of locking up the particular offenders caught, convicted and sentenced.[37]

We are forced to conclude that prison does not constitute a

very effective or constructive way of dealing with criminals or reducing crime. We have not thought of anything better for dangerous, violent, serious offenders – and prison has force as a symbol of the importance of keeping the law and of society's condemnation of those who offend against it. But we would do just as well to use it much less and make it a much more constructive experience. We can ask the question, would it make any measurable difference to levels of crime, peace on the streets and social well-being, if the prison population, instead of being say 50,000, were 35,000, 30,000 or even 20,000 (the rough equivalent for England and Wales of the Dutch prison population)? Probably not – but it would make a great deal of difference to those left inside, who would experience much better conditions, and to prison staff, who could then do a really decent job, develop a real welfare role, go on training courses, get out of the institution to work with community organizations, innovate and experiment.

5   The Custodians

Prison officers – their perspective

What we have seen since then (January 1985) is deterioration of our conditions, insane financial controls, broken promises and agreements, complete disregard for health and safety of staff and inmates alike ... I accuse the Department of having a pre-planned, pre-meditated, organized attack on prison officers and on the POA ... I'll tell you why they did it. It is really very simple. They did it to cover up their own incompetence and their own inaccuracy. That's what they've done. If they were in outside industry, they would have been sacked years ago for incompetence. 'We reserve the right to manage,' they said. God in Heaven, if only they would. We are sick and tired as prison officers of propping up their lousy system because they can't get it right ... Wormwood Scrubs prison had £6 million spent on A wing, hospital and kitchen, and when all the boffins from head office with their brief-cases and their bowler hats and their pinstripe suits cracked the champagne and toasted the success of the mission we moved into A wing. You couldn't drink the water – it was contaminated. You couldn't wash the trays because the sewage came up in the sinks. That was just for starters. They spent nearly a million pounds on the hospital. They will now look you in the eye and say: It's not going to open. A million pounds. No problem. A beautiful new eighty-bed hospital ...

For too long the prison service has suffered from crisis and isolated management. Career civil servants have used us as a political football for their own gain. We are governed by people who have never seen a prison. They come from the

> Ministry of Agriculture, Fisheries and Food and they get
> promotion and they're telling us what to do. They've never
> seen a prison but it's OK because they're civil servants and
> they've got it right.
>
> Delegate from Wormwood Scrubs speaking to the POA
> Annual Conference, 20 May 1986.

The prison staff are at the very centre of any discussion
about change or improvement in the prison system. They see
prisoners every day, talk to them, listen to their complaints
and problems, and help them, or ignore them, as the case may
be. They, and not prison administrators, even the most committed and progressive prison administrators, determine the atmosphere of a prison, the level of day-to-day fairness and freedom
from harassment that prevails. They decide whether well-inten-
tioned reforms will be carried through or subverted.

A lot of people work in prisons, as well as the management
(the governor class) and the workers (the prison-officer class).
Probation officers, who technically still work for their own
probation service, are seconded to the prison for a spell of two
or three years. Chaplains from the Church of England, and
Roman Catholic and Methodist churches, work directly for the
prison service and have their own head administrator, the
chaplain-general at Prison Department headquarters. Doctors
also work for the Prison Department (although many are part-
time and normally work in the NHS) and have their own head
at headquarters, the Director of Prison Medical Services. Teachers technically work for the local education authority and are
seconded to the prison. There is also a Chief Education Officer
at headquarters. There are 2,600 industrial staff, for example,
drivers, stokers, caretakers, mechanics, fitters and car park
attendants, and around 130 psychologists.

The specialists are numerous, but their influence is not great.
At least, one assumes it is not. It is hard to imagine that any of
those from professions concerned with the health of the body
and mind, the condition of the soul, the stimulation of the
intellect or the social welfare of prisoners would wish the prison
system to be as it is. The real power to determine the culture,
ethos and atmosphere of a prison comes from a negotiation

between the governing staff and the prison officers. On 1
August 1988 there were 19,135 prison officers: 18,060 men
and 1,075 women. Figures for the numbers of black prison
officers are now being collected. Of those filling in the forms in
1988, 0.6 per cent were black.[1] However the response rate
was below 50 per cent, so no one really knows.[2] However
most observers would agree that apart from a few black women
officers at Holloway, a black prison officer is a rarity. It would
also be very hard to find a black governor.

Mixed staffing has been slow in coming and fiercely resisted
in some places. Although there has been flexibility for some
time with governors and dog handlers, in September 1988
only 138 officers were working in prisons where the prisoners
were of the opposite sex.[3] The appointment of the first two
women officers to Dartmoor gave rise to press coverage. The
Daily Mirror greeted the news with the words 'Stand by your
beds, Jailbirds! Petticoat power has arrived at Dartmoor. So
from now on you had better mind your language.'[4]

The prerequisite for a constructive and humane prison
system would seem to be well-trained and committed staff who
get satisfaction from their work and feel that the difficult and
sometimes dangerous job they do is understood and appreciated
by those in authority over them. Unfortunately the reality is
rather different. The history of industrial relations in the prison
service is a history of failure going back many years. No one
should have been surprised at the way the industrial relations
problems of the prisons burst into the headlines in April 1986
and have rumbled on ever since. The potential for such a
breakdown has been there for a long time.

At the 1985 POA Annual Conference the Home Secretary
was received with a great lack of enthusiasm. Responding to
his speech the General Secretary, David Evans, said: 'Home
Secretary. You have been received in this Hall with some scepticism. We are not rude people but we have been let down so
often ... We have suffered for years from people making
nothing but empty promises to us.'[5]

Until 1987 the prison service staffing structure was organized on a quasi-military model with a 'lower ranks' force of
prison officers, going up to the rank of chief officer, and an

'officer' class of managers, consisting of non-uniformed governor grades with direct entry for those coming from higher education. In 1987 the service was unified on the model of the police force with only one point of entry (the bottom) and the same career prospects for all entrants. The distinctions between management and managed have thus been softened although structurally the unification has not made much difference. Staff wear uniforms up to a certain level and then move at chief officer level into civilian clothes. The notion that all staff including governors should go into uniform was floated but rejected, much to the disgust of the POA. A POA official attacked the decision, accusing the Home Office of fearing the unity a wholly uniformed service would create. This is why, he says, 'they directed that not only would governors continue to wear civilian clothing but also that two of the senior prison officer ranks should also wear civilian clothing in future. Thus they succeeded in creating a further division rather than healing an existing one.'[6] A prison officer from Manchester prison put his feelings about the change into verse.

> Chief Officer One, Chief Officer Two
> Whatever has become of you?
> Where are the men who led the staff?
> They've gone and joined the other half.[7]

The old structure persists in the trade union organization also. The former prison officer grades are organized through the Prison Officers Association. The governors are in a different association. Until 1987 they constituted a small section of a large civil service union, the Society of Civil and Public Servants. They then broke away and formed the Prison Governors Association, a trade union outside the TUC. This widened the gulf still further, as the POA refused to sit down with them.

Such a structure reinforced feelings about inferior status. According to a government survey concluded in 1982, many prison officers 'believe that others view them with suspicion, as though the miasma of prison clung to them outside and deflected otherwise good intentions. Others felt looked down upon or, . . . felt they were seen as bullies, hard and unfeeling, even brutal.'[8]

The current atmosphere of suspicion and resentment between the Prison Officers Association and prison management
goes back many years. The 1970s was a decade of bad industrial relations in prisons, characterized by regular disputes with
staff. For example in 1976 there were thirty-four incidents of
industrial action by POA branches; in 1977 there were forty-
two and in 1978 the number was 119. At the end of that year,
in November 1978, the Home Secretary, Merlyn Rees, set up a
Committee of Inquiry into the United Kingdom Prison Services
under Mr Justice May. The Committee finished its report in
1979. In that year industrial action took place in thirty-nine
prisons. Some incidents lasted only a day – others up to twelve
months. The Prison Officers Association told the May Committee:

In 1976 the Government ordered a cut in man hours equal to a
saving of £2 million . . . A number of branches felt . . . they had no
alternative but to take industrial action and this attitude was subsequently vindicated by additions to the manpower budget.
This gave the outward impression that industrial action was the
only effective means of securing common-sense decisions from 'management' and since that time its use has formed part of the fabric of
industrial relations in the Prison Service.[9]

In its report, the May Committee made some damning observations on the industrial relations record of the prison service:
'. . . the prison officer unlocking forty criminals on a wing in
an establishment as much as three hundred miles from London
saw the headquarters of his service as a faceless monolith
caring not for human beings . . .'[10]
The Committee felt that perhaps the prison officer had got it
right. They concluded: '. . . at the very least there seemed to
have been a failure at the centre to carry the service along
with it and that the lack of clear, identifiable, effectively communicating leadership had played its part[11] . . . That something
has gone wrong with relations between staff and local and
central management is undeniable – evidence of distrust, alien-
ation and suspicion occurred too frequently for the reality of
that to be seriously in doubt.'[12]
An understanding of the industrial relations background is

essential to an understanding of why even the most obvious reforms in our prisons have been so long in coming: why, for example, the majority of prisoners' letters are still censored, even in cases where there is no security argument for doing so; why the idea of prisoners being able to use the telephone to keep in touch with their families has provoked such a hostile reaction among staff; why prison officers resent prisoners having access to a range of good education provision.

What is a prison officer's job really like and how do prison officers feel? In response to the criticisms of the May Committee that there was a great gulf between the staff working in the prisons and the Home Office management of the prison service, the Home Office commissioned the Social Survey Division of the Office of Population Censuses and Surveys (OPCS) to look into staff attitudes in the service. The survey was carried out in 1982 and the analysis in 1983. The Report was eventually published in March 1985.

The survey found that the majority of prison staff have a background in the armed forces, and most of these as regulars. Of discipline prison officers (that is, the non-specialist prison officers) 40 per cent have no educational qualifications and only a very small number have any full-time education after the age of seventeen. Three out of ten have O-levels and a number have trade qualifications. The report concludes that prison officers are: 'a remarkably homogeneous group of people. The great majority are middle-aged family men . . . The majority share some kind of military background in an age where such a background is becoming increasingly rare. They have the kind of educational and previous employment background usually associated with manual workers − but few other social characteristics that would place them as members of the working-class community.'[13]

Their separateness is reinforced by the circumstances of their jobs. Officers who live in prison houses (about one in three) often live in remote places, for example near Dartmoor or at Haverigg in Cumbria, with other prison officers for company. Even those who own their own houses often live in prison-dominated communities because of the remote locations of many prisons. Being what the Civil Service calls 'mobile', and therefore likely to be moved on anywhere in the country in the course of a career, must contribute to the prison officers' dependence on other prison officers for social and community life.

A strong sense of being undervalued by the organization that employs them emerges from the OPCS survey. Most prison officers feel that 'the people who make decisions should give more consideration to the personal lives of staff (89 per cent)'.[14] Most prison officers agree that management does not care enough about prison staff, that officers are not supported when criticized (86 per cent), that the authorities are too frightened of public opinion (80 per cent) and that society cares more about prisoners than staff (84 per cent).[15]

Prison officers live with a very wide gap between what they know the purpose of their job is officially meant to be, that is rehabilitation of prisoners for a good and useful life, and reality. A majority mention rehabilitation as a purpose of prison but a majority also say prison is 'not at all successful' at rehabilitating prisoners. However, nearly all prison officers think prison is partly or very successful at looking after prisoners humanely.

They seem also to be insecure in their relationships with the outside world. Nearly half say they prefer not to tell people they meet socially that they work in the prison service. Prison officers feel that people outside are suspicious or guarded if they know they are prison officers. A large minority feel people would look down on them. The police are the prison officers' most important reference group and references to the police are frequent in prison officers' views of their own status and role. A majority feel that being a prison officer has affected them – by making them more cynical and suspicious of others.

Women prison staff were surveyed separately as their numbers are much smaller. Generally their views are similar to those of the men but they are likely to 'take a somewhat more vocational view of their work' and are 'less ambitious'.[16]

The researchers summed up their findings on prison officers' views of their job as being generally jaundiced. 'It is,' they said, 'a feeling that contains an odd mixture of bravado, cynicism, resentment and, it must be said, *fear*.'[17]

More clues as to prison officers' attitudes emerge from the *POA* magazine, called *Gatelodge* (the gatelodge is the entrance to the prison where staff assemble before and after duty). Each prison has a branch of the Prison Officers Association, which puts in notes about local events which they feel colleagues in other prisons would be interested in. These, and the readers' letters, are a rich source of information about what is going on in prisons and how officers are feeling about them. Complaints always feature, sometimes it seems well-founded, about the seeming lunacy of those in charge, for example from Gloucester prison in February 1988:

Well, the £3 million 'White Elephant' gatehouse still sits at the end of our drive, lit up like a Christmas tree at night, but the only people to occupy it are workmen at present. I suppose eventually it will be fully operational sometime in 1988/89/90. Who knows?[18]

A similar line appears in a letter from Grendon:

It has to be said, and will probably cost me dearly, but what sort of a tinpot outfit do we all work for? I am now the proud owner of a new style tunic that doesn't fit and has no insignia, two caps with no badges and a promise of some trousers to match the tunic sometime in the future.[19]

Feelings of bitterness and cynicism about the whole purpose of the job emerge from a contribution in the February 1988 issue from Wetherby youth custody centre:

It's all about cost cutting, economy, savings etc., and the neverending form filling to perform. The inmates have dropped off the agenda, because the people who need to deal with them are all being enrolled as SPAR form compilers. SPAR used to mean somewhere that one acquired cheap groceries from. Maybe that's where they hit upon the word SPAR. CHEAP!! (SPAR stands for staff planning and reporting system.)[20]

Another abiding and pervasive gripe is that prisoners get more attention than staff. From Ranby prison in April 1988 comes the sharp comment:

The new hotel, sorry, prison is nearly finished and it's likely by the time these jottings are published the first inmates will have been issued with the keys to their rooms . . .[21]

And, more worrying, from Buckley Hall detention centre:

We open with the very disturbing news of the dismissal of colleague and P O A member . . . Briefly, a D C boy made an allegation of assault and although patently untrue, the department believed the boy. Twenty-three years of service down the drain on the word of a convicted DC boy. Despite the fact that there was no evidence, the department did their level best to make an example of the officer. This dictatorial attempt by management to keep their 'serfs' in order has only succeeded in exacerbating an already difficult atmosphere.[22]

However, it must be said that prison service matters do not occupy the bulk of the Branch News columns. Most of the material consists of descriptions of social events. Postings, illnesses, bereavements and achievements figure prominently. There is also a strong emphasis on charitable work, for example a Sponsored Jail Break from Kingston prison in Portsmouth in aid of the Great Ormond Street Appeal.

Overall a picture emerges from the magazine very akin to that revealed in the OPCS research of a close-knit group of mainly family men – looking to each other for social life and support, feeling misunderstood, unappreciated and looking at life with a semi-humorous, semi-bitter, cynical pessimism – a group where breaking ranks in any way is very difficult, because the bonds are strong, professionally, socially and culturally. The attitudes of women prison officers, as revealed in the contributions from the women's prisons, are remarkably similar in tone and ethos. The prison officers found themselves particularly isolated at the 1980 TUC Congress. Their motion in favour of a referendum on the subject of re-introducing capital punishment was introduced by the POA chairman, Colin Steel:

My colleagues will tell you that there is not a more onerous duty, a worse or more horrifying duty, than sitting on the condemned cell duty . . . We are not seeking the restoration of capital punishment because there is something in it for us . . .[23]

There was no seconder. The motion fell.

A prison officer's job has elements in common with a number of other professional groups – psychiatric nurses, for instance, or the police. But it has unique features – none of those a prison officer looks after are there voluntarily and they need attention twenty-four hours a day. Few other jobs require the postholder to supervise the emptying of several hundred chamber-pots several times a day. And, of course, the prison population of around 50,000 contains, as well as petty offenders, unsuccessful burglars and fine defaulters, some of the most violent, difficult and dangerous people there are. One prisoner, who has killed two other prisoners, spends his day in a specially constructed cell within a cell which allows him to watch television or play chess without involving the large number of staff which are felt to be necessary whenever his cell door is opened.

Fatal assaults on prison officers are fortunately very rare. During the past forty years two prison officers in England and Wales have been murdered on duty – one in 1948 and the other in 1965 – a much lower figure than the one for the police. The figures for assaults on prison officers are more difficult to disentangle. In 1986 12 offences of 'gross personal violence to an officer', 37 attempts to commit 'gross personal violence' and 3,394 offences of assaulting an officer or attempting to do so were punished internally. However these figures do not distinguish between assaults leading to injury and assaults which are more an affront to the dignity of an officer or signal an impending breakdown of control which is ultimately contained. Also they do not show assaults where a case against the assailant is taken to an outside court. More useful as a measure may be the figure for assaults requiring an officer to be off work for more than three days. In 1985 there were 363.[24] An edition of *Gatelodge* chosen at random (August 1988) lists 40 assaults on staff in one month.

As prisons are so different, so the likelihood of being assaulted varies considerably. It is illuminating to look at the assault rates of two of the dispersal, i.e. top security prisons. At Albany on the Isle of Wight in 1986, there were two attempts to do gross personal violence to an officer and 53 other assaults on officers. At Long Lartin there were none of the most serious assault offences and twelve other assaults. The Chief Inspector reports from an inspection of Liverpool prison in 1987 that: 'there had been nine assaults by prisoners upon staff during the preceding 12 months'.[25] Northallerton, a youth custody centre, experienced two assaults against staff in 1986–7, neither of them serious.[26] At Ford prison in 1986 'there were more assaults on staff (6) than at any other open prison'.[27] At East Sutton Park, a women's establishment in Kent inspected in 1987 'there had been no record of assaults upon staff for over two years'.[28]

Individual assaults are one problem. Collective action by prisoners is a different, and more frightening, one. The British prison system has its history of riots – involving groups of prisoners, extensive damage to prison buildings, assaults on officers, and on occasion retaliatory action by staff. The riot at Parkhurst in 1969 was a portent of things to come. The official report on it was never made public and the Prison Department's Annual Report for 1969 notes only that 'on 24 October a serious disturbance occurred at Parkhurst in which a number of prison officers were injured; nine prisoners were subsequently committed for trial'.[29]

The peak year for prisoner demonstrations was 1972. The Annual Report of that year says: 'The prison service experienced a year of disruption on a scale not previously encountered', but goes on, reassuringly: 'It is nevertheless proper to keep these events in perspective . . . In the many other aspects of the Department's work a year of solid progress can be recorded.'[30]

In fact a series of demonstrations started at Brixton early in May and ended with demonstrations at twenty-nine prisons at the end of August and beginning of September. 'During the intervening months, while the incidence of demonstrations was uneven, there was never a period of more than a week or so – and often only a few days at a time – when one or more of the forty-one prisons concerned did not experience some demonstration.'[31] On 4 August twenty-eight demonstrations were taking place involving 5,500 prisoners. As the year wore on the protests grew violent, culminating in serious incidents at Albany at the beginning of November, and Gartree at the end of November, where damage was done to the buildings.

Even more serious was the riot at Hull in 1976 between 31 August and 3 September. Damage amounting to £750,000 was caused. Five months after the riot a police inquiry began into assaults on prisoners by prison officers at the end of the riot. In May 1977 the National Prisoners Movement PROP, a radical group of prisoners and ex-prisoners, set up its own public inquiry into the events, chaired by an eminent QC. On 4 April 1979 eight prison officers were found guilty of conspiring to assault prisoners and were given suspended prison sentences.

Trouble blew up again at Gartree on 5 October 1978 and lasted throughout the night. Three of the four wings were taken over by prisoners and extensive damage was done. A total of 150 prisoners had to be transferred.

In 1979 there was trouble at Parkhurst again when five prisoners caused damage estimated at £50,000 and made two wings of the prison unfit for use. However, the Parkhurst trouble was overshadowed by the much-publicized incident on 31 August at Wormwood Scrubs which first introduced the public to a till-then secret new development in the prison service, the MUFTI teams. MUFTI stands for Minimum Use of Force Tactical Intervention and means specially trained prison officers in riot gear, brandishing sticks.

The Wormwood Scrubs incident did more damage to prison service credibility than any other incident in recent prison history. It was from beginning to end a saga of incompetence, fear, secrecy, deception and brutality. The facts are by now more or less clear, although it took two and a half years for some of them to emerge officially. Relationships between staff and prisoners in D wing, the long-termers' wing at Wormwood Scrubs, had been deteriorating for some months. Prisoners felt particularly aggrieved that POA demands for increased staffing had led to the closure of their education centre. On the night of 31 August a non-violent demonstration by prisoners was broken up by squads of prison officers in riot gear. The following day the Home Office reported that no prisoners had been injured and the whole thing had been over in a few minutes. On 7 September the National Prisoners Movement (PROP) began picketing outside the prison and handing out a leaflet saying that injuries to prisoners were 'numerous and some of them serious'.[32] On 10 September the Home Office admitted that five prisoners had been slightly injured. On 27 September

PROP held a press conference at which it was alleged that about sixty prisoners had been hurt, and many of these had head wounds which needed stitching. In October two voluntary prison visitors from the prison appeared on television to say that there had been a cover-up and many prisoners had been injured. Their status as prison visitors was subsequently withdrawn. On 22 October the Home Secretary in a written parliamentary answer admitted that a total of fifty-four prisoners and eleven prison officers incurred injuries.[33] In October a prison official, Keith Gibson, was commissioned to investigate the incident and report. This struck many as a strange decision as Keith Gibson was the Regional Director with operational responsibility for Wormwood Scrubs and had initially praised the staff for regaining control. In 1980 the investigation came to a halt because Keith Gibson reached the conclusion that there had been 'criminal assaults on prisoners by prison officers'. The police were then called in to investigate but no charges were brought because the police concluded that 'difficulties of identification and absence of independent corroboration'[34] meant there was insufficient evidence. This decision cleared the way for the finalization and publication of the Gibson Report, which was eventually published in 1982.

At the time of its publication some described it as a 'whitewash'. However, although it left many questions unanswered – could the Home Office really have been so inept in finding out how many prisoners were injured? – it nevertheless revealed quite a shocking set of events. Apart from Keith Gibson's conclusion of evidence of assaults on prisoners by prison officers, the governor seems to have given out inaccurate information about the incident for several weeks afterwards. The Principal Medical Officer gave inaccurate information to the prison's Board of Visitors, a group of lay people appointed by the Home Secretary to act as a watchdog for the prison, as late as October.[35] After the incident the prison officers imposed a total clampdown on the wing. No visitors were allowed for two weeks. Chaplains, probation officers and psychologists were not allowed in. Voluntary prison visitors were kept out for three months. Prisoners had no exercise for three days. No bathing facilities were allowed until 6 September. Those prisoners involved in the incident were not allowed to work for seven weeks. Education staff were not allowed in to do Open University tutorials until the middle of October. Prisoners were not allowed out of their cells for association until January of the following year. The governor did not try to stop this. In fact there were strong indications that 'the Governor came under pressure from the POA so severe that some of the policy decisions affecting the wing that he made at the time were against his own better judgement and the advice of his own most senior advisers'.[36] At a regular heads of department meeting on 12 September, one of the psychologists asked why there seemed to be a discrepancy between the published figures of injured prisoners and the higher numbers in the prison records. After this, the local POA branch took industrial action against the Psychology Department in the form of total non-cooperation. This lasted until 1 January 1980. No questions about or criticisms of the higher echelons of prison management appeared in the Gibson Report however. Prison officers may well have felt that perhaps not all of the blame should have been directed at the foot-soldiers. What about the generals, bringing up the rear? Perhaps they gave the wrong orders.

After the trauma at Wormwood Scrubs relative calm was maintained until 1983 when in May a serious riot took place, yet again at Albany. The riot lasted from 19 to 25 May and damage estimated at £1 million was done.

Also in 1983, in June, another disturbance took place at Wormwood Scrubs, where:

Twenty-five inmates took control of the upper landings and threw mops, buckets, cell doors and furniture at staff on the ground floor. With great presence of mind and considerable courage the wing Principal Officer immediately led his staff on to the landings where they drew their staves when confronted by inmates armed with broken furniture. Staff quickly regained control but twenty-five of them received minor injuries and six inmates required medical treatment.[37]

In 1984–5 things were more peaceful. There were thirty-seven acts of 'concerted indiscipline' (which is about the normal level in a year), usually involving refusing to work or refusing food. The style of protest more common in Northern Ireland prisons, the 'dirty protest' which involves prisoners smearing excrement over the interior of their cells, also came to Wormwood Scrubs. Six prisoners in the segregation unit started a 'dirty protest' in January. At Gartree discontent erupted for four days in February, starting with a complaint about food and ending with a refusal to work. Also at Gartree, a prisoner spent most of the winter on the roof, climbing up on 24 November 1983 and not coming down until 21 February 1984. And the under twenty-ones, at Glen Parva Youth Custody Centre, made their contribution by 'concerted banging of doors and shouting'.[38] Some of the young prisoners then smashed furniture and windows, and threw burning material out of the windows. Thirteen rooms were damaged.

April 1986 saw a fusion of these two interconnected facets of prison life, that is, prison officers' fears and dissatisfactions and prisoners' resentment at the conditions of their imprisonment. Prison officers imposed a work-to-rule because of a dispute with the Home Office on who decides manning levels. Prisoners in eighteen prisons reacted to the situation by going on the rampage, causing £4.5 million worth of damage and putting one prison completely out of action. And it goes on. 1988 has seen a new phenomenon, disorder in low security Category C establishments. In May there was trouble at Rollestone, on Salisbury Plain, an army camp converted to use as a prison only a few weeks before in response to the March population crisis. In June serious trouble erupted at Haverigg, a prison for 250 men in Cumbria. In July a riot took place at Lindholme, the old RAF camp in Yorkshire, bought and opened very quickly during the 1985 population crisis.

Since the early seventies there has been a continuing pattern of prisoners and prison staff reacting in their own way to discontent: staff by industrial action and prisoners by disturbances. Each incident served to heighten the tension and make the next outbreak more likely. Prison officers reacted defensively to prisoner disturbances by clamping down. Prisoners reacted to the clampdown by demonstrations and so the cycle went on becoming less and less retrievable as time went by.

The major incidents in the top-security prisons left behind a legacy of bitterness and resentment. The prison service has a very long memory and all these events have sunk very deep into the prison service psyche.

It is fundamental to any institution where one group of people is responsible for keeping another group in against their will, preventing them from doing what they want to do – and making them do what they do not want to do – that an outbreak of violence against their lot by the incarcerated is always a possibility. Those who run prisons know this and have to develop policies to guard against it, to run prisons as far as possible with consent and to minimize the dangers to their staff. For prison officers this is crucial. If they feel safe and in control they can be expected to listen to new ideas, be interested in change and in improving what they do. If they live in a constant state of fear of losing control, they will resist ideas for change and put their energies into fighting for more protection, for example by having more staff on duty at any one time, more riot-control training, more restrictions on prisoners, more oppressive security hardware.

Some threat of violence is inevitable in a prison setting. But some environments provoke violence and others defuse it. The special unit at Barlinnie Prison in Glasgow, where some of the more violent male prisoners in Scottish prisons have ended up – playing snooker with prison officers, doing painting and sculpture, and entertaining most eloquently a stream of interested visitors – contrasts sharply with, for example, Albany on the Isle of Wight where the architecture, the living conditions and the culture all lead to tension and fear between one prisoner and another, and between officers and prisoners.

Various ways of dealing with and defusing violence can be taught. Courses could be laid on for prison officers on this and other subjects. Unfortunately training for prison officers is one of the lowest priorities in the prison service – the first area to be cut when the cash limits begin to bite. The OPCS researchers found a heavy demand for better training. The Prior Committee on the Prison Disciplinary System* noted:

We were surprised by the low priority apparently given to *staff training*, both initial and in-service, and the lack of proper manage-

* The author was a member of this Committee.

ment and support structures for prison staff. Prison officers receive only twelve weeks basic training. They are then exposed to one of the most difficult and sometimes dangerous jobs people in our society are asked to undertake.[39]

Recent reports by the Chief Inspector suggest that training continues to be the poor relation. At Liverpool prison, for instance, he found staff training 'at a low ebb ... The twin restrictions of cash limits and low staff in post figures had all but removed any possibility of local training'.[40] Commenting on Ford prison the Chief Inspector says 'until financial restraints began to bite many prisons could afford to run high-quality, innovative and useful training programmes.'[41]

The prison administrators in Head Office therefore face quite a tricky problem. Not only do they have to contain too many prisoners in overcrowded conditions, some dangerous, some sick, many in need of help, while watching their backs for any political scandal, they also have to control a work-force of nearly 20,000 officers who feel undervalued, cynical and defensive. For many years they just about achieved this, but at a cost – in money and in an acceptance of inflexible working practices.

Before 1987 the way the prison service organized its workload was so complex that no uninitiate could understand it. An example of an event described in the *POA* magazine illustrated how working practices developed. A prisoner absconded from Ford open prison. He was caught and put in the cells. Arrangements were then made to have the cell-block staffed for twenty-four hours a day until Monday afternoon when the case against the prisoner for absconding could be heard by the Board of Visitors. Presumably he was the only prisoner in the cell-block and without him it would have been closed for the weekend and staff would not have been needed. The deputy governor, conscious no doubt of the pressures on him to save money, arranged for the prisoner to be dispatched to Lewes prison, where cells were staffed already and there would therefore be no extra cost. The staff at Ford were enraged at this decision since they had already fixed the weekend shifts, told their families and were ready for work. They rang their colleagues at Lewes who agreed not to let the prisoner in if he was brought. The staff at Ford then met and agreed that 'if the Dep. [prison service language for deputy governor] went ahead with his daft scheme' they would refuse all overtime. The outcome was, as reported, 'our Dep. decided perhaps, on reflection, he had made a mistake and we should keep the inmate here at Ford . . . It only goes to show . . . this Association is a force to be reckoned with.'[42]

This was the background to the introduction in 1987 of an entirely new working system, optimistically called Fresh Start by the Home Office. Overtime was abolished. New working practices were introduced. Proper management lines were established and prison officers were given specific jobs to do with some continuity.

Such a radical change would have been hard to introduce in a good industrial relations climate. In the climate of the prison service it soon ran into difficulties. The package was agreed by the POA in May 1987. Then the Home Office and the POA fell out over how many extra staff were needed to make up for the hours lost by the abolition of overtime. The POA claims it put the package to its members after assurances that 400 more staff would be recruited. After the ballot, a POA official says, 'came the deceit. The Home Office decided further efficiencies were required, to the tune of 15 per cent. Instead of continuing with recruitment, the Home Office stopped the programme when only 160 staff had been obtained.' He goes on, 'Officers now feel that yet again they were foolish and naive to expect that the Prison Department would keep their word.'[43]

Addressing the 1988 National Conference a year after acceptance of the new deal, the POA Chairman said, 'I turn now to the issue of Fresh Start . . . Everyone tells us how much they have done for us, how much they have spent on us and now how satisfied we are. If this is so, why do we have a mandate for national action and why are so many branches in dispute? The answer we know is that the agreements we entered into in good faith are being ignored and distorted.'[44]

And industrial troubles did indeed break out, at Wormwood Scrubs, Wandsworth, Norwich, Parkhurst, Camp Hill, Pentonville, Brixton and Holloway, where the bulk of the staff walked out. For seven weeks in the summer of 1988 Holloway prison was run by a skeleton staff of twenty officers, governor grades brought in from all over the country, and volunteers – reputedly very happily.

The quasi-military tradition of the prison system is beginning to look less and less appropriate to a prison system in the late twentieth century. A prison officer is recruited with no qualifications except basic literacy and numeracy and certain personal qualities. After twelve weeks' training it is straight into the prison. After two weeks' induction the officer is operational. Informal supervision takes place but it can be patchy. Soon the raw recruit has become a prison officer, guardian of the lives and rights of a landing full of diverse, difficult and unhappy human beings, deprived of most of the pleasures of life, stuck with companions not of their choosing, and wishing they were elsewhere in place and time – not just from nine till five but all day, every day, Christmas Day included.

It could be argued that this is all the training and preparation a prison officer needs – because the difficult tasks, the counselling, the welfare work, the care of souls, is done by the psychiatrists, probation officers and the chaplain. What a mistaken idea that is. First, it is impractical. There are not enough specialists and they are not available all day every day. Secondly it is undesirable to take away from the people who are closest to the prisoners the opportunity to do the rewarding, worthwhile parts of the job. The OPCS researchers found that nearly three quarters of prison officers agreed with the statement: 'Prison Officers are the best people to look after prisoners' welfare.'[45] Indeed the gradual erosion of the welfare role is often seen as one of the major factors in prison officers' loss of morale and growing discontent. In 1963 the POA passed a motion at its Annual Conference calling for prison officers to have a much more active role in prisons than the merely custodial, a role in rehabilitation and after-care. Following this a joint Working Party was set up with the Home Office on the Role of the Prison Officer. The Working Party met for many years and never got anywhere. It was eventually disbanded in 1981. In 1966 it was decided that probation officers should come and work in prisons to be 'prison social workers'. Gradually all the activities except those connected with the basic mechanics of living seemed to pass from prison officers to specially qualified people. More sophisticated prison industries required more trained people to run them and civilian instructors and an industrial manager were brought in. Outside teachers came in greater number. Psychologists were employed on diagnostic testing and regime development.

An attempt to counter prison officers' gradual distancing from the tasks given to the specialists has been made through a project called Social Work in Prisons. Started in 1977 the project has tried out various ways of involving prison officers in welfare work with prisoners. It has had some limited success, but it is not easy to break down well-established habits. A revealing insight comes from an article in the *Prison Service Journal* about how in Leicester prison a new way of working was introduced which involved prison officers in welfare work. This required prison officers to go on a training course. The course was open to all prison officers. The author, a probation officer, writes: 'Initially only six men applied and they were subjected to a considerable amount of ridicule and criticism, some of it in a good-natured way and some less so.'[46]

Some knowledge has accumulated about the likely effects of making a lifetime career of working in institutions full of people to whom society accords low status and who are kept there against their will. You would expect them to become institutionalized. Their view of the world would get narrower and narrower. The smooth running of the institution would become an end in itself. Cynicism would set in as people saw only their failures, that is the prisoners who came back, not the ones who gave up crime. Resistance to change would become a predominant attitude. That is what you would expect. This is what we have got. Yet if you were to ask the Home Office, what steps do you take to counter institutionalization among staff, to get them out working in the community, to allow them to maintain contact with trends in social and penal thinking?, the answer would not even fill one of the terser paragraphs in a Prison Department Annual Report. And if you asked, what do you do to counter cynicism and give prison officers a chance to succeed?, the answer would also not take long to give.

Elsewhere thought has been given to this. In an address to the Annual Conference of Boards of Visitors in October 1984, Hans Tulkens, head of the Dutch prison service from 1975 to 1984, described the methods used in Holland to transform the prison officer's role:

The sixth step is to broaden the job of prison officers in a professional way. So far we added the aspects of care, the humane and understanding way of dealing with prisoners, to the task of maintaining order and security. These are not additional duties in a material sense, but a change of attitude and a different approach. Because this was a particularly important and difficult change it had to be accompanied by structural changes in the organization of the institution: the formation of small groups of prisoners, of teams of officers, the introduction of work consultation and the changing of management structure and methods.[47]

The prison officer is at the centre of the system. And the prison officer's job is crucial to a humane and civilized prison system. This is where reform has to start.

6   Doing Time

What is it like to be a prisoner?

> They treat you like a human being. They say 'Enjoy your
> meal', 'Good morning'. They treat you like a man, they let
> you do things the way you like, they're not always looking
> up your arse for drugs, they don't guard you when you see
> the governor, with two warders either side. Even when you
> go to solitary, you take yourself there. You think 'It can't be
> true, there must be a catch' but there isn't. I just can't
> believe they don't despise you because you're a criminal.
>
> In England, they punish you for being a criminal. Then
> they punish you while they're punishing you. Then you're
> punished for the rest of your life.
>
> English prisoner in a Dutch closed prison, from *Contrasts in
> Tolerance: Postwar Penal Policy in the Netherlands and England
> and Wales* by David Downes.[1]

We have seen in Chapter 5 that life in the prison service is not
all that satisfactory for prison officers. Not surprisingly it is even
less so for prisoners – and while most of them have one great
advantage over prison officers (they will not be staying very long)
they also have some great disadvantages. They cannot go home
at night. They are stuck with the conditions twenty-four hours a
day – and they are at the bottom of the power heap. Prison officers
may feel that they are ignored and undervalued by those above
them. At least they have someone below them to establish their
place in a hierarchy. Prisoners are at the bottom, without many
defences, in a world almost totally closed off from public scrutiny.

When you enter prison to serve a prison sentence many things are taken away from you – not just your personal belongings, your clothes (if you are a man), any tablets or medicines you may be taking, but also your uncontrolled access to the outside world and much that goes to make up your identity. You are given a number, which accompanies you on a file around the system, gets on to a computer at HQ and goes on a little card fixed on to your cell door.

When you arrive at the prison in the evening with lots of others, you are put through a reception procedure conducted by a group of people, prison officers, doctors, who have a lot to get through in a short time. Audrey Peckham, a deputy headmistress sentenced to prison for 'incitement to murder', wrote a book about her experiences in the English penal system. She describes the reception process at Styal prison in Cheshire:

... it was the usual performance: take all your clothes off, put the dressing-gown on, leave all your clothes, go back and wait. Clothes are searched, you are searched, body, feet, hands. Right, get dressed again. Go through the property, trousers, jeans, shirts, three bras, three pants and so on. I had many letters which had been sent to me at Pucklechurch after my trial, and which I had not yet been able to answer. I asked if I might take them, but was told that I could only have two recent letters: that the rest must stay in my property.[2]

You will probably start your prison career in a local prison – most people do – so you will find yourself plunged straight into the worst conditions the prison system has to impose, rather on the lines described by the Chief Inspector of Prisons in his 1984 Report. Overcrowding, he writes,

results in most of these inmates having to use their pots in the presence of one or two other inmates in the confines of a small cell. When the time for slopping out comes the prisoners queue up with their pots for the few toilets on the landing. The stench of urine and excrement pervades the prison. So awful is this procedure that many prisoners become constipated – others prefer to use their pants, hurling them and their contents out of the window when morning comes.[3]

This may comes as rather a shock.

What you do all day will depend on whether or not you are one of the lucky few to get work. If, for instance, you were in

Birmingham prison during the week ending 27 May 1988 you
would have had to be very lucky. Out of the 1,063 prisoners
there, 244 got out of their cells to work, 91 to do 15 hours'
work that week in the workshop, or 23½ hours in the laundry
and 153 doing catering, stores, maintenance duties or clean-
ing. Similarly in Leeds, holding 1,332 prisoners, 318 were
working that week. So your chances of working were about
one in four. However it might have consoled you to reflect that
in Leeds there are only 451 work places anyway so even if
they were all filled your chances of working would only go up
to one in three. If you ended up in Wandsworth your work
chances would be a little better – 31 per cent of prisoners had
some work to do.

The problems of smell linked to the absence of proper sanitation would not be helped by the bathing and clothes-changing
arrangements. In Birmingham, Leeds, Manchester, Wandsworth and Pentonville you would get one bath or shower a
week, unless you were lucky enough to get a dirty job which
entitles you to a shower a day or to use the gymnasium, which
carries a similar bonus. Clothes too have to keep their freshness
for some time. At Wormwood Scrubs and Birmingham you
would get one clean shirt, one T-shirt and two underpants,
vests and pairs of socks each week. At Leeds, Manchester,
Wandsworth and Pentonville you would get two of each.[4] In
Wandsworth prison in 1987 you would frequently have had
to 'paddle through other men's urine towards the end of the
"slopping out" sessions'.[5] You might also have had one plastic
bowl for washing your face and shaving, washing your hands
after using the slop bucket and washing your knife, fork and
spoon after eating.[6]

The prison timetable on p. 83 shows how you would spend
a typical day. If you are serving a short sentence, this is
probably all you will do every day. If your sentence is longer,
you will in due course be moved to a training prison where
there is a programme of work, activities and education.

If you are a black prisoner you will no doubt meet additional
difficulties. Researcher Jennifer Monahan says of prison life:

Casual racism is not just the norm but the fashion . . . And calling a
prisoner 'you black bastard' tends to be regarded by supervisory staff

A Typical Day in a Local Prison for Men

This routine is typical of a day in the life of a male prisoner in one of Britain's local prisons.

7.30 Cell unlocked. Prisoners get hot water and slop out (empty plastic chamber-pot). Razors are handed out and applications to see the governor, probation officer, doctor, etc. are made.

7.50 Prisoners collect breakfast from the hotplate and are locked in their cells to eat it.

8.30 Unlocked. Breakfast trays collected and slop out. Back to cells and details of work shouted out. Prisoners taken to exercise, where they walk around a small garden or yard for an hour.

9.45 Prisoners who are working go to their workshops or other place of work. Unemployed prisoners return to the wing and are locked in their cells.

11.45 Working prisoners return to their wings. Dinner served at the hotplate and eaten in cells. This is the main meal of the day. Cell doors remain locked for the prison officers' lunch break.

2.00 Slop out and return to work. Unemployed prisoners remain in the cells.

4.00 Working prisoners return to the wings and collect their tea which is eaten in their cells. They are also given a small cake which they can save for supper. They then slop out – the last opportunity until the next morning – and are locked in their cells.

6.30 Some prisoners may be allowed out of their cells for a recreation period. Facilities are very restricted and this tends to be a privilege allowed only to those who have been there for some time.

8.00 Recreation period ends. Supper (a cup of tea) is sent to everyone in their cells.

9.30 Lights out.

From a leaflet produced by the Prison Reform Trust, 'Prison: Facts and Figures'.

as only joking. Yet, according to one black inmate, 'They laugh and smile at you but deep down in their heart, deep down in their heart, you know that they mean what they're saying.'[7]

In August 1983 a Memorandum on Racial Comments in Parole Reports[8] was issued to prison governors. The chairman of the Parole Board had drawn to the Prison Department's attention the Board's concern about a number of cases in which prison reports on parole candidates had included offensive, prejudicial or irrelevant references to racial or ethnic origin. The purpose of the Memorandum was to alert governors to the need for particular vigilance in ensuring that inappropriate racial comments were excluded from parole reports.

The courts have held that the law does apply to racial discrimination in prisons. In a hearing at Southampton County Court of a case brought by the Commission for Racial Equality in December 1984, a judge held that a prisoner can bring a complaint under the Race Relations Act 1976. The case concerned a black prisoner, John Alexander, who alleged that he had been refused a job in the kitchen at Parkhurst prison on racial grounds. Rejecting submissions by the Home Office that prisons were outside the scope of the Race Relations Act the judge held that sections 20 and 21 of the Act do apply to prisoners seeking jobs allocated by the prison labour board.

Following the ruling that an action could be brought the case against the Home Office began in December 1986. Passing judgment in May 1987 the judge said that:

white prisoners ... would not accept black prisoners working in the kitchen ... the prison staff ... were not prepared to remedy the situation.

He concluded:

In this respect the Home Office as the employer failed in its responsibility to ensure fair treatment for black prisoners.[9]

In reaching the decision the judge took into account the Induction Report written by the induction officer at Parkhurst prison which said of Alexander:

He is an arrogant person who is suspicious of staff and totally anti-authority. He has been described as a violent man with a very large chip on his shoulders which he will have great difficulty in removing. He shows the anti-authoritarian arrogance that seems to be common in most coloured inmates.

The judge decided that 'at a key point in his prison life at Parkhurst those comments had the effects of not treating Mr Alexander as an individual but as a damaging racial stereotype'.[10] He therefore concluded that unlawful racial discrimination had taken place and awarded John Alexander £50 for injury to feelings, £68.15 special damages for lost earnings in the kitchen, and costs. Subsequently the Court of Appeal was asked to consider whether the sum awarded was too low. In their ruling allowing the appeal the Court commented on the 'high-handed conduct, persistent abuse of power and attempts to justify the plaintiff's [John Alexander's] treatment, and conspicuous want of any withdrawal or apology'[11] on the part of the Home Office. The judge, they said, could have taken this into account. They increased the sum awarded to £500.

A black prisoner, then, is likely to find prison life even more full of unpleasantness than the average white prisoner. All prisoners, black and white, will find it hard to avoid being absorbed by what the professionals call 'the inmate sub-culture'. The prison sub-culture is described very graphically by a governor, Philip Wheatley, in the *Prison Service Journal*,[12] the magazine where governors and others can place thoughtful articles about the prison system. Prisons are about power, he says. Locking people up subjects them to economic, social or sexual restrictions which any reasonable person would find unpleasant. So prisoners, quite reasonably, spend much of their time trying to make up for these deprivations. The 'prison sub-culture' provides a framework for prisoners to mitigate their deprivations. The job of the staff is to control or stop this. So life in prisons must be a power-struggle between staff and prisoners. To make this workable staff and prisoners between them devise unwritten rules about how things will be done. The staff have perks to give out, for example, prisoners who get jobs in the laundry can have the best pressed shirts; kitchen workers can get themselves better food. These perks will be given out according to these unwritten rules. The way staff draw the limits on what is allowed and what is not is also governed by unwritten rules. Prisoners know this. Staff know it. Governors and other senior staff often do not know the unwritten rules or take a while to find out. In the course of their careers governors move much more frequently than staff so they are at a disadvantage here.

Prisoners produce a 'sophisticated inmate power structure'. Those at the top of it have most of whatever worth having is going in the institution. Those at the bottom get least. There is a place in this power structure for the prison bookmaker, the tradespeople, those who buy and sell anything, the brewer who makes illicit liquor. According to Philip Wheatley, the sub-culture is a helpful thing to have in a prison: 'It is an excellent form of time filling, the battle to beat the system and come out ahead can fill the prisoner's day with excitement and interest. It is obviously much more enjoyable than the boredom of the official routine.'[13] The job of the governor is to recognize it, to control it, and use it to ensure the smooth running of the prison.

Looking inwards, this is what you as a prisoner will need to understand and handle. Looking outwards, you will also discover a multitude of restrictions on continuing your relationships with the outside world that probably never occurred to you beforehand. If there is no work and you are stuck in a cell all day with nothing to do then you might as well use the time by reading or writing letters to your acquaintances. Unfortunately all that is not easy. The rules about books are an interesting example of how nothing should be taken for granted. Standing Order 4 contains the rules on books. Prisoners can have twelve books at any one time, apart from library and approved textbooks, without the approval of the governor. When a prisoner's 'total holding' of books reaches eighteen, the governor can refuse permission for another book until 'the holding' has been reduced below eighteen. The method of reducing a prisoner's 'book holding' is to give one away to a visitor, or send one out, or donate one permanently to the library. Even having eighteen books is not a right however. The standing order says: 'If conditions in a particular establishment dictate, the governor has discretion to reduce the number of books which an inmate is permitted to retain.'[14] Also, the governor has the power to stop the prisoner having a book if it is considered to be a threat to good order and discipline or 'likely to have an adverse effect on the inmate from a medical point of view'.[15] Finally, on books, prisoners may not give books to each other without permission and the transfer of the book, if permission is given, must be recorded.[16]

Writing and receiving letters is also complicated. Prison Standing Order 5 states:

> It is one of the roles of the Prison Service to ensure that the socially harmful effects of an inmate's removal from normal life are so far as possible minimized and that his contacts with the outside world are maintained. Outside contacts are therefore encouraged especially between an inmate and his family and friends.[17]

Regrettably these admirable sentiments do not translate so easily into action. A number of obstacles come between a prisoner and all attempts to keep contacts with family and community. First is geography. Prisons are not built for the convenience of prisoners and their families. Most prisoners come from the big conurbations – most training prisons are in remote rural areas. Prisoners who are sentenced to eighteen months or more will usually be allocated from a local prison, probably reasonably near home, to a training prison within an area covering one quarter of the country. Some prisoners are sent to prisons even further away if they are in a particular category and there is no suitable place in the region for them. So prisoners from London can end up in the far reaches of Norfolk or on the Suffolk coast where public transport is minimal or non-existent and to get there and back in a day requires great stamina and considerable expenditure from the visitor. London prisoners also end up in the Isle of Wight prisons – which have the complication of a ferry-crossing added to the travel arrangements. For women it is even worse. At least male prisoners usually stay within one of the four prison department regions – so a male prisoner from Birmingham remains in an area called 'the Midlands' big enough to include Bedford, Lincoln and

Shrewsbury, but still only one quarter of the country. As there are only twelve women's prisons, London women can end up as far afield as Durham or Styal in Cheshire.

The women's prison system is not divided into security categories or into local and training prisons. Women's prisons are either open or closed. Top-security women prisoners are put in a special wing, H wing, at the men's prison at Durham, rebuilt as a county gaol in 1881. The conditions in H wing are some of the worst of all the long-term prisons. In 1965 and 1966, after the spectacular escapes, the Prison Department set up three special units to hold top-security prisoners at Parkhurst, Leicester and Durham. Lord Mountbatten said in his report that these units should be regarded as for temporary use only. He went on: 'The conditions in these blocks are such as no country with a record of civilized behaviour ought to tolerate any longer than is absolutely necessary as a stop-gap measure.'[18]

The Radzinowicz Committee also looking at top-security prisons did not think much of the units either. They called them 'miniature prisons within prisons' and added:

no one regards the containment of prisoners in such small confined units as anything other than a temporary and most undesirable expedient. The physical limitations of the buildings preclude any major improvements in the conditions ... the regime of the units is unsatisfactory for men who have to be in them for long periods ...[19]

Writing to the campaigning group Women in Prison a prisoner in Durham described the conditions she lived in every day:

The lack of fresh air and daylight, and the artificial light, mean most women have found their eyesight has suffered since they came here. Restrictions of space: we are never off this wing for anything other than the dentist; everything is on here too, i.e. Church, gym, workshop. There is not enough physical exercise; we get the absolute minimum ...[20]

At the end of April 1988, thirty-seven women were there, two of them aged under twenty-one, from all over the country. Three of them were Category A, defined as requiring the high security that Durham provides.[21] None of the others were deemed to need such high security and were there to allow the three Category A women to be 'dispersed' among them. One of them had been there for fourteen years when she was transferred in 1988.

When the Chief Inspector inspected Durham H wing he noted that half of the women prisoners were from the South, making contact with their children, relatives and friends very difficult to keep up.

If you come from London and are sent to a prison on the Suffolk coast or on the Isle of Wight you may hate it so much that you are prepared to put up with much worse conditions, for example those at Wandsworth, in spite of the cockroaches, in order to be nearer home or family. In his 1983 Report the Chief Inspector wrote: 'Many prisoners in these local prisons were prepared to tolerate the over-crowded conditions and impoverished regimes because they preferred to remain in an urban location and one which was reasonably accessible to their visitors.'[22]

It is not just geography that makes contact with the outside world difficult. Writing and receiving letters is also a complex process governed by rules and depending on what category of prisoner you are. But as a newly arrived prisoner in a local prison you will be allowed to send a minimum of one statutory letter a week on which postage is paid by the authorities (second class). First-class post is allowed for your first letter when you arrive, a letter written when you are transferred and letters about an appeal. You will also be allowed one extra letter but you will have to pay the postage out of the money you earn. You may be allowed to write extra letters postage paid where necessary for the welfare of you or your family. You may also get an extra one in place of a visit, if for some reason your family cannot visit you or if you are involved in legal proceedings. Normally your letter cannot be more than four sides and is usually to be written on instantly recognizable lined prison paper with your number in the corner. At Christmas you can write an extra letter on plain paper and buy up to twelve Christmas cards. If you are still waiting for trial and have not yet been convicted you can send and get as many letters as you can afford but as they will all be censored you will be encouraged not to write more than four sides so as not to make too much work for the censors.

Whom can you write to? As the result of changes described in detail later in this chapter you can write to almost anybody – so long as the letters sent and received are acceptable to the authorities. You need permission from your and the other person's governor to write to someone in prison.

And what can you write about? Everything except, not surprisingly, information about escape plans, anything that would assist or encourage a disciplinary or criminal offence, anything prejudicial to national security, descriptions of weapon-making, poisons etc., coded messages, threats, blackmail, obscene material or information which would cause anyone to come to harm. You cannot make a specific complaint except to a lawyer about something that has happened to you, unless it has been made through the internal channels at the same time, but you can make complaints of a general nature about overcrowding or what it is actually like in prison or how you feel about it. You can also write to the newspapers if what you are saying 'consists of serious representations about conviction or sentence or forms part of serious comment about crime, the processes of justice or the penal system'.[23] If you write a letter which breaks these rules it will be stopped. You will be told and given a chance to have another go at it, so long as you keep the rules this time.

So your letter-writing will be considerably confined, in number, length and what you can write about. Also, you will no doubt be conscious as you write that your letter will not only be read by the person you are writing to, but also by a third party. You will probably therefore not want to give much away about your feelings or discuss any private matters.

Also, you will not be able to make a phone call, unless it's an emergency of a welfare nature, or you are lucky enough to be at an open prison, or at a specified low security women's or young offenders' institution and therefore a beneficiary of the new Prison Department regulation that prisoners in prisons can make phone calls using specially purchased phone cards (the amount limited by how many phone cards you can buy from your earnings, plus £2 a month from your private cash), on specially adapted phones which cannot take incoming calls. This small concession comes after many years of debate and attempts to install telephones in prison. We still lag well behind other countries. In the USA and Canada prisoners have had access to telephones for some years. In Holland all prisoners have access to telephones. In Dutch open prisons there are telephone boxes. Sometimes, in closed prisons for security reasons the prison officer makes the connection and the call is then transferred to the prisoner in a private booth. In Scotland in 1984 pay phones for use by category C and D prisoners were installed in all open prisons and three closed prisons.[24] The rules on writing letters are also much more relaxed in other systems. In Holland prisoners may write as many letters as they like. The authorities can read letters from prisoners on remand or in closed prisons when there is reason for suspicion. Letters to and from prisoners in open and semi-open prisons are opened in the presence of the prisoner and checked for contraband but not read.

The other method of keeping in touch with the outside world you have left behind is through people coming to visit you. You are entitled to at least one visit every twenty-eight days of a minimum of thirty minutes – six and half hours a year altogether. If you are under twenty-one you can have a half-hour visit every two weeks which makes thirteen hours a year. Of course, there is discretion and some prisons allow more frequent and longer visits – but in the overcrowded local prisons the statutory minimum is sometimes all they can manage to provide, especially when they also have to cope with un-convicted prisoners who are allowed a visit every day of at least fifteen minutes.

The visits' process also involves a lot of red tape. As a con-victed prisoner you must send a visiting order (VO) to your prospective visitors. Your visitors must bring the visiting order, which is valid for twenty-eight days, with them. Without it, they will not get in. Up to three adults and children are normally allowed, though some prisons have to restrict num-bers because of pressures on space. All visits must take place within the sight of but, other than in exceptional cases, not in the hearing of a prison officer. You will be allowed to embrace your visitors. Your visitors can take notes during the visit but have to get permission to take them out with them. If the visit takes place in a visiting room you and your visitors must sit at a table. In some visiting rooms the WRVS provides toys for restless children and refreshments. In special circumstances you may only get 'closed' visits, which means you are sitting in an individual cubicle and are separated from your visitor by perspex or a grille. In allowing people to visit, priority is given to close relatives. Governors can refuse visits from prisoners' friends, less close relatives, and anyone not known to the prisoner before custody. Visits by journalists and authors in their professional capacity are not normally allowed. If you have the stamina to go without visits for several months and your relatives have problems in travelling long distances, you can accumulate up to twelve visits and be moved to a local prison near home to take them all at once.

In some other countries the rules for visits are more relaxed. In Canada local prisons allow two visits of twenty minutes each week within visiting hours of 1–4 p.m. and 5.30–7.30 p.m. Some Canadian federal prisons where prisoners are serving two years or more provide small houses or portakabins within the grounds, so that prisoners who are not allowed home leave can spend forty-eight hours with their families once every three months. Those with no family are also allowed to use the facility for a weekend just to get a respite from prison life.

Swedish open prisons allow prisoners to have keys to their cells and to entertain visitors there in private. Swedish maximum-security prisons provide visiting areas where each room has a bed and visits can take place in private. In the Netherlands prisoners are allowed weekly visits of one hour, or two hours if they are in a closed prison and have six months or more to serve. Prisoners serving more than six months are entitled to an unsupervised visit at least once a month.

In 1979 a Home Office initiative to allow mothers at Styal prison to be visited by their children with adult female escorts, staying in caravans within the prison perimeter for thirty-six hours or so, received such strong opposition from the Prison Officers Association that the idea was scrapped.

Miss Parsons, Chairman of the POA Committee at Styal prison, told the MPs of the Expenditure Committee: 'The only point I would make is that they will not get through the gate. The staff will not allow them through the gate. They are unanimous; they are all standing together. It is not just the staff of Styal prison.'[25]

Home leave is one of the most important ways in which prisoners can keep in touch with home and family. In 1982 the Council of Europe recommended that member states should grant home leave 'to the greatest extent possible'.[26] But as a prisoner in a British prison you will not get very much home leave. A Home Office committee pointed out that our practices on home leave are 'markedly more cautious than in the rest of Europe'.[27] In 1985 4,440 home leaves were granted to adult prisoners. New regulations have increased the chances slightly. In 1986 men in open prisons serving two years or more, and women serving eighteen months or more, became eligible to apply for a two-day home leave every four months after completing one third of the sentence. In 1988 a new short home leave was introduced for prisoners in low security and some women's and young people's institutions. The numbers however are still very small. Many other countries have much better home leave allowances. In Northern Ireland home leave is granted more frequently than in Great Britain.[28] In West Germany, prisoners can take twenty-one days' leave a year, which they are entitled to after serving their first six months.

So a prisoner's right to keep up contact with the outside world is quite constrained, and considerable effort has to go into keeping relationships alive through censored letters and half-hour visits in crowded visiting rooms. The prison is closed off from the outside world in other ways too. If you are ill and seek medical attention you will be treated not in the National Health Service but by the Prison Medical Service, a separate medical service working for the prison authorities.

There have been medical services in prison since 1774 when an Act was passed 'for preserving the health of prisoners in gaol' and the local justices were required to appoint an experienced 'surgeon or apothecary' to work solely in the prison. The main aim of this new development was to stop the typhus in the prisons spreading to the law-abiding folk outside.[29]

The prison system in England and Wales is the only one in the western world to have a large and self-contained Prison Medical Service.[30] In recent years the Prison Medical Service has been subject to a great deal of debate and indeed criticism, so much so that in 1986 the Social Services Committee of the House of Commons decided to conduct a far-reaching inquiry into the service. The controversy about the Prison Medical Service centres on two main criticisms, put well by John Gunn, Professor of Forensic Psychiatry in London. The Prison Medical Service, he says, 'is regarded by some as an arm of the law misusing medical techniques to control prisoners and by others as providing a poor standard of care'.[31]

The proceedings of the Select Committee provide some useful glimpses into what is usually a closed world, that of prison medicine. The doctors themselves, appearing before the Committee, seemed to have doubts about the quality of the care they can offer to prisoners. Dr Trafford, Senior Medical Officer at Bristol prison, told the Committee that staff shortages affected what he was able to offer his patients. He said that sometimes when doctors asked for a prisoner patient to be brought to them for examination, 'We are just told "Sorry, no staff, sir. Try again tomorrow."' And he concludes: 'It is a funny way of delivering medical care.'[32]

The Prison Medical Association, which Dr Trafford represents, also said in its evidence that 'prison reception medical examinations are frequently hurried and often neglected with the result that the medical record . . . is valueless'.[33] Dr Trafford suggested that the Committee should go and visit 'Brixton prison on a Friday night, at about nine o'clock in the evening, when there may be seventy or eighty new receptions coming in, when the police cells are being cleared for the weekend and the staff are all anxious to get away, as is the doctor who happens to be on duty. To take medical histories and conduct full examinations of that number of patients really is an almost impossible task.'[34]

The heart of the controversy about prison medicine comes under the heading of what the doctors call 'Ethics'. The essence of this controversy is that prisons are places where people are made to do what they do not want to do and doctors should not be part of the structure that imposes this control. As the Prison Medical Association says: 'The doctor's primary responsibility must be to the patient and it is to the detriment of the doctor/patient relationship that the doctor is also seen to be involved in management.'[35]

The problem is perhaps put most starkly by Dr Benjamin Lee, explaining in the *Lancet* why he resigned from the position of medical adviser to the Chief Inspector of Prisons. Dr Lee notes the 'difficult problems peculiar to prisons' that may arise in the 'grey area blurring the boundaries between disciplinary sanction and medical treatment'.[36] Doctors have to get on with the governor and the staff or they will not be able to do their jobs; but they have to remain 'on the ethical qui vive' if they are 'not to function merely as a rubber stamp on behalf of management'. Doctors are particularly involved in the medical management of prisoners – inadequate, psychotic or psychopaths – who should not be in prison at all. Such prisoners may show 'noisy un-cooperative or violent behaviour'. Dr Lee goes on: 'The medical management "for his own protection" of a prisoner may in reality involve intimidatingly severe additional deprivation.'

What it may involve is this:

The prisoner is isolated in a bare cell, containing one object only – a chamber-pot. He is usually put into a two-piece garb of untearable Terylene and perhaps given an indestructible sheet. On one occasion I saw a patient who had been put naked into the special cell. There is no furniture and during the day no mattress. He must eat his food either standing or off the floor. The prison doctor is required to ratify these procedures, but his decisions may be modified by several layers of influence and pressure acting upon him in the closed, strange, prison world.[37]

The doctors are clearly unhappy about the position they are in. The Prison Medical Association recommends 'a review of the medical officer's managerial role in the prison, and of whether or not he/she requires to be directly accountable to the Home Office in clinical matters'.[38] Dr Trafford says, succinctly, 'After all, the patient should be our first concern, not the Home Office.'[39] The ambivalence of the prison doctor's position is highlighted by the way the prison medical service responds to prisoners who are HIV positive. On the one hand the Home Office policy statement on AIDS/HIV says 'government policy is strict on the need to preserve medical confidentiality in relation to AIDS/HIV antibody positive cases'.[40] On the other hand the prison doctor is required to pass on information about HIV positive prisoners to other members of staff 'with a need to know'.

So as a prisoner you could well feel that your relationship with the doctor treating you is rather a strange one. You may also feel that because you are at the bottom of the power heap – and relatively defenceless, living in a closed world – there will be a panoply of protections and systems for ensuring that the power the system has over you is not abused. Having power over others, as anyone in a powerless situation in even a small hierarchy knows, is a great temptation, even in broad daylight, in the outside world, in circumstances fully exposed to the eyes of the public and the media. A person who wants to throw his or her weight about tries it. The prison world is even more vulnerable to misuse of power – because it is so shut away from other people – and because it contains some people who have committed such totally unacceptable crimes that their safety will always be in jeopardy.

Prisoners and the law

But the expected panoply of rights and protections is not there. The prison rules do not seem to confer rights on prisoners. The issue of rights never seems to get anywhere near the top of prison administrators' agendas. Management, industrial relations, the latest crisis, propping up buildings, what sort of new building to have, even what prisoners should do all day, take up most of prison administrators' time. Prisoners' rights intrude much less often. There is no reason to attribute this neglect to a conscious wish to oppress or allow people to feel oppressed; it arises more from a remoteness from the realities of power – a power which must look so much less threatening when filtered through the civilized language of liberal civil-service intercourse in a carpeted, air-conditioned office than it does on the echoing landing of a tense and overcrowded prison or behind the two thick doors of a strip cell. It is interesting that in the new definition of its task, drawn up by the Prison Department and published in the 1983 Annual Report, and discussed in Chapter 4, safeguarding prisoners' rights is not mentioned, even in passing. Also interesting is that the Control Review Committee, a committee made up of senior governors and Prison Department officials, drew up their own definition of the tasks of the prison service. Their list is more exhaustive than the official one. Their first objective was 'to ensure that prisoners' lawful rights are respected'.[41] Perhaps the Prison Department is not such a monolith after all, but harbours a wide range of opinions about its priorities. Perhaps also everyone joining the prison administration should be required to spend a week in a position of total powerlessness, completely at the mercy of others' rules and systems.

Rights for prisoners have been slow in coming. Those that are established have had to be fought for, sometimes as far as the European Court of Human Rights. The law has moved in ten years. In 1972 Lord Denning said: 'If the courts were to entertain actions from disgruntled prisoners, the governor's life would be made intolerable. The discipline of the prison would be undermined.'[42] In effect how ridiculous it would be if prisoners could take their jailers to court – how could anyone manage a prison in such circumstances. In 1979 came the famous case of St Germain, where Lord Justice Shaw said:

The rights of a citizen, however circumscribed by a penal sentence or otherwise, must always be the concern of the courts unless their jurisdiction is clearly excluded by some statutory provision. The courts are in general the ultimate custodians of the rights and liberties of the subject whatever his status and however attenuated those rights and liberties may be as the result of some punitive or other process ... Once it is acknowledged that such rights exist the courts have function and jurisdiction.[43]

In 1982 Lord Wilberforce set out the principle again: 'Under English law a convicted prisoner, in spite of his imprisonment, retains all civil rights which are not taken away expressly or by necessary implication.'[44] A prisoner does after all have some rights and, the corollary of that, the courts will have to ensure they are respected. But these are rights held by all citizens and not taken away by Parliament. They are *not* rights conferred on prisoners by the Prison Rules. The St Germain case is important because it establishes that if prisoners think they have been treated unfairly in a disciplinary hearing before a Board of Visitors they can ask the court to examine the proceedings and rule if they have been fair or not. If they have not been fair the decision can be quashed.

As it is in relation to the disciplinary system that the few but important advances in prisoners' rights have been made it is worth going into a little more detail here. The prison disciplinary system is basically quite simple. There is a set of rules, that is things you must not do, and if you break them, there is a series of punishments you can be given, and a procedure through which you are accused, heard and sentenced, so to speak. (In prison service language the punishments are called, rather oddly, 'awards'.) The things you cannot do are fairly obvious, and are set out in Prison Rule 47. You cannot mutiny, assault anybody, escape, be absent from where you are supposed to be, have anything you are not allowed to have, sell anything you were allowed to have for yourself only, damage anything, make 'a false and malicious allegation against an officer' (of which more below), be indecent or insolent or idle at work, or refuse to work, or disobey an order or try to do any of these things. Also you cannot do anything which 'in any way offends against good order and discipline' – a controversial element because it looks as if it could be used to cover anything which those in authority do not like.

If you do any of these things you may be charged. If it is not very serious (for example being late for work or losing your socks) you will be dealt with by the governor. If it is more serious or more complex or is felt to need heavier punishment (fighting another prisoner, being in possession of drugs or assaulting an officer, for example) you may be put in front of the Board of Visitors. If it is more serious still and also a crime in terms of the criminal law, for example an assault on an officer

causing physical injury, the police may be called in and then it
will be dealt with as crime is dealt with in the outside world.

The punishments you could get are losing your privileges
such as being allowed to buy items at the canteen, attendance
at films, lectures or classes (a punishment which is only applicable in prisons which have these privileges), not being allowed
to go to work with other prisoners, not getting your earnings,
which are on average £2.23 per week,[45] or being confined to
a cell. Being confined to a cell is one of the severer punishments.
In the Home Office's own words it means:

the inmate remains by himself in a cell containing only a table, stool
and chamber-pot. Work should be provided if available, but this is
often not possible; in any case the inmate is not permitted to use his
bed during the day on the ground that other inmates are working
(the bed may in fact be removed until the evening) ... The inmate
must be observed by a prison officer at least once an hour ... Depending on the local arrangements, the inmate may or may not come into
contact with other inmates undergoing segregation.

The Home Office goes on to say:

The Prison Department has always maintained that cellular confinement does not amount to solitary confinement, but the degree of
isolation can be considerable. It is for this reason that the punishment
may not be awarded unless the medical officer has certified that the
inmate is fit to undergo it.[46]

Losing remission is usually regarded as the most serious
punishment of all. Providing more than five days have been
served, every prisoner, is entitled to one third remission, that
is, a prisoner can expect to serve two thirds of the actual
sentence imposed, unless some of this one third remission is
taken away as punishment for breaking the rules. It is the
existence of this punishment that has brought the courts into
the workings of the disciplinary system because a prisoner has
a legitimate expectation of getting remission. Removing it thus
constitutes a deprivation of liberty.

The case of St Germain has already been mentioned. The
roots of this case go back to the Hull riot of 1976 (see Chapter
5). After the riot 185 prisoners were charged with offences
against prison discipline. After the hearings, at which quite

severe punishments were imposed – one prisoner lost 720 days, that is nearly two years, remission – seven of the prisoners went to court to get the decisions quashed, arguing that the Boards hearing the cases had not observed the principles of natural justice. They went to the Divisional Court which ruled against them saying that prisons were rather like the armed services where decisions had to be taken quickly and put into effect at once. The courts could not interfere with that.

The prisoners then went to the Court of Appeal and won. The Court of Appeal decreed that Boards of Visitors have to act judicially and according to fundamental principles of natural justice. Once this had been decided cases began to trickle through and decisions made by Boards at hearings against prisoners were overturned. The next significant landmark however did not come from a British court but from Europe, from the Commission of Human Rights, and concerned the cases of Mr Campbell and Father Fell. Also arising from a riot, this time the Albany riot of 1976, these two prisoners were charged with offences. Mr Campbell lost altogether 570 days remission for incitement to mutiny and gross personal violence. He then complained to the European Commission that he had been denied his rights under Article 6 of the European Convention on Human Rights which says that anyone charged with a criminal offence shall be tried by an independent tribunal and have all the requirements of a fair trial including the right to be represented by a lawyer. The Commission ruled in May 1982 that since the amount of remission taken was so substantial, the hearing in fact amounted to a criminal trial and therefore Mr Campbell should have been allowed legal representation. Father Fell's complaints related to other matters.

In the meantime another case was making its way through the courts, that of Mr Tarrant. A case arising yet again from the incident at Albany in May 1983, Mr Tarrant along with others was found guilty of mutiny and punished severely. The prisoners had asked the Board of Visitors if they could have lawyers to represent them but the Board said they had no discretion to grant it. The prisoners sought judicial review of the decision and the court ruled that although they had no right to legal representation there was a discretion and the

Board of Visitors should have considered whether or not to grant it. The court also suggested guidelines that the Board should take into account when deciding whether or not to grant it.

This all came as something of a bombshell to all the parties involved. The Home Office had always maintained that Boards did *not* have discretion to grant legal representation, and had squashed any suggestion from Board members or elsewhere that this advice might be wrong. The decision to let the lawyers in caused considerable consternation and upheaval. The Home Office eventually responded by setting up the Prior Committee to look into the whole disciplinary procedure.

One of the pieces of work commissioned by the Committee was some research into how participants in the disciplinary system felt about it. Prisoners' views were also canvassed – quite unusual in prison research. All parties, prisoners, governors, and prison officers, were asked their opinions on the fairness of the prison disciplinary system. The researchers found: 'Inmates clearly believed that the adjudicatory system was heavily biased against them and that the inclination of both governors and Board members was to believe staff, rather than them.'

Prisoners felt that the key factor was the extent to which they 'were able to put their side of the case'. The factors that prevented this were 'lack of representation, the intimidating nature of the experience and failure to investigate fully the circumstances of the offence'.

The Report goes on: 'all three groups criticized the Boards of Visitors for being poorly trained and out of touch with prison life'.[47] The Chief Inspector also has doubts about Boards of Visitors conducting disciplinary hearings against prisoners: 'This is because the majority of inmates, in our experience, regard Boards of Visitors as part of the establishment.'[48]

The Prior Committee recommended that Boards of Visitors should no longer preside over disciplinary proceedings. A new independent tribunal to take over the task was proposed. However, a White Paper published in October 1986 rejected the idea of independent tribunals, proposing instead new Home-Office-appointed bodies. This rejection is not surprising. The

Home Office has never been very keen on allowing agents not under its control to operate on its territory. When the May Committee asked the Home Office for views on the idea of an independent Inspectorate, the reaction was most unenthusiastic.[49] Whenever it is suggested that medical services in prison should be provided by a non-Home-Office organization, namely the National Health Service, the Home Office has made the case against it with a range of arguments about the need for central control which are not very convincing.[50]

However, in spite of the outcome of the Prior Committee proposals, the intervention of the courts in prison disciplinary matters has brought about some real changes. In the years before the St Germain case a prisoner at a hearing would often be brought in to stand before the panel of the Board of Visitors in a position known as 'eyeballing'. This means that the prisoner stands facing the Board and standing very closely facing him or her – one looking at the right side of his or her face and the other at the left – are two prison officers. When the prisoner is small and the officers are more substantial, all the Board can see of the prisoner between the prison officers' peaked caps is a small triangle in the middle of the face, the nose and a little bit of the top of the head – not an ideal position from which to convince a group of people of the truth of your version of events, or to consult notes, if you have written any. Nowadays it is usual for prisoners to sit at a table where they can make notes and, if they are granted a lawyer, they can sit and consult with the lawyer when necessary. However, such good practice is obviously not universal. In his 1987 Annual Report the Chief Inspector said 'the conduct and process' of adjudications gave him cause for concern and added, 'As a matter of course inmates and their escorts should always be comfortably seated, with pen and paper provided for those who need them.'[51]

So the courts have had some impact on one area of justice in prisons. The other where their impact has been marked is that of prisoners' access to lawyers and correspondence. It is here that the European Convention on Human Rights has made most impact. The first shock to the system was the Golder case. Mr Golder was accused by a prison officer at Parkhurst of having assaulted him during a disturbance at the prison. He wanted to consult a solicitor about bringing an action against the officer for defaming him but was stopped from doing so. Both the European bodies, the Commission and then the Court, held this to be against Article 6 of the Convention (which sets out the standards to be followed if someone is charged with an offence) and Article 8 which says: 'Everyone has the right to respect for his private and family life, his home and his correspondence.'[52]

A very broad condemnation of the British government for human rights abuses came in 1980 when the Commission ruled in the case of Silver and Others that the stopping of fifty-eight letters from prisoners by the prison authorities was against Article 8 of the Convention. The Commission also found breaches of Article 6 which protects access to the civil courts, and of Article 13, which requires that there should be an effective way in the UK of seeking redress for alleged breaches of the Convention. The very critical nature of the Commission's findings highlighted the extent of the arbitrary power that the system exercised over prisoners.

The British government argued that it respected the provisions of Article 8 allowing freedom of correspondence and only stopped letters when there was a good reason. Article 8 allows letters to be stopped when 'it is in accordance with the law and is necessary in a democratic society in the interests of national security, public safety, or the economic well-being of the country, for the prevention of disorder or crime, for the protection of health or morals or for the protection of the rights and freedoms of others'.[53]

The UK government argued that all the letters that had been stopped fell within this definition. One of the main planks of its defence was the 'prior ventilation rule'. This rule required that no complaints could be made outside the prison until all the internal channels had been used. This was the basis of stopping letters to Members of Parliament and legal representatives.

The Commission argued that none of this would do. The prior ventilation rule does not appear in the published prison rules, only a secret standing order; and it is quite unreasonable to apply secret laws that no one could predict existed. Also the internal complaints system takes a very long time (Mr Silver petitioned the Home Secretary in 1972 and it took five months for him to get a reply). The requirements of the UK government could as well be met by a 'simultaneous ventilation rule', so complaints could go inside and out at the same time. Therefore the stopping of letters to Members of Parliament and solicitors was against the Convention.

Letters to other people including some from prisoners to their wives were stopped because they contained complaints about what was happening to them in prison. The UK government argued that this was necessary to maintain staff morale, and for the prevention of disorder. The Commission asserted in reply, 'there is a basic human need to express thoughts and feelings, including complaints about real or imagined hardships. This need is particularly acute in prison, as prisoners have little choice of social contacts, hence the importance of having access to the outside world by correspondence.'[54] The Commission went on to argue that stopping these letters was against Article 8.

A number of letters to people other than relatives or friends were also stopped. The Government argued that this was necessary 'for the prevention of disorder'. The stopped letters included letters from Mr McMahon to the Secretary of the IBA asking for the name of the producer of a television programme which Mr McMahon felt might have a bearing on his case, to the barrister about his case, to the presenter of 'Panorama', to Professor Cross and to the Mayor of Islington. The Commission felt that the letters were not likely to lead to disorder and that stopping them was a violation of Article 8. Mr McMahon was subsequently released from prison early – the rest of his sentence was remitted – because of doubts about his guilt.

One letter to Devon County Court was stopped because Prison Rule 34(8) required a prisoner to get permission from the Secretary of State before writing on any legal matter. The Commission accepted that stopping the letter was within the law but decided that the prison rule itself was a violation of Article 8 of the Convention. The Commission also ruled that stopping all letters from prisoners for publication in the media without distinguishing which might cause harm and which might not was also a violation as was the stopping of a letter from a prisoner to his wife, allegedly because it contained 'material deliberately calculated to hold the prison authorities up to contempt'.[55] The Commission was 'unable to discern how such a letter, addressed to Mr Tuttle's wife, would have the effect of undermining prison staff morale with consequential adverse effects on prison order and discipline'.[56] The Commission also ruled the stopping of a letter to the Lord Chancellor about a prisoner's trial was a violation.

The only aspect of the case where the Commission agreed with the UK government was in the stopping of four letters from a prisoner to his mother whom he obviously did not like and which contained a range of abuse, insults and threats to her.

After this thorough trouncing in Europe, the Home Secretary, William Whitelaw, got to work on improvements and in December 1981 the standing order on correspondence was amended to take account of most of the Commission's findings and, in a remarkable volte-face from the earlier secrecy, published. Those expecting much to be revealed were, however, disappointed. The real information about how to interpret standing orders is centralized in Circular Instructions, which remain mostly secret. In fact, getting hold of even those documents you are entitled to see may be difficult. Joyce Plotnikoff, in a study of the prison rules, points out how little of the mountain of documentation prisoners are actually allowed to see. She adds 'it is therefore disquieting to discover that even this is sometimes withheld'.[57]

The 'simultaneous ventilation rule' continued but before long it was modified when applied to writing to lawyers. In 1982 the House of Lords ruled that the governor of Albany prison was in contempt of court for stopping Mr Raymond from applying to the High Court to commit the governor to prison for contempt of court.[58] In 1984 the case of Mr Anderson finally established that the 'simultaneous ventilation rule' was an impediment on a prisoner's access to the courts and was therefore unlawful.[59] Thus, nine years elapsed between the European Court in the case of Golder ruling that prisoners

should be able to complain to the courts about their treatment
and the Home Office finally accepting the ruling of the Divisional Court here that impediments to access to court should
not exist.

However, there is still a long way to go. Whole areas of
prison life are still untouched by the intervention of the courts.
Prisoners still have few, if any, rights which would allow them
to complain about the conditions under which they are held.
For example, a prisoner who took the Home Office to court in
1981 for keeping him in the control unit which he claimed
was run in breach of the prison rules did not win his case.[60] In
1984 a prisoner complained to the court that he had been
moved unlawfully from one prison to another. The court
decided that the Home Office's argument, that he had been
moved for 'operational security' reasons, was acceptable even
though it was agreed that he had been moved without warning
to a prison where it was very difficult for his invalid parents
and legal advisers to visit him.[61] In 1988 a prisoner complained
to the courts about the Home Secretary's decision to end the
rule that allowed remand prisoners to have food brought into
prison for them. He asked for judicial review 'on the ground
that the Home Secretary had no power to deprive unconvicted
prisoners of civil rights including the right to consume food of
their own choice'.[62] The court dismissed the complaint saying
that Parliament had entrusted the making of rules for running
prisons to the Home Secretary and if he wanted to change
them that was Parliament's affair, not a matter for the courts.

One aspect of prison life that has worried civil libertarians
for a long time is the use of Prison Rule 43. To people in the
prison world Rule 43 has many connotations wider than being
the rule that stands between Rule 42 and Rule 44 in the prison
book. Rule 43 is something a prisoner can be *on* – or it can
describe prisoners themselves. A circle of prisoners exercising
in a tiny yard with wire mesh all round and overhead are
probably 'the Rule 43s'. Rule 43 comes in the section of the
prison rules called 'special control and restraint' and says: '(1)
Where it appears desirable, for the maintenance of good order
or discipline or in his own interests, that a prisoner should not
associate with other prisoners, either generally or for particular

purposes, the governor may arrange for the prisoner's removal from association accordingly.'[63]

Rule 43 allows the prison authorities to take a prisoner out of the general population of prisoners and keep him or her separate, in some type of segregation. There are two reasons for 'going on Rule 43', as it is called. One occurs when the prisoner asks for it and wants to be kept separate, from fear of being attacked by other prisoners, either because of the offence committed (sex offenders are particularly vulnerable) or because of attempts being made to settle old scores, or because the prisoner has fallen out with a stronger prisoner.

The other use of Rule 43 is more controversial. This is the use of segregation to maintain 'good order and discipline' (GOAD). Figures are hard to come by but it is known that on 31 March 1985 seventy-five male and six female sentenced prisoners were segregated to maintain good order and discipline, that is .16 per cent of the male population and .39 of the female. This use of Rule 43 is controversial because it allows the authorities to inflict on a prisoner conditions which are almost indistinguishable from the conditions given as a punishment after a proper hearing – but without any safeguards such as a hearing, a chance for the prisoner to hear why this is being done or make out a case against it. Once a prisoner is on Rule 43 the conditions are likely to be those of a cell in the segregation block. Unlike prisoners being punished, a prisoner on Rule 43 can keep the mattress in the cell during the day and may have a radio and books. Otherwise the conditions are very similar to those of prisoners segregated as a punishment.

The use of segregation for good order and discipline is, in effect, an informal disciplinary system, a way of keeping order without having to go through the proper procedures – or to use on occasions when the proper procedures would not work. There could be many reasons for this – maybe whispers suggest that the prisoner is planning some illicit action although it has not been done yet. Maybe what the prisoner is suspected of doing cannot be proved, because it has reached the ears of the authorities through sources they cannot reveal, an informer for instance, or evidence would never come out at a hearing because witnesses would be too frightened to appear.

Its use as an unofficial informal disciplinary system, a system to use when the regular system will not work for some reason, is admitted. In fact in its evidence to the Prior Committee the POA said:

... the courts have opened up the prison disciplinary system to public scrutiny and judicial review. They have liberated prisoners from many artificial constraints but in doing so they have also thrown the disciplinary system into crisis and seriously depressed the spirit of the prison service. One possible consequence – one that we deprecate – will be to drive the disciplinary system 'underground' and replace formal adjudications with administrative segregations, relocations, adverse parole reviews and so on. We can see something of this happening now and it is a disaster for our service. It will destroy the morale of the prison population and make prisons even more dangerous places for Prison Officers to work in. It will vindicate our antagonists (who argue that there is no justice in prisons) . . .[64]

The Chief Inspector, who devoted resources to a complete study of how Prison Rule 43 is used, is not happy with the present system. He argues that:

... more elaborate safeguards were required for dealing with inmates who were segregated in the interests of good order, or for their own protection but against their wishes. Currently, such inmates are subjected to restricted regimes, while having little chance to argue their case or even hear the case against them. Moreover, a significant minority can be held for weeks and even months in inferior conditions at the prison governor's discretion, provided that a member of the Board of Visitors or a senior member of staff at regional office (neither of whom is likely to dissent) provides formal authorization.[65]

As the Chief Inspector points out, the authorization by the Board of Visitors or the senior member of staff is rather a rubber-stamping exercise. The only major study of how Boards carry out their duties, by Mike Maguire and Jon Vagg, published in 1984, found that the authorization process was somewhat perfunctory. It was not the general practice to see a prisoner before authorizing segregation. Some felt that their signature amounted 'to little more than a token gesture of involvement'. Many Board members agreed that the system worked well but they still felt that 'there were too many men in segregation and that the periods of segregation were often too long'.[66] The Wandsworth Board of Visitors admitted in its 1985 Annual Report that the present system of authorization may well be 'something of a charade'.[67]

Another way of dealing with prisoners that the authorities feel are troublesome is through the use of Circular 10/74. (Following prison service style, prisoners subject to it are called 10/74s.) The Control Review Committee set up by the Home Office summed up very well how governors can react to troublesome prisoners:

At present, if a prisoner is causing trouble governors have three options: They can try to have him transferred to the prison hospital (if he is mentally disturbed); they can send him to the segregation unit on punishment or Rule 43; or (in the case of dispersal prison inmates only) they can transfer him to a local prison for 28 days under CI 10/74.[68]

CI (Circular Instruction) 10/74 says that a dispersal, that is high-security, prisoner can be transferred to a local prison under Rule 43 for a cooling-off period of twenty-eight days. The process involves the prisoners no one wants (described by the Home Office as 'subversive') being constantly on the move, going from one prison to another for the statutory twenty-eight days and then being moved on – or, as it is put by the Home Office: 'A very small number of inmates are so disruptive that they cannot be held at any establishment for any length of time and may spend much of their sentence being passed from one establishment to another.'[69]

The Wandsworth prison Board of Visitors is not very happy with these arrangements. They say of prisoners they receive under Circular 10/74:

During the 28 days the prisoner is allowed two visits. He may not work, go to the gym or take part in classes; ... his is a deprived existence, he cannot associate at all with other prisoners. He has a basement cell with no natural light. His one hour daily exercise is spent alone in a small unkempt area with wire netting above and around it, like a large cage ... The Board's main concern is that no formal procedure exists for the transfer of these prisoners and safe-guarding of their rights, except Circular Instruction 10/74. It seems that the Home Office have devised forms of administrative punishment which avoid use of the Prison Rules.[70]

The regulation of these powers by some system of independent scrutiny and some requirements on the authorities to record reasons for them is clearly desirable. Maguire and Vagg suggest that Boards should develop guidelines to assist them in deciding when a prisoner should not be held on Rule 43. They also recommend that: 'Board members should not sign automatically, without seeing the prisoner as soon as possible. They should also follow up complaints by men who are held under the Rule against their will more carefully than is the case in most establishments.'[71]

The Chief Inspector recommends that authorization should be done by 'the body that adjudicates on the more serious disciplinary offences',[72] which is currently the Board of Visitors. The body should have powers to call for evidence and when it reaches a decision it should pass the decision and the reasons for it in writing to the prisoner. If segregation goes on for as long as three months the authorizing body should find out why a transfer cannot be arranged. Any segregation for longer than six months should be reviewed by a higher body independent of the Prison Department. The Chief Inspector's recommendations were received by the government in 1985. Three years later a response was announced. The recommendations were to be 'taken into account in a general review being undertaken by officials of the management of prisoners segregated for reasons of good order and discipline or for their own protection'.[73]

Also in need of an overhaul is the complaints system. While prisoners now have access to the courts, many causes for complaint arise in prison which are not serious enough to call for legal intervention but nevertheless matter considerably to a prisoner. In the closed world of a prison, where so many of the distractions of normal life are shut out, small things loom very large. The Prior Committee argued that an important element in controlling prisons is the 'fairness of the procedures', and concluded: 'If prisoners feel they are completely powerless, and are merely objects to be moved around and disposed of according to the will of the authorities, with no opportunity to ask for a reason or argue their case, a sense of grievance will soon build up into something explosive.'[74]

At the moment the complaints procedures are cumbersome and unrewarding. If you were a prisoner, and wanted to complain about some decision you felt was wrong, if, for example, you were on Rule 43 segregation for your own protection and had been refused permission by the governor to have a small pot plant in your cell because this might 'make you too comfortable and encourage you to stay on Rule 43' you could take the following steps. You could complain to the Regional Director of Prisons or the Deputy. However, this is not in practice a very useful procedure since regional directors' visits to each prison are occasional. Prisoners (and often staff) do not know when they are next coming. Although they must be told of the complaint, they need not see the prisoner if they do not want to, and they have no duty to inquire into the complaints they receive. So you might decide it is better to go to the Board of Visitors. This is not terribly straightforward either. Maguire and Vagg found that boards varied greatly in how easy they made it for prisoners to make complaints to them. Some allowed prisoners to talk to them when they did their routine rounds. In other prisons this was not allowed. Some have very formal systems where all complaints or requests have to be put to a full meeting of the Board. In any case, Boards have no power to make decisions and only a limited power to investigate anything. You may in any case have your doubts about putting your complaint to the Board because they are also the people who you came up before on a disciplinary charge and you cannot imagine they will be particularly pleased to see you again or grant you any favours.

So having decided that these two avenues are not very promising you may decide to petition the Home Secretary. The Home Secretary of course has not got the time to deal with your complaint himself or herself. In practice officials in the Prison Department will deal with it. They will ask the governor for the facts of the case, even though it is often the governor's decision that the petition is complaining about. There is no independent input. This process will take some time to carry out. For years the length of time it takes to deal with a petition has been a cause of complaint. Successive ombudsmen have criticized the

Home Office for delays in answering petitions.[75] The last ombudsman was assured that systems for monitoring the progress
of petitions had been introduced. These procedures require
prisons to send a reminder to the Home Office if a reply is
outstanding after two months and a further reminder if it is
still outstanding after five months. So you might get a reply
within five months. But by then, probably, your plant would
have withered and died.

You could have written to your MP, provided you also complained through one of the internal channels. This could work,
but only if your MP is active and persistent. If not, you will
probably get a standard reply. Your MP would not be able to
pass your complaint on to the ombudsman because it was
about unfair treatment, not maladministration.

If your complaint was not about something like a pot plant
but about something much worse which involved you in
making a complaint about the behaviour of a prison officer,
you would then come up against a real problem – that it is an
offence against the disciplinary code to make 'any false and
malicious allegation against an officer'.[76] This could well deter
you from making your complaint even it if was genuine. If
you could prove it that would be fine. If there was any doubt,
then you might well feel it was not worth the risk. The Prior
Committee noted: 'a very strong body of evidence from our
outside witnesses that the offence should be abolished, both
on principle because it is held to be inconsistent with attempts
to create and operate a fair and open grievance system and
because there is some evidence that it does discourage prisoners from putting forward complaints which may be ... justified'.[77] In 1987 the Chief Inspector recommended that the
offence be abolished. 'The police,' he said, 'who face similar
problems in this respect to prison officers, do not have such a
rule – nor do a number of other penal systems.'[78] In 1988 a
survey of Boards of Visitors showed 70 per cent in favour of
abolishing the offence on the grounds that it intimidates prisoners to the extent that they are afraid to make legitimate complaints.[79]

Complaints procedures in other countries are much more
developed. In the Canadian federal system, for instance, there

are five internal levels at which a complaint or grievance can be heard and an attempt made to resolve it. One of these involves putting the complaint to a prison committee made up of three prison staff and two prisoners. The final internal level is to a prison official, the director of inmate affairs, who represents prisoners' interests in the headquarters administration. Finally the grievance can go to the Correctional Investigator who is a prisoners' ombudsman. In Holland a Central Advisory Council for Prisons, the Care of Criminal Psychopaths and Rehabilitation was established in 1953. It has a prisons section which hears appeals by prisoners against decisions to place them in a certain prison, transfer them, refuse to transfer them, or place them in a national segregation department. The decisions of this appeals committee are binding on the Minister of Justice, who is responsible for the prisons.

In this country the only appeal against such decisions is by petition to the Home Secretary whose officials made the decision in the first place. So if you came to prison with the feeling that it is an unfair world, and with a certain amount of anger and bitterness, your stay may well increase it. The Justice Report *Justice in Prison* puts it thus:

The standards of open and impartial justice required by the rule of law are specially needed by prisoners because of their vulnerability, in the closed world in which they live, to abuse of power, humiliation and degradation ... our system fails to provide satisfactory procedures. That failure increases the tensions of prison life. It creates an atmosphere of greater uncertainty, arbitrariness, unfairness and resentment. Condemned for infringing the law, the prisoner finds himself in a society ruled not by law, but by arbitrary power. It is small wonder if at the time of his release the contempt for law, justice and the rights of others is greater than it was before he was imprisoned.[80]

Unfortunately, it is not prisoners' rights that preoccupy the time and energy of those who run our prisons. Mostly it is money: use of resources, cash limits, staffing-levels, building contracts, trying to provide a service while having no control over the numbers of those using the service and only the most rough and ready ways of predicting how many customers there will be in any given year. It is to these questions that we now turn.

7 Two Hundred and Seventy-five Pounds a Week

Resources and the prison system

> We have become decreasingly able to meet virtually any of the objectives expected of us other than the simple 'incapacitation' of the offender for the period of his sentence.

> Dennis Trevelyan, Director-General of the prison service 1978–83.[1]

There is no doubt that prison is a very expensive business. Running any establishment where people have to live and be looked after by others twenty-four hours a day is always very costly. When those being looked after are not there voluntarily, the costs are even higher. The average weekly cost of keeping someone in prison, £275 per week in 1987–8, is a tidy sum. The capital cost of a new prison cell at £87,500[2] is much more than the cost of building a new three-bedroomed house in expensive inner London. And it all seems to have got more expensive over the years.

Some facts to start with. For the financial year 1988–9 £915 million has been set aside to spend on running and maintaining prisons, as well as for the design and construction of new prisons. How does this current expenditure break down? Staffing takes 83 per cent; 10 per cent goes on costs like heating, maintenance and so on; 7 per cent on 'inmate-related costs', for example, food, clothes, education, welfare services, earnings, discharge grants and laundry. Losses on industries and farms, which are intended to be self-financing but usually make a loss, account for 3 per cent – £16 million in 1986–7. Travelling and transport, and miscellaneous items, took 3 per cent.*

Some parts of the system cost more than others, as Table 10 shows. The table shows a wide range – from an average of £557 for a high-security dispersal prison to £184 for an adult open prison. Even within each category there are wide variations, as Table 11 shows.

Some of these variations are easy to explain, for example, the difference between Parkhurst and Wakefield. At Parkhurst there are 1.75 prison staff to each prisoner, at Wakefield only 0.82. Why there should be these staffing differences is not so clear but is no doubt rooted in history. What the figures do show is how overcrowding helps to bring the average costs down. Durham, which is 60 per cent overcrowded, has staff costs of £222 per prisoner per week. Leeds, which is 108 per cent overcrowded, has staff costs per prisoner per week of only £185.

These figures average out at £275 per week for the year ending March 1988. The figure for Scotland in 1986 was much lower at £222 per prisoner per week.[3]. The figure for Northern Ireland was much higher at £941 for 1987/8.[4] Top security is obviously very expensive.

The average figure for the cost of a prisoner per week is often bandied about and compared with the cost per week of various other residential establishments, such as Eton College or Claridges Hotel, to show how expensive prison is – which indeed it is. It is however an oversimplification to suggest that by refraining from sending Ms X or Mr Y to prison this amount of money is liberated for some more worthy venture such as community service or worthwhile activities for unemployed young people to keep them off the streets. The marginal cost of keeping Ms X or Mr Y out of, for example, Leeds prison would be little more than the cost of feeding one more person, that is, £6.36 per week.[5] Sending fewer people to Leeds prison would vastly improve conditions there but would not save much. Great savings would certainly come from being able to close an establishment but this would require a big change in sentencing habits, or, as the Prison Department puts it: '. . . only

* Items are rounded separately and do not therefore add up to 100 per cent.

Table 10 Average weekly net operating cost by type of establishment, year ended 31 March 1988

Type of establishment	£ per prisoner per week
Dispersal prisons	557
Female establishments	385
Open youth establishments	361
Closed youth establishments	298
Category B training prisons	277
Local prisons and adult remand centres	248
Category C training prisons	233
Open adult prisons	184
All establishments	275

Source: Based on *Report on the Work of the Prison Department 1987–8*

Table 11 Variations in the net weekly operating costs of different types of prison establishment, year ended 31 March 1988

Type of establishment	Highest cost per week	£	Lowest cost per week	£
Local prisons and adult remand centres	Brixton	396	Leeds	185
Dispersal prisons	Parkhurst	733	Wakefield	348
Category B training prisons	Kingston	335	Blundeston	256
Category C training prisons	Blantyre House	964	Featherstone	135
Open adult prisons	Campsfield House	839	Rudgate	116
Closed youth establishments	Feltham	498	Stoke Heath	219
Open youth establishments	Hollesley Bay Colony	395	Lowdham Grange	262
Female establishments	New Hall	734	Drake Hall	240

Source: Based on *Report on the Work of the Prison Department 1987–8*

minor savings can be expected to accrue from a fall in the prison population unless it is of sufficient magnitude to enable the Department to close down complete establishments'.[6] Not opening a planned new one would also yield substantial savings.

A number of controversies surround the way the Prison Department has used its resources over the years – prompted mainly by the question, does it use its resources wisely or not too well? The first controversial area is staffing. The facts show that the number of staff has gone up steadily – much more rapidly than the number of prisoners. In 1965 there were 2.95 prisoners to one member of staff. In 1975 the ratio had fallen to 2.21 prisoners to one staff member and in 1985 to 1.8. So in twenty years prison staff increased by 136 per cent and prisoners by 46 per cent. Between 1979 and 1986 the number of prison officers increased by 22 per cent whilst the increase in the number of prisoners was 11 per cent.[7]

These facts were not very different, though less stark, when the May Committee looked at them in 1978–9. In their evidence to the May Committee the central departments (the Treasury, the Civil Service Department and the Central Policy Review Staff) raised some questions about the use of resources in the prison system. They noted that the Home Office argued that the increase in prison officers was needed because of growth in commitments (simply more prisoners to deal with), tighter security (more intensive work, more searches, more procedures), improvements in the regime for prisoners and arrangements for parole and allocation procedures (it is not entirely clear what improvements are referred to here), and improvements in conditions of service of staff and changes in attendance schemes (meaning a reduction in hours required to be worked and more holidays).

Another factor was prison officers' overtime. The amount of overtime prison officers worked was legendary. At the time of the May Report the average was about twelve hours a week. The May Committee was not very happy with the overtime arrangements, commenting that:

. . . high levels of overtime can have a most deleterious effect, not only on individual officers and their families, but also on staff/management relationships generally . . . staff become reliant on a standard of living dependent on a degree of overtime . . . It is even said that some officers known as 'overtime bandits' take maximum advantage of available duties and have not been above attempting so to manipulate affairs that it is possible to retain high levels of overtime.[8]

The Committee had to conclude that the position was far from satisfactory. They complained that they had not been given:

figures which state unambiguously what total manning-levels should be in order to eliminate dependence on overtime and what they in fact are ... Over the entire area there appears to rest a pall of uncertainty, if not incomprehension ... the general situation was one not prone to generate confidence that management at all levels was firmly in control.[9]

This view of management failures in the sixties and seventies is widely held. An experienced governor, Brendan O'Friel, wrote in the *Prison Service Journal* in July 1988 of 'mistakes made within the Prison Service in the late sixties and seventies. One of these was to allow the uniformed staff to become excessively dependent on overtime'.[10] The nettle was finally grasped in 1985 when the Government called in consultants to look at prison officers' work systems. The consultants' report said nothing new, but said what it had to say quite starkly. Shift systems are 'complex', not understood or controlled by management, 'rigid and unresponsive'.[11] Task lists depend not on what is needed to run a prison well but on how many prison officers want to do overtime.[12]

The service 'has become overtime driven'.[13] The Report recommended new pay systems and a changed work organization which would help managers to manage.[14] Thus was laid the basis of the 'Fresh Start' system, launched with much publicity, with videos and regular bulletins on progress. For each prison it meant an analysis of the tasks to be done and construction of a new way of doing them. Overtime was abolished; prison officers' working hours were gradually reduced. One of the outcomes was to be an improvement in what is available for prisoners. Such an improvement is certainly necessary.

Take, as an example, the number of prisoners with nothing to do, neither education, nor training, nor work, on the day, 30 June, that the census is carried out in prisons. In 1967 11 per cent of prisoners had nothing to do all day. In 1972 14 per cent, in 1977 20 per cent and in 1982 25 per cent were in that position. So, while the number of staff went up between 1967 and 1982 by 84 per cent, and the number of prisoners went up by 25 per cent, the number of those prisoners who could be kept occupied went down from 86 per cent to 75 per cent. In 1987 the figure was even lower, at 68 per cent.

Another measure, the number of hours worked by prisoners in a year, also shows a dramatic deterioration. In 1974–5 17.07 million hours were worked. In 1984–5 the number had fallen to 9.13 million. Even those with work to do have a very short working week. The average hours worked per week in a prison workshop in 1986–7 was 19.4. Between 1985–6 and 1986–7 the number of employment places in workshops was cut from 14,204 to 12,863. The number of prisoners who worked fell from 9,279 to 8,431.[15]

The Chief Inspector of Prisons has consistently criticized the inadequate educational facilities at some prisons and the lack of access to those that do exist. At Dorchester prison he discovered that the accommodation provided for education was so sub-standard that the Local Education Authority had threatened to withdraw its education service from the prison.[16] Reporting on Risley remand centre he found that no evening classes were being held and that four out of the five wings of the prison had no classroom accommodation. In the women's part of the prison the dining room was used for education. 'More often than not, however, discipline staff were not available for supervision so even this meagre facility was frequently denied to inmates.'[17] At Pentonville prison, 'following months of sporadic cancellation of classes because of lack of discipline officer cover, both the main day classes and all evening classes had virtually terminated for a period of 6–8 weeks in September and October.'[18] In June 1988 the minister with responsibility for prisons, Douglas Hogg, reported on the situation at Bullwood Hall, a prison for women in Essex. 'In the nine weeks following Easter, only 43 class sessions were made available to inmates out of a total of 125 sessions planned for the period.' He went on, 'The establishment is in dispute with the Prison Officers Association regarding the level of prison officer cover for education classes and it is not possible to state when the matter will be resolved.'[19]

One explanation for the deterioration in services to prisoners, at least in local prisons, is the court commitment. In England and Wales (but not in Scotland where the task is done by the police) the role of prison officers is to escort prisoners to magistrates' courts (outside London), escort all prisoners to crown courts and staff the docks there. The cells at the Crown Court are staffed by prison officers and often two prison officers sit in the dock with each defendant.

All this costs a lot of money. In 1976 it was estimated that these duties took two million prison officer hours and cost £6.8 million.[20] More recent estimates suggest that escort duties take between one fifth and one quarter of staff time in local prisons and about 7 per cent across the service as a whole.[21] The total cost in 1985–6 was estimated at £33m.[22] David Faulkner, the civil servant responsible for prisons' operational policy in 1980, told the Home Affairs Select Committee with unusual frankness: 'escort work has a place in the hierarchy of expectations of prison officers which is not necessarily in the interests of the Prison Service . . . Large sums of money are to be gained from it and staff are less interested in doing the work back in the establishment – in running a decent, well-ordered establishment within the gate.'[23] The impact of the court commitment on local prisons can be dramatic.

The Chief Inspector inspected Birmingham prison in 1981 and reported:

The more we visit local prisons the greater becomes our concern at the way in which the demands of the courts not only prevent the development of existing regimes but actually strangle them, until establishments are reduced to being human warehouses and nothing more.[24]

The Prior Committee commented:

We found that several governors, on the day we visited them, had to close workshops and suspend activities because of staff shortages. Usually, the reason for this was that priority had to be given to escorting prisoners to and from court and manning the dock in the Crown Court.[25]

Staff have clung to the court commitment for obvious reasons. Although it is no longer financially beneficial to them since overtime was eliminated, they get out of prison for a day or two. What goes on in court can be quite interesting. It adds variety to a job with not much variety.

Here we see yet another example of one of the abiding

problems of the prison service. Something is wrong. There is widespread agreement that it is wrong. All the arguments are deployed cogently and regularly. And nothing at all happens. The Chief Inspector summed it up in his 1983 Report:

> This problem of escorts has, in our view, for too long adversely affected the regime of too many prisons. Next to overcrowding it is the biggest single problem affecting the quality of life in local prisons. It is a problem which affects the Prison Service, but which the Service itself cannot solve, and for which it is not responsible. Proposals for change have, however, been put forward over the years by various bodies including the May Committee. So far nothing has resulted.[26]

Sorting out the escort problem is back on the agenda, this time in a novel context, the context of privatization. In July 1988 a Green Paper came out asking for comments on the proposition, amongst others, that the private sector could be involved in handling escort duties.

So the prison system has more staff than ever before, provides more impoverished services as the years go by, and is still dogged by staff shortages. The Chief Inspector said of Liverpool prison, which he inspected in November 1987:

> The inmates' regime is impoverished and urgent steps should be taken to improve work, education, activities and association. Fresh Start should provide this opportunity but more prison officers will be needed to meet the shortfall.[27]

Are any of these shortages caused by staff time being devoted to pointless tasks? Certainly many commentators have questioned how staff time is used, for example on censorship of mail. In 1978 the House of Commons Expenditure Committee recommended the lifting of censorship for most prisoners in most prisons. The extra privacy for prisoners would be good for relationships inside and outside prison. Also, they added: 'We are keenly aware that by ceasing to scrutinize all prisoners' mail a significant number of staff would be made available for other more interesting and constructive duties.'[28]

The Government's reply to this recommendation with suitable adaptations could stand as a reply to many sensible proposals for prison reform made over the years. First of all, they agree that it's sensible: 'The Government agrees that some

further relaxation of censorship is desirable.' Then they modify
that agreement by genuflecting to some hard-liners that they
fear are lurking in the political woodwork. 'But policy in this
area has to maintain a balance between the needs of security
and good order on the one hand, and, on the other, the entitlement of prisoners not to have their correspondence interfered
with unnecessarily.' And anyway, the Government reply goes
on, we shall never get it through the trade unions, or as it is
put officially, 'Censorship of domestic mail has already been
suspended in open establishments, apart from a 5 per cent
random check. A recent proposal to introduce a similar procedure experimentally in four Category C prisons foundered for
lack of cooperation by local branches of POA . . .'[29]

In April 1988 a circular was issued, bringing censorship
in Category C (low security) prisons to an end except for a
random 5 per cent. So a policy decision, a timid decision, well
within the limits of the possible, made by the appropriate
Minister in the proper way, has been implemented after a
delay of ten years.

The central departments, in their submission to the May
Committee, also asked some pertinent questions about levels of
security:

What risks would the system run by reducing the present level of
security?
Would those risks be justified in relation to the likely savings that
would follow?
What changes have there been in the make-up of the prison population?
Is the present categorization of prisoners satisfactory?[30]

These questions are worth pursuing in any consideration of
resources because security costs money – and higher security
costs more than low security. So the more secure your prison
system is, the more it will cost. The buildings cost more in the
first place and the running costs are much higher. Long Lartin,
a top-security, that is dispersal, prison catering for an average
of 406 prisoners cost over £11m. to run in 1987–8 whereas to
look after a similar number at Ranby, a lower-security prison,
cost £4.5m. per annum.

The security question is one of the most contentious in the prison system. The contention goes back to 1966 when a spy, George Blake, escaped from Wormwood Scrubs. George Blake's escape was the final straw, following soon after the escape of Charles Wilson (a Great Train Robber) from Birmingham prison in 1964 and Ronald Biggs (another Great Train Robber) in 1965. The Home Secretary of the time, Roy Jenkins, asked Lord Mountbatten to carry out an inquiry into the escapes and make recommendations for the improvement of prison security. Lord Mountbatten finished his report in six weeks and made a series of recommendations. Prisoners should be divided into four main categories according to their level of security risk. For prisoners in the highest category, whose escape would be highly dangerous to the public or the State, a new maximum-security fortress-like prison with room for not more than about 120 prisoners should be built on the Isle of Wight as soon as possible. If necessary a second such prison should be built after a study of how many prisoners really need maximum security. Once prisoners are allocated to categories the allocation should not be fixed for all time but continually reviewed.

The Home Office did not react at all favourably to these proposals. They very rapidly commissioned another report from a sub-committee, chaired by the criminologist Professor Radzinowicz, of the Advisory Council on the Penal System. The sub-committee, whose report was published in 1968, took quite a different line from Mountbatten. They 'became increasingly doubtful about the possibility of establishing a satisfactory regime within a fortress-type prison in which all maximum-security prisoners were concentrated'. Instead they recommended 'that these prisoners should be ... dispersed among three or four larger prisons with strengthened perimeter security'.[31]

The sub-committee argued for a very high degree of perimeter security to the extent of having armed guards in the watchtowers or on the perimeter fence. One member of the four-person sub-committee and seven members of the full committee, including the chairman, Sir Kenneth Younger, dissented and this recommendation was not implemented. But the rest were – and the dispersal system was born.

Instead of being in one or two high-security prisons the high-security prisoners should be dispersed round a number of prisons, all therefore needing high security, but mixed, diluted perhaps, with lower-security prisoners. They would then become, it was argued, easier to handle and less explosive than if they were all together. Dispersing them would reduce the chances of an attack from outside and the possibility of liberating a lot of very dangerous prisoners at a stroke, reduce the scope for plotting and manipulation among big-time gangsters and lessen the likelihood of a fortress-like mentality developing among prisoners. On the basis of these arguments the more expensive option was chosen, providing top security for thousands of people, for the benefit of hundreds. At the last count (March 1988), 390 convicted prisoners designated Category A were dispersed in prisons with room for 2,968. The rest of the places were taken up by Category B prisoners, many of whom by definition could as well be in Category B prisons. In the Midland region in 1987–8 the dispersal system could mean placing a Category B prisoner in Gartree costing £546 a week or in Nottingham at £283 per week – quite a difference, and due of course to the staffing-levels. In 1987–8 the average cost of the manpower for each prisoner was £483 for Gartree and £245 for Nottingham.

The May Committee, while not going into much detail, were sufficiently convinced by the evidence of two leading academic experts on prison matters, Rod Morgan and Roy King, that the policy had disturbing features, to say 'we are not satisfied that the Home Office has struck the right security balance'.[32]

Developing this theme in a lecture in 1983, Rod Morgan showed how much scope there was for reducing prisoners' security categories so they could be housed in less prison-like conditions which cost less to run and provided a much better environment. His analysis showed an extraordinarily close relationship between the categorization levels in each Prison Department region and the prisons in that region. For example, in the Midlands, which had only 7 per cent of its accommodation at Category B level and 53 per cent at Category C, 12 per cent of its prisoners got categorized as B and 55 per cent as C. In the South-East where 22 per cent of the accommodation

The Story of Albany Prison

1961
In February £1 million is earmarked for a new secure prison. In May a site is approved at Albany Barracks on the Isle of Wight. In August the plan is announced for a medium-security prison for 480 long-term repeated offenders to replace Dartmoor.

1964
Building begins with a completion date of 1966.

1966
Security standards are reviewed after escapes of two Great Train Robbers. Plans are made to strengthen windows and skylights. In October the spy Blake escapes from Wormwood Scrubs and the Mountbatten report is commissioned. In December Lord Mountbatten visits Albany and criticizes the inadequate security and lack of access to lavatories at night.

1967
In January the first governor starts work. In February another committee under Radzinowicz is set up to look at maximum-security prison regimes. It is decided that the 12-foot-high fence round Albany should be replaced by a 17-foot-high fence. In April the first forty-one prisoners arrive. In October work begins on converting the brand-new prison to an electronic unlocking system that will allow prisoners access to lavatories at night. The whole prison has to be re-wired so one or other of the five halls is out of use for the next five and a half years.

1968
In July a new governor replaces the first governor, who is moved on.
   In October Home Secretary James Callaghan announces that Albany is to become one of the new dispersal prisons, recommended by Radzinowicz, and will take Category A prisoners. In November six dog handlers and their dogs come to work at Albany.

1969
In January the new 17-foot-high fence is finished. Work begins on a new security fence, 20 feet inside the first. In October the sounds of the riots at nearby Parkhurst prison are heard in Albany.
   In December the 1968 Prison Department Report is published. It says 'gloomy predictions that increased emphasis on security would seriously affect the development of liberal regimes in closed prisons' have not been fulfilled.

1970
The second fence and strengthened gate-house are completed. TV cameras, high-mast lighting, geophonic alarms and a control room are installed. In September the segregation unit is completed. In October the first Category A prisoners arrive. In December the first incidents of arson take place.

1971

By March the number of prisoners asking to go into segregation as a protection from other prisoners is double the October 1970 figure. In April the governor leaves for a new post. In May a new governor, the third, arrives.

In September there are disturbances and several injuries to staff and a prisoner.

1972

In June more than a hundred prisoners demonstrate. In July disturbances take place in dining halls. Between 25 and 28 August there is a riot and extensive damage is caused. The *Daily Mirror* on 28 August talks of SIEGE AT THE JAIL OF FEAR. In September the dining hall is abandoned and prisoners have to eat in their cells. In November fifteen prisoners in segregation since the August riot break down the partition walls in the segregation unit.

1973

In June the partition walls in the segregation unit are reinforced. The perimeter fence is solidified into a wall. In October prison officers picket the prison calling for firm action against troublemakers.

1976

Six prisoners carry out a sit-down protest in a corridor. In the struggle that follows a number of people are injured. Two of the prisoners, Mr Campbell and Father Fell, go before the Board of Visitors for serious offences and lose 570 and 590 days of remission respectively. They claim abuses of human rights and take their cases to the European Court.

1983

A riot takes place between 19 and 25 May. The MUFTI squad is called in. Damage is estimated at £1 million.

Prisoners are charged with disciplinary offences. A number of them, including Mr Tarrant, go to court and argue they should have been allowed to have legal representation. The court decides that prisoners can have legal representation at a disciplinary hearing, at the discretion of the Board of Visitors.

1984

In January it is announced that £3.7 million will be spent to repair the damage done in the May 1983 riots and for other improvements.

The European Court rules that the disciplinary hearings against Mr Campbell and Father Fell were contrary in some respects to the European Convention of Human Rights.

1985

In September five prison officers need hospital treatment after a riot in B wing. The *POA* magazine in October reports that over forty staff have been assaulted since January and eighteen of them are still off work, two are seriously injured and one may not work again.

1988

Dartmoor has not been replaced.

Source: Roy D. King and Kenneth W. Elliott, *Albany: Birth of Prison, End of an Era*, Routledge & Kegan Paul, 1977.

was Category B, 25 per cent of the prisoners got classified that way; Category C was 34 per cent and 39 per cent of prisoners were categorized as C. Either prisoners are more dangerous in the South-East than in the Midlands or prisoners are being classified to fit the accommodation. This danger was seen from the very beginning. In 1966 the Prison Department said in its own Annual Report: 'Any attempt to segregate different categories of prisoners requires surplus accommodation for each category if the size of groups is not to be dictated by the limits of the accommodation.'[33]

Rod Morgan goes on in his lecture to show that many millions of pounds could be saved if all regions did their security classifications as they are done in the Midlands. The Chief Inspector endorses this analysis. In 1984 he wrote: 'many prisoners are being held in unnecessarily secure conditions. For many of the 2,000 or so Category B men in the dispersal system such elaborate precautions are probably not necessary to prevent their escape.'[34]

Apart from questions of how the staff are actually used and how much security there is and should be, a few other points about resource use cannot be ignored. There are the dreams that never came to fruition – for example the Zuckerman woodworking machine bought in 1980 for £144,000 and installed at Frankland prison at a cost of £6,000, used only for trial periods, and then offered for sale by tender and which would cost £2,000 to move. The purchase had been based on 'an error of judgement about the market for furniture assembly work carried out in prisons'.[35] At Stocken prison, as the Chief Inspector tells us, the 'shell of a large industrial workshop' has been empty for two years. 'Various plans for its use have been cancelled. During this time the workshop has had to be heated and the ventilation windows have allowed birds in.'[36] And the mistakes – a new kitchen completed in 1977 at Liverpool prison which is 'too small and on the wrong level',[37] building special cells at the new Feltham youth custody centre 'without either windows or ventilation',[38] so they had to be modified after completion, cell doors dropping off their hinges in the refurbished K wing at Liverpool, an increase in the costs of building Littlehey prison of £274,000 because the spacing between staircase railings was wrong,[39] a hospital at Acklington prison, built 'lavishly and elegantly some ten years ago'[40] which has never held an in-patient because it is too expensive to run and an operating suite in the hospital at Liverpool prison, not in use in spite of large sums of money spent on it over seven years because it was 'clinically unacceptable'.[41]

There are questions, too, about the resource implications of prison industries, once known by the trade-name for prison-produced goods PRINDUS, then called Directorate of Industries and Farms, and now renamed Prison Service Industries and Farms. The frequent change of name may well be an indication of a deeper confusion about the role of work in prisons and the fate of what was intended to be a commercially viable enterprise. Embarrassment was caused when evidence of 'serious irregularities'[42] came to light in 1983–4 which caused the head of the Home Office, Sir Brian Cubbon, to be summoned before the Public Accounts Committee to explain 'losses and bad debts of up to £25 million'.[43] He assured the Committee that measures were now being taken on all fronts to produce 'a different system and a different climate'.[44]

In 1988 he appeared again before the Committee to discuss the performance of prison industries and the large losses they make. He assured them:

We have reduced the operating loss on prison industries from an actual loss in 1985–86 of £22 million a year to an actual loss in this year of probably around £17 million and a forecast loss for next year of about £16.5 million ... On rather optimistic assumptions, in two or three years time it could be down to about £14 million.[45]

All in all then it would seem that the prison system spends a lot of money and many question marks hover over how it is spent. It is also worth looking at how prison expenditure compares with other parts of spending on criminal justice – what sort of priority does it get? Prisons are expected to cost £1,140 million in 1989–90. This can be compared with £4,014 million on the police and £269 million on the probation service. However prisons are the fastest growing part of government spending on law and order. Between 1986–7 and planned expenditure in 1989–90 expenditure in cash terms on the police will increase by 31 per cent, will increase on probation by 28 per cent and increase on prisons by 64 per cent.

The prison system has always maintained that it has been starved of resources. This may be so in absolute terms, but relatively, compared with other areas of public expenditure, prisons have done very well. A pioneering study, carried out for NACRO by Stephen Shaw, currently Director of the Prison Reform Trust, looked at the cost of penal sanctions and the relative position of prisons.[46] The study established that between 1956 and 1978 police expenditure grew thirteen times, or nearly three times in real terms, and prison expenditure twenty-nine times, or over six times in real terms; between 1947 and 1965 the number of prison officers increased threefold, while the number of police increased by little more than half; and between 1956 and 1978 public expenditure as a whole grew 2.5 times in real terms compared with the over six-fold growth of expenditure on prisons.

Finally, if we come back to where we started – to the average cost of prison per person per week – and make comparisons in that form, prison is by far the most expensive option, twice as costly as the dearest alternative. A week of prison, on average, costs £275. A probation order for a whole year cost £780 in 1985–6. A community service order lasting a year cost £690 in 1985–6. A place in a voluntary hostel could cost £69.75 a week, and in the most expensive resource of all, a probation hostel, £156 a week in 1986–7. A year's worth of intensive intermediate treatment for a youngster under seventeen costs £2,000 a year. Three weeks' prison therefore costs more than a whole community service order, or a year on probation.

International comparisons of the resources and cost of prisons in various European countries were made by the Dutch Ministry of Justice in a report The Price of Prisons Compared, published in 1984. The number of staff per 100 prisoners varied greatly between countries, from 38 in Austria to 147 in Sweden. In England and Wales 53 staff were employed for every 100 prisoners. In Holland the figure was 96. A figure was also calculated for how much the prison system cost per year for each person in the total population. In Sweden the prison system cost £15 per head. In Holland, because of the very small number of prisoners, the cost per head of the prison system was well under £6. In England and Wales it cost £12 per year for each of us.[47] The conclusion cannot be escaped that prison costs a lot of money. Everything else the law allows as a penalty is very much cheaper. The case was made in Chapter 5 that prison is not really very effective. Why then do we seem to find it irresistible, so irresistible that at a time when universities are being restrained, the building of public housing almost stopped, schools closed and capital expenditure on the Health Service reduced, spending on the prisons is shooting ahead? The answer, of course, is politics, and it is to the politics of prisons that we now turn.

8   No Votes in Prisons

Politics and imprisonment

> In seeking to ease the prisons crisis by creating fewer prisoners Mr Hurd might like to reflect that it ill becomes the party of law and order to stop sending criminals to jail. If there is more wickedness, there are bound to be more people who deserve prison, and it should not be denied them.
>
> *Daily Telegraph*, 28 April 1986.

If the popular press is to be believed, the thirst for punishment among the public is very great. An outcry against what are imagined to be lenient sentences is easy to produce. Indignation against the luxurious conditions that prisoners are supposed to be living in is not difficult to manufacture. It has always been so. In 1820 Lord Eldon, arguing in Parliament against the removal of capital punishment for 'stealing privately in a shop to the amount of five shillings', agreed that 'it appeared a harsh thing to condemn a man to death for stealing privately in a shop to the amount of five shillings'. However, he said, we must remember that a small shopkeeper could be ruined by such a theft and went on: 'If hereafter it should be found, that shop-lifting became universal, and that many persons were reduced to misery by this crime, he hoped it would be remembered that he had suggested the consideration, whether this law which had so long existed was not wise and politic.' As a compromise, he intended, he said, to propose an amendment that anyone stealing to the value of more than ten pounds should still be subject to capital punishment.[1]

In the early 1860s, as prison replaced transportation for convicted criminals, public anxiety rose. Geoffrey Pearson, in his book *Hooligan*, describes how Victorian England reacted to the reformed criminal justice system:

It was immediately much regretted that the death penalty could not be applied to burglars and footpads, and the prison system was the object of particularly fierce criticism. *Punch* regularly indicated 'the mildness of magistrates' and the 'luxurious' convenience of a snug cell in prison which 'unless the Government interfere to make the living less luxurious . . . will be popularly looked upon as one of the most comfortable ways of spending life'.[2]

This was at a time when prisoners were kept in total solitary confinement, forbidden to speak and required to operate a treadmill for hours on end.

These themes, of reckless leniency by judges and magistrates, and luxury living-conditions in jail, still run strongly through public debate and the media, and return to haunt reforming politicians. When a new prison was opened in Norfolk in 1985 and local councillors were invited to view it, the response was not unexpected: FURY OVER 'HOLIDAY-CAMP' JAIL and ALL-MOD.-CONS JAIL IS JUST LIKE BUTLINS said the headlines.

There are supposed to be 'no votes in prisons' and no political prizes for doing something about them. Any politician brave enough either to tell the truth about them or grasp the nettle and try to change the way they are run is likely, so it is believed, to run into difficulties with public opinion.

Yet the evidence that exists does not support the view of a vindictive public thirsting for more and harsher punishment. In a study published by the Prison Reform Trust in 1982[3] a rather different and more credible picture emerges. The study reports on a National Opinion Poll survey commissioned by the *Observer* newspaper into public attitudes to crime and punishment. One very interesting fact to emerge from the poll, worth pondering by politicians, is that the public is not actually very clear about the basic facts of imprisonment. When asked how many people were in prison in the UK only 12 per cent picked a figure in the correct range of 45,000 to 54,999. One in five thought it was below 25,000 and 18 per cent thought it was more than 75,000. Nearly a third thought that half the prison population went inside for crimes of violence (the correct figure is one fifth). Even when asked if the Government should respond to the high prison population by building new prisons or reducing the prison population, over a third advocated reducing the prison population as against half for building new prisons. Less than half, 47 per cent, wanted immediate imprisonment for burglary. Substantial support, 85 per cent for and 12 per cent against, emerged for more community service instead of prison sentences and 65 per cent were for and 28 per cent against an amnesty for those in prison for minor crimes.

These findings are not a fluke. A National Opinion Poll on public attitudes carried out for the *Mail on Sunday* in 1985[4] included questions on Law and Order. When asked if it would be better to spend more money to build prisons, or should prison numbers be reduced by giving non-prison sentences for minor crimes, the supporters of a liberal approach were in a clear majority. More prisons were wanted by 40 per cent. Non-prison sentences were advocated by 53 per cent. In a study of burglary carried out by the Oxford criminologist Mike Maguire, victims of burglary were asked what they wanted to happen to the person who had burgled them. Fewer than three in ten wanted 'their' burglar sent to prison. Most victims favoured restitution or reformation and the most commonly expressed view was that prison was expensive and ineffective. The author concludes: 'we were surprised by the lack of vindictiveness among victims'.[5]

Questions about public attitudes to sentencing were also asked as part of the Home Office's major research study, *The British Crime Survey*. For the study 11,000 people were interviewed about their experiences as a victim of crime, their feelings about crime and their attitudes to punishment. The First Report to come out of the study, published in 1983, described the attitudes of victims of crime to the punishment of 'their' criminal. It appeared that:

Only half felt that, if caught, 'their' offender(s) should be brought before the courts. Ten per cent of victims favoured a prison or borstal sentence; this figure rose for victims of burglary and car theft to 36 per cent and 31 per cent respectively . . . The most favoured sanction (mentioned by a quarter of victims) was a fine; a fifth wanted a formal caution from the police or some sort of less formal reprimand; 15 per cent mentioned some sort of reparation, either community service or direct compensation by the offender. Twelve per cent felt that no action was called for at all.

The Report concludes that 'the findings are at odds with the impression which opinion polls tend to give of a thoroughly punitive public'.[6]

In the second *British Crime Survey*, carried out in 1984, questions on punishment were asked 'to see whether popular opinion and court practice are in step'.[7] The researchers set out to establish whether the public really is dissatisfied with the decisions of the courts, whether people want the courts to be tougher. The replies show that first of all people overestimate how lenient the courts actually are. Two thirds of those replying thought that only one in three burglars are sent to prison. In fact, one in two is the correct figure. People were also asked to say how they would sentence certain criminals, for example, a 25-year-old with previous convictions found guilty of car theft. Of those questioned 23 per cent favoured prison. The courts are in fact tougher than this. They send 31 per cent. For robbery 85 per cent of those questioned advocated prison. The courts are tougher here too. They actually sentence 92 per cent of 25-year-olds found guilty of robbery to prison. In reply to more general questions 86 per cent favoured community service for some non-violent offenders, and 69 per cent favoured shorter sentences for people guilty of non-violent crimes. The researchers conclude from their findings 'that policy-makers and courts can treat with a degree of scepticism the claims often made by the media that public opinion demands a tougher line with offenders . . . there is probably leeway to introduce more lenient or heavier sentences without losing public support'.[8] However, they add that support for more lenient sentences would be more likely if the public knew more about what court decisions actually are. A poll carried out by National Opinion Polls for London Weekend Television found the views of the public to be 'some way from the "hang 'em and flog 'em" attitude'. Over half those questioned believed no non-violent offenders under the age of sixteen should be locked up in custodial establishments. Three quarters favoured reducing the prison population by substituting community service.[9]

These surveys would seem to support the consensus that ruled policy on prisons from the time when Roy Jenkins was Home Secretary in 1966, up till the General Election of 1983. During this period Home Secretaries of both parties took the view that prison should be used more sparingly, both through fewer people being sent there and through giving shorter sentences. They all encouraged the more frequent use of non-custodial penalties. Dealing with prison overcrowding by building more and more prisons to contain more and more prisoners was not admitted to be the central policy plank of either Labour or Conservative Home Secretaries.

A consensus also seemed to govern a conspicuous inaction on improving prison conditions. The agendas of neither Conservative nor Labour Home Secretaries contained crash plans to give prisoners access to lavatories, to remove the host of petty restrictions that governed prisoners' lives, nor to respond to prison officers' wishes to have more and better training and a more satisfying job of work to do. Looking back over the record it is evident that prisons are a remarkably undivisive issue. No pattern of performance on prisons emerges which would enable an observer not knowing which party was in power to say, 'Ah, that must have been under the Conservatives,' or 'That was clearly Labour.'

This lack of commitment to prison reform does not reflect broken promises. Manifesto commitments since 1966, if they existed at all, have been vague and flabby. For instance in 1966 Labour concluded: 'Our prisons can only provide a useful reformative influence when we close the doors on some of the worst survivals of mid-nineteenth-century England and transfer the inmates to more modern surroundings where they can do work of some social value.'[10] The Conservatives said even less. They would: 'Train those in prison to become useful members of the community.'[11] In 1970 the Conservative manifesto promises to 'restore the prison building programme'.[12] The

Labour manifesto talks of 'penal reform', and 'our approach to rehabilitating the prisoner' not just for the sake of the prisoner but for society as a whole.[13]

In neither February nor October 1974 were prisons mentioned in the Labour or Conservative manifestos. In May 1979 a reference is made. The Conservatives talk about sentencing and promise 'a tougher regime as a short, sharp shock for young criminals'[14] in certain detention centres. Labour promises 'more resources for the prison and probation services'[15] and the Liberals promise to modernize the prisons.[16]

In 1982 a Labour Party discussion document, *Prisons*, set out a programme for reducing the use of prison and improving prison conditions. Much of this document is reflected in the Labour manifesto for 1983, where, for the first time, Labour makes a series of commitments, including reducing the prison population, bringing in new legally enforceable prison rules incorporating minimum standards, cutting down on unnecessary restrictions such as censorship, refurbishing urban prisons, handing over specialist services to normal community agencies, establishing independent disciplinary and complaints procedures, and improving training and job opportunities for prison officers.[17]

In the same year (1983) the Conservatives asserted 'there must be enough prison places to cope with the sentences imposed by the courts'[18] and promised to complete a building programme to provide 4,800 places in ten new prisons. There is no mention of prisons in the Liberal and Alliance manifesto.

Even those groups within the political parties that produce discussion documents and hope to influence policy have not devoted much time and effort to prisons. In September 1983, the Tory Reform Group, at the progressive end of the Conservative spectrum, published a pamphlet calling for a radical reform of prison conditions and management style in prisons to bring them into line with best practice in other West European countries.[19]

In 1984 the Adam Smith Institute, a right-wing monetarist group, produced a paper, *Justice Policy*, containing a chapter on prisons. Their favoured solution is privatization.[20] Since, they say, there are plenty of security firms and hotel chains in the private sector and running prisons requires only a combination of these two talents, it should not be difficult to find contractors to take on the task. The way the prisons should be run could be set out in standards attached to the contract 'in the same way that local authorities set out standards with private refuse firms – in the contract conditions'.[21] In 1987 the Institute followed up their earlier paper with a whole document devoted to privatization called *The Prison Cell*. *The Prison Cell* argues for privatization from the most humanitarian of motives – 'In a humane society we should not seek to brutalize prisoners.' British prisons are characterized by overcrowding, violence and decline. The solution is to end the state monopoly. An element of competition in the prison business should 'increase supply, improve quality and reduce cost'.[22]

Also in 1983, the Fabian Society, an organization of Labour Party supporters, published a pamphlet, *Law and Order: Theft of an Issue*, by David Downes. On prisons, the pamphlet concludes: 'By comparison with most other Western societies, imprisonment in Britain is nasty, brutish and long ... The solutions to these problems have been reiterated time after time ... what is lacking is the political will to put things right.'[23] Four years later emerged a second document. *Conviction Politics: a Plan for Penal Policy* by Stephen Shaw. He concludes 'there are unlikely ever to be any votes in a rational penal policy'.[24]

The Tawney Society, the think-tank of the Social Democratic Party, has also produced a pamphlet, *Crime and Punishment: A Radical Rethink*, by Sean McConville and Eryl Hall Williams. This calls for more involvement of the private sector in prisons, for example by providing catering or court escort services; decentralizing the prison system towards a national system of high-security prisons for long-term prisoners and local prisons run by local boards for the short-termers; an ombudsman to hear prisoners' complaints and access to the telephone for every prisoner.

The absence of any document more substantial than a pamphlet from any of the main parties underlines the lack of party-political interest in prisons. The record of politicians between 1964 and 1979 shows clearly the consensus at work. During the period of the Labour Government 1964–70, there were three Home Secretaries, Sir Frank Soskice, Roy Jenkins and, from November 1967, James Callaghan. In those years substantial legislative changes took place. In 1966 a prestigious advisory body, the Advisory Council on the Penal System, was set up and given two remits: to examine reparation by offenders to victims and to study non-custodial and semi-custodial penalties. In 1967 a new Criminal Justice Act brought in suspended prison sentences and introduced the parole system which allowed prisoners to be considered for release on supervision after serving one third of their sentence or twelve months, whichever was the longer. The aim of the Government in introducing both these measures was to reduce the prison population. The years 1964–70 also saw the security scares caused by notorious prison escapes (see Chapter 7) and the publication of Lord Mountbatten's report. During this period eleven new purpose-built and two adapted prisons were opened. Reforms within prisons were notable for their absence. In 1968 it was agreed that women prisoners could wear their own clothes. Otherwise progress was minimal.

In the 1970–74 Conservative administration Reginald Maudling (until 1972) and Robert (now Lord) Carr filled the post of Home Secretary. In 1972 a Criminal Justice Act brought in community service orders, allowed the courts to send offenders to a day training centre operated by the probation service and to order an offender to pay compensation for injuring someone, and allowed the police to take a drunken offender to a treatment centre rather than to court. During the period five new prisons were opened. The punishment of putting prisoners on a bread and water diet was abolished.

1972 was also the year of widespread prisoner unrest and disturbances, which was followed by the development of a plan to set up control units at Wakefield and Wormwood Scrubs for disruptive prisoners.

The idea of the units was to separate 'really persistent and serious troublemakers who appear to be capable of mending their ways' from other prisoners. The units were frankly punitive. It was the aim to make the prisoner realize that it was 'in his own interests to mend his ways' so the regime was 'intentionally austere'.[25] For the first ninety days prisoners were to be segregated from others apart from at exercise and in church. If they behaved for ninety days they would pass on to a second stage, slightly less 'austere', for another ninety days. If they misbehaved they would have to go back to the beginning and start the process again. The plan was highly controversial and brought forth an outcry from concerned groups and prison reformers.

In February 1974 the Conservatives were replaced by a Labour Government and Roy Jenkins returned to the Home Office to be succeeded by Merlyn Rees in 1976. During this time reforms into the system of granting bail were introduced and enshrined in the 1976 Bail Act. The use of parole was increased. A Working Party to look into the training and information provided for the judges was set up. The Labour Lord Chancellor, Lord Elwyn-Jones, addressing the Magistrates Association, suggested that when they had a prison sentence in mind they 'might well consider whether imprisonment might not be for a shorter period than they have been inclined to give up to now'.[26] The Advisory Council on the Penal System was asked to look at maximum sentences. Four new prisons were built. Control units were abandoned and have never been reintroduced. After a very troubled period of industrial relations in the prisons, the May Committee was set up in 1978.

So both Conservative and Labour Governments brought in measures which they hoped (in some cases their hopes were in vain) would reduce the prison population, for example, suspended sentences, parole, community service orders, day training centres, the Bail Act. All of them built new prisons, although there was a hiccough in 1974 when the projected capital expenditure on prisons was reduced by £43 million. They built new prisons steadily and without seeming to conduct any substantial public analysis of what buildings really were needed, where they should be and what they should look like. None of them seemed to have come into office with a plan to humanize prisons, either by looking at how they were staffed or how prisoners were treated. Slight improvements seemed to pop up, for example the experiment in relaxing censorship of letters in an open prison in 1969 under Labour or the increase in privileges for unconvicted prisoners in 1972 under the Conservatives. But there is no sign in the record of anything more energetic than an acceptance of the odd, very small step towards more normality in prison life.

During this time the parties were also united by a consensus about reducing the use of prison. It has been shown in Chapter 3 how successive Home Secretaries advocated this policy. Throughout the 1970s official and parliamentary reports stressed this view. The inquiry commissioned by Roy Jenkins in 1966 on Non-Custodial and Semi-Custodial Penalties reported in 1970, saying: 'Imprisonment is not only inappropriate and harmful for many offenders for whom it is used; often it is also a wasteful use of limited resources.'[27]

In 1976 a major review of criminal justice policy was published by the Home Office. This listed all the policy objectives which had guided the activities of the Home Office during the years 1966–75. One of the 'particular preoccupations' listed was 'to reduce the size of the prison population and the proportionate use of imprisonment as a court disposal'.[28]

In 1977 the Advisory Council on the Penal System which had been asked in 1975 to look at the maximum penalties available to the courts produced its Interim Report. This expressed the view that the length of sentences passed on ordinary offenders 'are longer than they need to be in the interests either of society or of the offenders'.[29]

In 1978 a House of Commons committee, the Expenditure Committee, produced a report *The Reduction of Pressure on the Prison System*. They suggested that courts should consider very carefully all the evidence that suggested short sentences could be as effective as longer ones and short ones could be replaced by an alternative and went on: 'The question we have to ask, in the light of all the evidence cited, is whether in this country we should maintain the level of sentencing which has become customary and indeed whether it is necessary to do so in order to prevent or reduce crime.'[30]

In June 1980 the Parliamentary All-Party Penal Affairs Group, an all-party group of MPs and peers, issued a report *Too Many Prisoners* making forty-eight recommendations aimed at reducing the prison population. And in 1981 the House of Commons Home Affairs Committee continued this consensus with its conclusion: 'On the basis of the evidence presented to us, we have concluded that the public interest would not suffer from a diminished use of imprisonment, both by frequency of committal and by length of sentence.'[31]

The May Committee was no exception. It endorsed the recommendations on shorter sentences from the Advisory Council and urged a reduction in the use of prison sentences for petty, persistent offenders. However, it had doubts that any such measures would do much good. It discovered a remarkable phenomenon called 'penal momentum',[32] resistant to all policy changes or population shifts, which meant that the prison population would just get larger and larger. The Committee noted that the proportionate use of prison was going up and the use of fines going down. They concluded from this that 'trends towards reducing the use of custodial sentences are now exhausted'.[33]

However, this view of sentencing as having a life of its own, immune from the effects of training, legislative change, exhortation or shifts in the current state of knowledge, is not widely held. It was certainly not held by the Home Secretary who received the Report of the May Committee, William Whitelaw. He went to the Home Office after the General Election of May 1979, an election in which the Conservative Party made great play of the law and order issue, including Saatchi & Saatchi advertisements drawing attention to the rise in crime under the Labour Government. The years 1979–81 marked the high watermark of Home Office efforts to hold in check the use of prison and showed the power of politics to override quite courageous efforts to face up to a long-running problem.

The tone was set by a White Paper published in June 1980 replying to the Expenditure Committee Report of 1978. The White Paper recognized that the central problem was too many prisoners and commended very strongly the conclusion that prison sentences should be shorter and prison used less often.[34] Developments were complicated and given a new twist by a dispute between the Home Office and the Prison Officers Association about payments for meal-breaks which lasted from October 1980 to January 1981. Prison officers refused to take in more prisoners than the certified normal accommodation. Over

5,000 prisoners, many on remand, were held in prison cells and temporary prisons. The prison population fell to its lowest level since 1974. A circular was sent out to magistrates in October asking them to consider very carefully whether they could avoid the use of prison by using fines or suspended sentences instead. Emergency legislation was rushed through Parliament allowing prisoners to be held in places other than prison, depriving prisoners of their right to appear at a weekly remand hearing if the court agreed, allowing the Home Secretary to release remand prisoners whom the courts had remanded to custody or to release sentenced prisoners up to six months before their normal release date, and to restrict the power of magistrates courts to imprison fine defaulters. To cope with the extra prisoners Frankland prison was brought into operation early and was run by prison staff and the army. In November an old army camp, Rollestone, also staffed by prison governors and the army, was brought into use for 350 prisoners.

The dispute brought some interesting lessons for prison reformers. Through a circular and emergency legislation magistrates and judges were given strong government encouragement to avoid the use of prison wherever possible. It worked. The prison population including prisoners held in police cells and temporary prisons fell by over 4,000. Over half of the fall came from a reduced use of prison for those getting sentences of eighteen months or less. Just under half was due to more people being let out on bail. Evidence also emerged that prisons which housed only the number of prisoners they were meant to house were safer and happier places. Giving evidence to the Home Affairs Committee, Mr Fitzpatrick, the Secretary of the Prison Governors union branch at the time, told the Committee that because numbers in the prisons were down to what they should be 'for the first time officers have the time to devote to the prisoners under their control, and they are building up relationships. Indeed, the atmosphere, paradoxically, is better and more healthy in many of our big prisons than it has been for years.'[35] Unfortunately these halcyon days did not last long. The dispute was called off and within a month the population was creeping up again, to reach a new highest-ever figure of 44,558 in September 1981.

Maybe the effects of the dispute gave all those concerned a glimpse of a happier state of affairs than it seemed might be within grasp. In any case, the Home Secretary continued his campaign to persuade the courts that they used prison too much. In a series of well-publicized speeches he advocated a reduction in the use of prison. In March he appeared personally before the MPs of the Home Affairs Committee to say: 'Building new prisons cannot by itself be a solution to the present pressures. Imprisonment is not a cheap way of dealing with offenders . . . Nor in many cases is it the most effective way . . . On the evidence it would appear that there could be a substantial fall in our use of imprisonment without any significant rise in the threat to individual safety.'[36]

The Home Secretary went on to excite much speculation by announcing that he was considering what further steps were open to him to 'supplement and reinforce the lead'[37] the judiciary had given in two celebrated cases, those of Mr Upton and Begum Bibi. In these cases the Lord Chief Justice, Lord Lane, sitting in the Court of Appeal, which reduced the length of the sentences passed on Mr Upton and Begum Bibi, declared that sentences should be as short as possible, consistent with the duty to protect the public and punish and deter the criminal. Six or nine months in prison could be as just and as effective as eighteen months or three years. In April 1981 the Prison Department published its Annual Report suggesting again that some new measure might be on the way.[38] In May the new idea emerged. The Home Office published *A Review of Parole in England and Wales*, floating the idea of a 'supervised release' scheme whereby prisoners serving sentences of under three years would be released after one third to serve the middle third of their sentences in the community under the supervision of the probation service. The proposal would have reduced the prison population by up to 7,000.[39]

It received a warm reception in some quarters. The Parliamentary All-Party Penal Affairs Group supported it. The Home Affairs Select Committee supported it, as did the Parole Board. The judiciary was less enthusiastic. As Lord Justice Lawton wrote to *The Times* in November, 'None of us liked this proposal.'[40] However, it was not the judges that dealt it the final death-blow. As Lord Lane pointed out in the House of Lords: 'May I try to explode one myth which recently has gained currency in the media: that the judges thwarted Home Office liberal penal proposals by threatening to increase sentences in retaliation against the proposals. They did nothing of the sort.'[41] It was the Conservative Party Conference. In October 1981 William Whitelaw faced the humiliation of having his law and order motion defeated by a conference which considered his policies were not tough enough. Shortly afterwards he announced he was not going ahead with the supervised release proposal.

This dealt a seemingly terminal blow to the idea of releasing short-term prisoners on supervision for the middle third of their sentences. It also marked the end of a real determination to deal with the prison crisis by restricting demand.

For one prison governor, John McCarthy of Wormwood Scrubs, it was the last straw. He wrote his celebrated letter to *The Times*:

As the manager of a large penal dustbin I wish to write about the latest proposal of the Home Secretary to reduce the prison population ... I did not join the Prison Service to manage overcrowded cattle-pens, nor did I join to run a prison where the interests of the individuals have to be sacrificed continually to the interests of the institution, nor did I join to be a member of a service where staff that I admire are forced to run a society that debases.

I am aware of the difficulties that the Home Secretary faces in reducing the prison population, but I find it difficult to understand why, if he genuinely wishes to reduce the prison population, automatic release on licence for short-term prisoners is not introduced.

As it is evident that the present uncivilized conditions in the prison seem likely to continue, and as I find this incompatible with any moral ethic, I wish to give notice that I ... cannot for much longer tolerate ... the inhumanity of the system within which I work.[42]

Two weeks later the governor of Manchester prison, Norman Brown, wrote to the *Daily Telegraph* on similar lines urging a reduction in the prison population 'or must we go on being ignored by Parliament and the courts while they carry on talking about overcrowding for yet another thirty years'.[43] Early in December a sharply worded memo went out from the

Home Office reminding prison governors that they were civil servants and could be disciplined for engaging 'in public discussion of matters of political controversy such as the suitability or otherwise of particular government policies'. Writing to the press without clearance would lead to disciplinary action. Shortly afterwards John McCarthy resigned from the prison service. The political moment for tackling the prison population seemed to have passed.

In June 1983 William Whitelaw was succeeded by Leon Brittan and a totally different tone of voice emerged. At the Conservative Party Conference in October 1983 new measures were unveiled which put into reverse the consensus of the 1970s. Leon Brittan told the Conference that those who murder police and prison officers, those who murder someone by shooting in the course of a robbery, and those who commit sexual or sadistic murders of children can normally expect to serve at least twenty years. He also announced that 'no one sentenced to more than five years' imprisonment for an offence of violence to the person shall be released on parole, except . . . in circumstances which are genuinely wholly exceptional'.[44] As part of a balancing act, he also announced that parole would be introduced for short-term prisoners, so anyone serving ten and a half months or more would be eligible for release on parole after one third of the sentence.

The ethos had clearly changed. Ministerial speeches no longer discouraged the use of imprisonment. The official view was: 'Where people have to be incarcerated it is the Government's job to see that places are provided.'[45] The Government was 'committed to the largest building programme in the history of the Prison Service this century' which held out 'the real prospect' of 'an end to overcrowding by around the end of this decade'.[46] With such signals being given to the courts the dramatic surge in the prison population, from 44,433 in June 1984 to 48,099 in July 1985, did not come as a surprise. What is surprising is that the surge was quite so substantial, given that in July 1984 the Home Secretary's extension of parole came into effect and 2,000 short-term prisoners were released in one go. Without this one-off reduction the figure in July 1985 might have been 50,000 rather than 48,000.

As it was, seasonally adjusted figures show an average rise from September 1984 to July 1985 of about 530 prisoners a month, enough to fill a new prison the size of Bristol every four weeks.

In September 1985 Leon Brittan was replaced as Home Secretary by Douglas Hurd. The Ministerial statements became slightly more circumspect. After the 1987 General Election a new team at the Home Office, with Douglas Hurd as Home Secretary and John Patten as Minister of State, took tentative steps away from the Brittan years and back towards the consensus, but a consensus refashioned in the hard tones of the late eighties. Use of prison should be reduced for the young, the lesser offenders, the unsuccessful repeat burglar. Prison is ineffective, a school for crooks. But there is a balance to be struck, a price to be paid. And the price is very high. For minor offenders prison may be unproductive. For serious offenders only the longest, most punitive sentences will do. And the basic position remains the same – a massive prison building programme of twenty-eight new prisons between 1985 and 1995 and additions to existing prisons producing over 25,000 more prison places. The questions that should be asked have been shelved – questions such as, do we need an increase of over a half in our capacity to lock people up? Are we building the right prisons in the right places? Will overcrowding really be eliminated? Will prisoners at last have access to lavatories instead of using chamber-pots? Will our prisons be nearer in 1995 to keeping prisoners in conditions of humanity and dignity with access to work or other activities in the spirit of the European Prison Rules?

The chapter that follows proposes answers to these questions.

9   Mortgaging the Future

Will current policies solve the problems?

> MR CAMPBELL-SAVOURS, MP: When will the last 'slopping out' in British prisons be? When will it all come to an end?

> SIR BRIAN CUBBON, PERMANENT UNDER-SECRETARY, HEAD OF THE HOME OFFICE: I do not know.

> MR CAMPBELL-SAVOURS: Even after this work has taken place will there still be 'slopping out' within the British prison system, even after all these places have been made available?

> SIR BRIAN CUBBON: Yes.

> MR CAMPBELL-SAVOURS: So that I can get it quite clear, the objective set by the Home Secretary in 1983 of eliminating over-crowding by the end of the decade in Britain's prisons will not end 'slopping out' – that will remain?

> SIR BRIAN CUBBON: Correct.

> MR CAMPBELL-SAVOURS: If that is the case, could I also have some figures as to your projection for the number of prisoners within the British prison system by 1991 who will still be required in your view to carry out that rather odd practice?

> SIR BRIAN CUBBON: It is over ten thousand but less than twenty thousand.

> Proceedings of the Committee of Public Accounts, Provision of Prison Places, Minutes of Evidence, 17 February 1986.[1]

In the preceding chapters a number of problems faced by the prison service have been identified. The list is familiar – there is overcrowding, appalling physical conditions for many prisoners, an unpredictable population, and a dissatisfied staff not able to give of their best and erupting every now and then into industrial action. The prison population is changing. There are increasing numbers of life-sentence prisoners, more prisoners serving very long sentences with very little to lose by causing trouble, prisoners who have been told they are unlikely to get parole as a matter of government policy, and a significant race dimension as the proportion of black prisoners increases. In spite of genuine efforts the problem of the many mentally ill prisoners has not been solved. The clear pattern of deterioration in what the system provides for prisoners by way of work, education, recreation and constructive outlets for use of time has not yet been reversed and, the absence of any real sense of purpose, as well as the petty and unnecessary restrictions on prisoners continue. As a background, there is the drive in government for efficiency in the use of resources, which means the Treasury is breathing all the time down the neck of the Prison Service demanding that they use their resources more efficiently. In early 1986 the then head of the Home Office, Sir Brian Cubbon, appeared twice in two months before the House of Commons Public Accounts Committee, a fate dreaded by those in the public service. First, in January, he was summoned to answer for losses of £25 million and accusations of inefficiency and bad management in the Home Office Directorate of Prison Industries and Farms. Then, in February, he was called to reply to a report by the Comptroller and Auditor-General on the programme for the provision of prison places which made substantial criticisms of the Home Office strategy on prison building. The exchange which stands at the beginning of this chapter comes from that encounter. The drive for efficiency came up against the dismal industrial relations history in the dispute in the spring of 1986 which led to the overtime ban and the prison disturbances.

The prison service is the direct responsibility of a junior minister at the Home Office who is responsible in turn to the Home Secretary. It is however the Prisons Board that carries responsibility for day-to-day management and for resolving the problems of the prison service. The Prisons Board is the top management of the service and sitting round the table of a board meeting would be found the Director-General, who is the head of the service and comes from the mainstream of Home Office civil servants; the Deputy Director-General, who comes from a career as a prison governor; four regional directors, who also come up through the prison governor side; three top civil servants, heading respectively departments concerned with prisons policy, buildings and activities, and how prisons are staffed and paid for. The Director of Prison Medical Services and two non-executive members, usually from industry, bring the numbers up to twelve. The introduction of outsiders on to the board in 1980 has meant that since then there has been one woman on the board recently increased to two, as one of the few women in the upper ranks of the Home Office hierarchy reached the board. This is the group that has to grapple with the range of intractable problems just listed. As they do so they are aware that they are not the first to be in this position. Others before them have tried and failed.

Some of the problems are new. But many are endemic. In 1952 the Estimates Committee of the House of Commons carried out an inquiry into prisons and produced a report. The points they made have a familiar ring. In Wandsworth prison more than five hundred prisoners were sleeping three to a cell and 'the situation is further aggravated by the acute shortage of discipline staff, which makes it necessary for the prisoners to be locked up from 5.30 p.m. until 7 a.m.'.[2]

Furthermore, it emerged in the evidence from the Chairman of the Prison Commissioners (the prison service was run by a prison commission until 1963 and not directly by the Home Office) that there were other problems in Wandsworth. Only about forty of the prisoners were able to eat together. The rest had to eat in their cells. Also in local prisons generally, the Commissioners regretted the low hours of work they could provide – only twenty-two or twenty-three hours a week.[3] The Wandsworth Board of Visitors would no doubt be jubilant if they reached half that figure in 1988. There was trouble with prison officers' working arrangements:

The present one-shift system leads to a considerable amount of overtime being worked by prison officers. They work regularly an extra hour per day, known as the 'Morrison hour' since it was instituted during the war when Mr Herbert Morrison was Home Secretary. The staff shortage was then more acute but it was never anticipated that this form of overtime would continue for another nine years.

And certainly not for another forty-two years after the war, one assumes. The Treasury would no doubt applaud the spirit of the Committee's conclusion: 'It is the view of Your Committee that the establishment of permanent overtime at special overtime rates is a very expensive form of labour and not conducive to efficiency.'[4]

The problem of court escort duties is also not new. This Committee 'formed the opinion that the heavy demands made upon prison officers, in particular upon women prison officers at Holloway who have to provide escorts for duty in eighteen counties, strain the administration in local prisons, result in a great deal of overtime at a heavy cost to the Exchequer and upset the continuity of prisoners' work, which is already far too short and limited'.[5]

The same point was made by the Holloway Project Committee in its report, written forty-three years later: 'Holloway serves a vast catchment area covering the South-East of England as far west as Dorset and as far north as Norfolk. This means that as many as seventy-five officers can be out of the prison on a weekday morning escorting prisoners to court.'[6]

What to do with difficult prisoners was a problem in 1952: 'Your Committee were told more than once during the evidence that in most prisons there is a hard core of trouble-making prisoners.'[7] The Committee went on to recommend the solution of 'a separate prison or prisons for psychopathic troublemakers'.[8] Providing sufficient and constructive activities for prisoners was not easy even then. Sewing mailbags by hand was criticized by the Committee as monotonous and demoralizing work – especially when there were sewing-machines available but the men were not allowed to use them because sewing by hand took longer and made the available work go further.[9] Mailbags were also the subject of a Chief Inspector's observation, in 1983. He reported that one of the causes of the riot at

Albany in 1983 had been the employment of prisoners on
sewing mailbags – 'an occupation many consider to be unsuitable for long-term prisoners'.[10]

The problems highlighted by the 1952 Estimates Committee
– overcrowding, lack of occupation for prisoners, overtime by
prison officers and handling difficult or mentally disturbed prisoners – have been recurring themes, never absent from the
minds of the administrators or the pages of official and parliamentary reports. In 1959 the Government White Paper *Penal
Practice in a Changing Society* summarized the position very
clearly: 'Apart from the gross overcrowding of this very mixed
population in unsuitable buildings, another serious disadvantage from which these local prisons suffer is shortage of work.'[11]
The White Paper also had no progress to report on mailbags.
The Estimates Committee's recommendation made seven years
earlier, on phasing out mailbags, had not yet been implemented. The White Paper reported: 'work such as the making and
repairing of mailbags, which is not unsuitable for some prisoners when done on machines, has had to be done by hand
while the machines stand idle in order to make the limited
orders for work last'.[12]

By 1969, ten years later, the hand-wringing had become
rather predictable. The White Paper *People in Prison* repeated
the well-known complaint: 'The fact that in our local prisons too
many are locked in their cells for up to eighteen hours out of the
twenty-four, and sometimes longer at the weekend, shows the
extent to which progress is still hampered by Victorian buildings,
designed for solitary confinement, and by shortages of staff.'[13]

Overtime was still a problem. The 1969 White Paper said: 'It
is a matter of great concern that prison officers must regularly
work overtime . . . to an extent which impairs efficiency and
may affect health and welfare.'[14]

By October 1985, when the Chief Inspector published his
1984 Report, the recital of the problems of the prison service
had become almost routine – no report on prisons would ring
true without them. The Chief Inspector cited shortage of staff,
the demands of court duties, the state and design of the buildings, only intermittent work and little access to education,
recreation or association with other prisoners.

So the Prisons Board faces a daunting legacy of problems, recited over the years to the point of becoming clichés, yet as real in 1989 as they no doubt were in 1952 to the woman or man locked in an overcrowded smelly cell for hours on end. As William Whitelaw wisely pointed out in his Foreword to the First Annual Report of the new Chief Inspector: 'The major problems to which HM Chief Inspector refers have been decades in the making and cannot be resolved overnight.'[15]

To these problems, as the years have gone by, have been added others, not dreamed of by the Estimates Committee in 1952. Officers have moved from a military style in their relationships with management towards an industrial approach. The long-running controversy on the ethics and practice of prison medicine has been thrown into sharp relief by the need to care for HIV positive prisoners. The involvement of the courts here and in Europe in determining prisoners' rights is only one pressure for a more rights-orientated prison system. The Report by the influential lawyers group, Justice, declared: 'Since prisoners have rights, it is essential that these should be recognized, and that the system should provide the prisoners with means of asserting them.'[16]

With the grossly disproportionate numbers of black people in prison the need to face up to and deal with racism in the prison system grows ever more urgent.

It would be quite wrong to think that those who run the service do not understand that they have these problems, do not care about them or have not tried to solve them. The system is littered with vestiges of good ideas that started with great hopes but never got incorporated into the system or led to major change. The prison service has never been short of pilot projects, imaginative and worthwhile, worked at by dedicated people. The fate of these projects is depressing. Either they die or their pilot status persists for years and years, never to influence the mainstream of practice, never to actually change how things are done across the system. Grendon Underwood psychiatric prison is a case in point – opened in 1962, it was set up to treat 'personality disorders in a prison setting'.[17] The idea is that much of the prisoners' time should be spent in therapeutic groups with medical staff, prison officers and outsiders. Visitors are made welcome. Open days and concerts are held and the atmosphere is quite different from the tension and oppressiveness that can pervade the more traditional adult male prison. Visitors are invariably impressed by the dedication and skills of the staff and the purposeful atmosphere. Yet the lessons of Grendon are not applied to the rest of the system. The efforts of reformers and supporters are dedicated to ensuring that Grendon is protected from the attentions of the cost-cutters and keeps its distinctive character. In July 1986 the House of Commons Social Services Committee concluded: 'the psychotherapeutic regime has been so diluted that Grendon is now little more than an ordinary prison run on tolerably humane lines'.[18] The annexe at Wormwood Scrubs, a special unit where drug, alcohol and sex offenders are treated, remains the only unit of its kind, most publicized when there are rumours it might be closed and outside supporters are mobilized to save it.

The young offender system is a fine example of an area where experiment and idealism flourished and were gradually squeezed out by the pressures towards uniformity. It has long been regarded as right to have a separate system for young offenders, that is those under twenty-one. The young offender system is run by a different part of Prison Department headquarters from the adult male system. Attitudes towards the young have always been more hopeful. Admittedly, a streak of the 'we need to wipe the smiles off the faces of the young thugs' approach has also been present, exemplified in the detention centre and more particularly the short, sharp shock (see Chapter 4).

On the other side of the coin has been a school of thought that regarded young men as worth working with, amenable to kindness tempered with firmness, and able to be influenced by understanding shown by sympathetic, substitute-parent figures. These aspirations have not unfortunately been borne out in better results. Undoing the work of eighteen years of deprivation with one year's good food, exercise, country air and firm kindness is an unrealistic aim. Probably the views of one of the first recipients of the new, revolutionary (as it was then) borstal training, are moderately representative. Arthur

Harding, who grew up in the underworld of London's East End
at the end of the last century, was sent to borstal in 1903. This
was his second prison sentence. At the age of sixteen he had
been given twelve months' hard labour at Wormwood Scrubs.
He describes his experiences thus:

> We were the first Borstal Boys and the governor . . . was keen to
> make the new system a success. He would visit the lads in their cells
> and urge them to do well in a trade. He was always immaculately
> dressed – he seemed to have a different suit on every day. We were
> also permitted more library books and the more backward lads were
> taught to read and write. I read *Oliver Twist* – that was the first time I
> came in contact with Dickens. You weren't kept in a cell. Every day
> there were physical exercises out of doors and these had a beneficial
> effect on my health . . . and I learnt a good deal of woodwork.

Arthur Harding was discharged after a year – literate,
healthy and good at carpentry. He says: 'Borstal had made me
fitter, stronger, taller. I was no longer a kid, and when I went
back to my old associates I found that I was something of a
hero.'[19] He became a pickpocket – having learnt pickpocketing
from a man he met in Wormwood Scrubs – and spent the next
ten years in and out of prison.

The spirit of borstal training infected the whole of the male
young offender system and allowed much that was worthwhile
to develop. Two examples are worth following through: the
involvement of the respected organization, Community Service
Volunteers, in providing volunteer programmes for young offenders in custody, and the neighbourhood borstal scheme. To
take first the Community Service Volunteers scheme, it started
in 1972 when the scheme was introduced into five establishments. The organization placed young men as volunteers in
mental hospitals, a Cheshire home and a school for handicapped children for a month near the end of their sentence. In
1973 the scheme was described as 'experimental'[20] but continuing, and by 1974 the number of participants had increased to
one hundred, where it stayed until 1979 when it reached 163.
In 1983 it reached 250 trainees each year. Now it is working
with sixteen young offenders institutions, with young men and
women and 'could work with the rest if sufficient resources

were forthcoming'.[21] But the implications, that it is desirable to involve outside agencies like Community Service Volunteers, that it is beneficial to get young people in custody to go into the community and get involved in something worthwhile, have not dented the structure or assumptions of the system. The project has remained a valued extra and has never become intrinsic.

A worse fate befell another worthy experiment – the neighbourhood borstal scheme. The idea surfaces in the Prison Department Report for 1972 which explains how much better it would be if young men from the same home area all went to the same institution – and that institution built up links with the home area which could be nurtured during the sentence and then brought into play for resettlement purposes when the young man went back home.[22] In June 1973 the experiment was introduced in two borstals, Hindley, near Wigan, and Hewell Grange, near Birmingham for young men from Manchester and Birmingham. It was hoped that 'the community itself should develop a better understanding of its offenders and feel a greater degree of responsibility for assisting in their training and in their successful re-establishment in society when they leave'.[23] In 1975 reports suggest the scheme was thriving although the emphasis suggested it was more an experiment about the prison and probation services working together, than about working with a community.[24] In 1976 the first signs of its likely demise are clearly appearing. The scheme, it is reported, continued to develop 'though budgetary control has affected the links with the community in both places'.[25] In 1977 the only report is of a new idea, to attach to the neighbourhood borstals hostels like one in Ipswich that had been attached to Hollesley Bay borstal since 1968. At the hostel young men from the borstal lived under supervision and went to work during the day for local employers. A site was found for such a hostel in Manchester but a public protest in Birmingham forced the Prison Department to withdraw from taking on a building there.[26] In January 1979 the Manchester hostel was opened but Birmingham continued to prove difficult. The report on the scheme in the 1978 Report makes it clear that its original aim of working with the community has been reduced to a more modest one – to find a better way of working with the probation service.[27] In 1979 a hostel in Birmingham had still not been found. Reports of the scheme then disappear completely. We never hear what became of the hostel in Manchester, or of that in Ipswich – or of the neighbourhood borstal scheme. Diligent research has revealed however that the neighbourhood borstal scheme fizzled out – it was costing too much – and the Manchester hostel was passed to the probation service. It now lies derelict and boarded up.[28]

The young offender system, of course, is subject to frequent reorganizations. In May 1983 Borstal was abolished and the old borstals became youth custody centres. The change in ethos shines through the rhetoric. In 1975 it was confidently asserted: 'the young offender system has a strong traditional commitment to the ideals of training, of providing offenders with an opportunity to examine and, if they choose, to change their lives and also of staff involvement in a caring as well as a controlling role'.[29]

In 1980 the tone is more tentative:

Young offenders, by virtue of their age and susceptibility, present the prison service with unique problems and opportunities. Traditionally these challenges have been met with a confident and pioneering spirit ... in some cases solutions to problems posed by young offenders paved the way for far-reaching reforms in other parts of the service. In recent years, disenchantment with apparently declining success rates and philosophical doubts about the purpose of custody have led to a general re-examination of many of the assumptions underpinning traditional methods.[30]

A highly symbolic death-knell of the 'confident and pioneering spirit' sounded in 1983 when 'in the interests of the unity and cohesiveness of the prison service as a whole, staff in discipline grades in young offender establishments who had previously worn civilian clothes went into uniform'.[31]

In 1988 another reorganization brought another change of mood. Young offenders are to be separated by age into under and over seventeens, and the ethos is to be one which emphasizes 'throughcare', 'staff-inmate relationships', 'personal officer schemes' and 'bringing about the will to change behaviour'.[32] The uniforms are to stay.

The juggernaut of the system moves on, squashing good little ideas and with an innate tendency to demand uniformity, which is so much easier to manage, if you are a harassed bureaucrat, than diversity. Uniformity in rights and standards would be worth having. A uniformity which represses staff initiative and enthusiasm impoverishes the system. The ability of the system, as a system, to stimulate and nurture change is not helped of course by the Civil Service system of moving civil servants on to another job at about the point – five years at the longest – when their attempts to influence developments would just be coming to fruition. Nor is it helped by the culture and ethos of the Prison Department which require new incumbents to cast a critical eye over the work of their predecessors and prove their independence of mind by changing everything.

There is ample evidence that those currently responsible for the prison service are not ostriches with their heads in the sand. They know what the problems are and are showing some determination to face up to them. They have a programme of work that is truly formidable. First, they are expanding at a rapid rate – new prisons are planned to come on stream every year: one in 1990, seven in 1991, five in 1992, two in 1994, two in 1995 and four yet to be decided. These new prisons have to be planned for, staffed, opened and run. Boards of Visitors and Local Review Committees have to be appointed to them.

Second, the Prison Service is feeling the effects of the Government's drive to provide services in a way which is efficient, effective and gives value for money. The facts set out in Chapter 7 about the use of resources, workshops built and never used, machines never operated and increased numbers of staff running ever more impoverished services for prisoners are well known to the Treasury. The implementation of the Fresh Start way of working with its abolition of overtime, its organizing of prison officers into groups and the creation of a more modern management structure has moved the Prison Service from the 1950s to the 1980s organizationally. A 1980s philosophy has also stimulated the proposals for privatization of some Prison Service functions. In 1987 the Conservative majority on the Home Affairs Select Committee visited some private prisons in the United States and came back enthused enough to recommend an experiment here. Subsequently in 1988, the Green Paper, *Private Sector Involvement in the Remand System* outlined possibilities for privatization. Management consultants, alongside 'criminal justice experts',[33] were to carry out an investigation to see how privatization could be done and what procedures were needed to do it.

Many of the recommendations made by the May Committee about how the system should be managed have been implemented. To create 'a greater degree of unity and identity',[34] as May put it, the Prison Department moved to its own building, outside Home Office headquarters. The Director-General works there near his staff, instead of in Home Office HQ near his ministers. The Prison Department has its own notepaper and logo. It has its own monthly newspaper, *Prison Service News*, full of news about policy, people and sport. A communications consultant has been brought in and the not very informative Prison Service Annual Report has been re-vamped to become more attractive, more comprehensible, but even less informative. The Prison Department now calls itself 'the Prison Service' to emphasize unity. The Prisons Board has approved the new statement of functions which is the basis to which governors are to work. In 1984 a circular instruction went out to all governors, called 'Management Accountability in the Prison Service', setting out a new framework of accountability. 'Regime monitoring' is being brought in. This means that information on how far a prison does what it is supposed to do – e.g. get prisoners bathed, ensure they get their letters, visits to the library, clean clothes and how many hours of activities, such as education or work, it provides – is collected every week and fed into a computer. Then those in charge can see how they are doing. Prison Service organization is being reviewed to 'improve effectiveness and value for money'[35] and see if there is scope, say, for more delegation of responsibility to individual prisons.

A new head of the Prison Medical Service, formerly a director of the World Health Organization at the United Nations, has come in and has taken an energetic look at the deficiencies of the prison medical services. He is particularly concerned about the shortfall in recruitment, and the low morale and the lack of understanding between the Home Office and the Department of Health and the National Health Service.[36] A major report on the control of long-term prisoners has provided the basis for some very slow change. Minor changes in the disciplinary system are being brought in following the Government's rejection of the main recommendations of the Prior Committee on the prison disciplinary system. Following a thorough-going critique of prisoners' complaints procedures by the Chief Inspector a review of complaints procedures has been launched. Following criticisms by the Chief Inspector a review of prisoners' pay has been established.

All in all, this represents a formidable programme of activity. But – a big but – where is it leading? Is it going towards a modern, humane prison system fit for the twenty-first century where prisoners are treated decently and staff have satisfying and worthwhile careers – or towards an expanded, more efficient, managerially less incoherent version of what exists today.

Regrettably the answer is very likely to be the latter. Many of the details of the programme are admirable. What is wrong with it is its priorities and its lack of a basic rationale and sense of purpose. The expansion of the system – the twenty-eight purpose-built new prisons – is a costly mistake. The efficiency drives and management initiatives are a hollow shell, the medium but not the message, because they fail to tackle the basic question – what is the system for? – and then concentrate on enabling the major resource of the service, that is the staff, to deliver it.

To look first at the expansion of the system – an expansion which is costing over a billion pounds for the twenty-eight new prisons and draining resources from the rest of the prison service – the arguments against the expansion come from several directions. Three questions need to be answered. First, will it succeed in its own terms? That is, will it eliminate overcrowding? Second, will it end bad prison conditions? Third, can it be justified in terms of benefit to society?

First, is it going to end overcrowding? Overcrowding would no longer be necessary if the number of prison places was slightly more (around 1,000–2,000 more) than the number of people in prison. Anyone who promises to end overcrowding by building more cells must therefore have an idea of what the number of people in prison is going to be when all the building is finished. However, predictions of the prison population are very difficult to make. In 1971, for instance, the Home Office projections were that by 1980 the population would be nearly 70,000. In 1972 that projection came down to 57,000. The actual population in 1980 was 42,300. Wisely, the method of projecting was changed in 1973 and the projection made in that year for 1980 of just under 42,000 was not far wrong. However, recent events have again thrown the forecasters into some confusion. Leon Brittan, asked on 19 July 1984 in the House of Commons by Alf Dubs, MP, what he expected the prison population to be in 1990, replied, 'Forty-seven thousand.'[37] There were more prisoners than that by the middle of the following summer and the population remained around 47,000 for much of 1985. In 1984 official Home Office projections for 1991 were just over 48,000. In April 1985 estimates were 49,600.

Also in April 1985, for the first time, at the suggestion of the Treasury, Home Office statisticians took account of the impending changes in the age-structure of the population. A substantial drop in the number of those in the age-group most likely to commit crime is already taking place. As David Riley points out in the *Research Bulletin* of the Home Office Research and Planning Unit, 'the size of the seventeen–twenty-year-olds' group is set to shrink from 1.7 million to 1.2 million between now and 1995'.[38] On a simple view, this ought to mean fewer prisoners, but the dynamics are not so simple. The same proportions could be arrested, convicted and imprisoned as now, which would certainly reduce the numbers in prison. On the other hand the system, to keep up its workload, could spread its net wider and draw in less serious criminals. Another possibility is that the smaller number of young people there will be in the early nineties will commit more crime than their predecessors did. No one really knows. So the Home Office now has what it calls a 'demographic projection' for the prison population in 1991, that is, a reduced one because of the drop in the numbers of young people, which is 47,500. In March 1986, as a result of the sudden, unexpected, and very substantial surge in the numbers in prison which took place in 1985 these projections were both revised upwards. The Home Office is now predicting 60,000 in 1991 and 69,000 in 1996 on the non-demographic model and 56,700 in 1991 and 63,000 in 1996 on the demographic model.

On the surface the figures look simple. The building programme will mean that by 1996 or thereabouts (if there is no slippage) there will be 61,000 prison places. However that forecast has to be seen realistically. It assumes that all the existing places keep going and remain usable, that nothing is burnt down or falls down or is destroyed, and no cells are lost by programmes of modernization and putting lavatories into cells. For example 800 places were lost in the disturbances of 1986. Also, it is planned to close Oxford prison. Lancaster prison, housed in a castle dating back to 1094, is on a lease from the Duchy of Lancaster which expires in 1991. The claim that the programme would, in Leon Brittan's words, 'put us on course for ending prison overcrowding altogether by the end of the decade'[39] has already been overtaken by events. In 1990 there will be 47,500 prison places.[40] The non-demographic projections for the number of prisoners is 57,300. If these projections come to pass it will mean that Leon Brittan's aim of eliminating overcrowding will have become overcrowding to match the highest level ever recorded, that is 20 per cent. The notion that overcrowding could be ended by 1990 received a drubbing from the Comptroller and Auditor-General, Gordon Downey, in a highly critical report published in December 1985. The Report concludes that: 'the building programme will not succeed in meeting their [the Home Office's] target objective of matching total available places with aggregate prison population by the end of the decade'.[41]

The Report noted that if eliminating overcrowding was the objective, the Home Office was going about it the wrong way. Overcrowding is concentrated in local prisons, yet the Home Office plan meant that: 'Most of the 3,100 extra places to be provided in local prisons, where overcrowding is worst, will not become available until 1989 at the earliest, and, even when they are all complete, they will be insufficient to eliminate the 1984–5 level of overcrowding.'[42] The Report also drew attention to the conclusion of the Home Office's own Working Group on Resource Strategy which 'drew attention to a possible excess of 2,000 inmates over prison places in 1991, due mainly to the planned temporary withdrawal of accommodation for refurbishment'. This Group also 'identified significant problems with local prisons which could continue into the next decade'.[43]

Sir Gordon Downey concludes with a profoundly depressing but very convincing analysis expressed in more forthright terms than one often finds in government documents. 'My more general conclusion,' he says, 'is that a high degree of risk attaches to the present programme.' And he goes on:

... these are fundamental uncertainties about the size of the prison population in the early 1990s ... unless the Home Office take special operational measures, the programme will fail to achieve their broad objective of matching total available places with total prison population by the end of the decade ... they do not have the more detailed objective of providing adequate prison places of the right categories and in the right locations ... at the end of the decade there may well still be overcrowding in some prisons and under-occupation in others.[44]

Five years after Leon Brittan made his promise Home Office officials were again before the Public Accounts Committee, explaining the prison building programme and what was being done about overcrowding. Sir Brian Cubbon explained the sequence of events so far with remarkable clarity. The Home Secretary had, he said, agreed in 1983 that the target should be set of eliminating overcrowding by the end of 1990. 'This was,' said Sir Brian, 'a valuable discipline because it meant that slippages in the programme would affect the target, and we were under pressure to find extra places within existing establishments. But the wild card in all this was the size of the prison population, over which the Home Office does not have control. It is the size of the prison population which has meant that the target has not been met.'[45]

However, Sir Brian assured the Committee that the Home Office still has the policy objective of eliminating overcrowding.

However 'eliminating overcrowding' has a subtle meaning. He was asked on an earlier occasion before the Public Accounts Committee by Sir Michael Shaw, MP, whether the Comptroller and Auditor-General had been right to suggest that overcrowding would remain. He replied:

> Yes. The objective has always been to match the average population with the accommodation'... Something like 1,000 to 2,000 extra places would be needed to cope with every possible level of population within the year ... we ... almost certainly will not have a total match between the categories of our accommodation and the categories of the prisoners at the time ... which explains that there will certainly remain overcrowding in some prisons and under-occupation in others. It would be much more expensive and not necessarily value for money to have the objective of always ensuring there was no overcrowding.[46]

So the answer to the question, is it going to end overcrowding, is no, it is not. It was not ever meant to. Eliminating overcrowding would not represent 'value for money'.

The second question that needs to be answered is, will the building programme lead to better prison conditions? For some prisoners, undoubtedly, in a physical sense, conditions will be better. The new prisons will have lavatories in the cells and good facilities for work, education and visits. But those who imagine that the prison building programme represents the modernization of our prison system, the end of prisoners using a pot in a cell shared with two others and then queuing up in the morning to slop out, are going to be disappointed. This is not so. As the extract at the beginning of this chapter makes clear, when asked a direct question by the Public Accounts Committee, will this still be going on?, Sir Brian Cubbon had to say, yes, it will. The Public Accounts Committee are not impressed. In their 1988 report they return to this theme with commendable persistence. And they conclude:

> We also note that in 1999 there will remain twenty-six establishments completely lacking in access to night sanitation. In all 14,500 prison places are affected, representing about one quarter of all prison places; and the Home Office admitted they knew of no other European country which had a worse situation.[47]

The Wandsworth Board of Visitors are similarly dismayed by the seeming inability to end slopping out. In their 1985 report they recount how warmly they welcomed the news that work would start in 1987 on providing integral sanitation in three wings. The Board saw this 'as a major reform, the most significant advance for many decades in civilizing the conditions of imprisonment in Wandsworth'.[48] When they heard that the project had been postponed, their disappointment was bitter. The reasons they were given for the change were shortage of cash, and the burgeoning prison population. In their 1987 report they write '1987 was to have been the year when integral sanitation came to Wandsworth. It has been postponed to 1991/1992 and there is no guarantee that it will begin then . . . the lack of proper sanitation in prison is possibly the greatest public health disgrace in this country. Prisoners and officers frequently have to paddle through other men's urine towards the end of the "slopping out" session as the drains cannot cope with the volume of use'. But pressure can bring rewards.[49] In 1988 a project began to bring running water and sanitation, as an experiment, to 8 out of Wandsworth's 1,254 cells.

The twenty-eight new prisons still to be built are not intended as replacements for the old decaying Pentonvilles and Brixtons. They are additional. By 1995 the system will include some of the most modern prisons alongside others that could well be turned into museums. On present form prisoners in 1995 will still be living in Dartmoor, a prison originally built by prisoners of war in the Napoleonic Wars in 1815 and used by them. First used as a prison in 1851, the 1959 White Paper said it was nearing 'the end of its serviceable life'.[50] It has been refurbished and propped up and it soldiers on.

Physical conditions for many prisoners therefore will be untouched by the massive expansion of the system and the new building that is being undertaken. Will the expanded prison system offer improvements in those aspects of prison life that matter particularly to prisoners – being near their homes and families, being able to communicate with the outside world, being prepared for release and enabled to keep their community links? Unfortunately not. The new prisons enshrine the philosophy – in so far as it can be called a philosophy – of treatment and training. The existing edifice of Category A, B, C and D, the division between local and training, the current wisdom about the right size of an institution, all remain. The first new prisons to be built are the training prisons and the top-security places. The real pressures are on the overcrowded locals. Even odder is the decision that 60 per cent of the people in these new local prisons will be housed not in cells on their own – but in cells for two. A decision has been taken to build cells for two, on cost grounds, even though the European Prison Rules first advocated a right to the privacy of a cell on one's own in 1973. To construct in concrete and brick twenty-eight purpose-built monuments to outdated penal theology – outdated even before the foundations have been excavated – over £1 billion is being spent.

There are other ways of running a prison system and other approaches to imprisonment. A number of Prison Department officials visited the USA and came back with a range of ideas, set out in *New Directions in Prison Design: The Report of a Home Office Working Party on American New Generation Prisons*. The Working Party looked at a number of 'new generation' prisons in the United States run by the Federal Bureau of Prisons and concluded that the UK could learn much from developments there. Particular design elements they singled out include a campus-type layout, provision of separate house units for about fifty–seventy-five prisoners with similar needs, with cells giving access directly on to a central living area, eating together for most of the prisoner population, and furnishings designed to produce a non-institutional atmosphere. Nearer home, in Sweden, through a radical turn-around in prisons policy that took place in the early 1970s, plans to build seven new maximum-security prisons were scrapped in favour of building small neighbourhood prisons, holding fifty or sixty short-term prisoners, where the whole basis of imprisonment would be contact with the local community and preparation for release. Seventeen of these prisons were needed.

No such radical rethinking has characterized the current prison building programme here. New prisons are to be built which will increase capacity since 1985 by 64 per cent. Yet how they are built and the principles that govern their design, location, style and appearance have not been the subject of intense consultation or debate, certainly not publicly and, one suspects, not internally either. The prison at Full Sutton, which opened in August 1987 and which will no doubt serve well into the next century, was 'based on an off-the-shelf design of the old style',[51] as the Director-General of the prison service told the Public Accounts Committee. Some 'new generation' prisons may be considered, but only in relation to two prisons at the very end of the programme, Doncaster and Milton Keynes. It would seem that decisions about what to build, how large and where, are taken on the basis of what was done last time, in accordance with building standards based on what is allowed to be spent, and without any evident analysis of how such prisons will be staffed, managed and controlled. The Comptroller and Auditor-General found, for instance, that Frankland prison 'is expected to need nearly 400 staff to run it, compared with 290 originally estimated in 1976; and Full Sutton is being built to the same basic design as a result of a Home Office decision in 1978, aimed at saving time in the design stage, despite their awareness that the design was manpower-intensive and would not minimize running costs'.[52]

So there is no reason to think that in 1991 the expansion will have improved our system very much. More prisoners will be living a long way from their homes and families, many in new buildings which replicate the institutional mistakes of the past, or deliberately ignore international standards, others still in overcrowded buildings more than a hundred years old, emptying their chamber-pots every morning. In 1964 a Labour Party Study Group report, *Crime: A Challenge to Us All*, made some comments on the prison building programme of 1959 which are depressingly topical. The programme, of eight new security prisons for men, costing many millions of pounds was, the Report said, 'largely misconceived' for several reasons:

The design of more secure buildings should be ... more flexible than it is: these buildings ought to be readily adaptable to meet possible future changes in prison regimes ... in their general aspect and architecture the new prison buildings show few signs of original thought: it does not seem to have occurred to those who designed them that a prison in 1970 might differ in any important way from a prison in 1870 . . . no attempt has been made to demolish and replace those gigantic nineteenth-century fortresses, in London and other cities, which are to most people a symbol of the prison system at its most hopeless.[53]

Perhaps though the last word on the inefficacy of a building programme should rest with the Home Office itself, who wrote in the White Paper of 1980 that to keep pace with the current projections of increase in the prison population would demand substantial expansion in the building programme. It goes on: 'to increase the number of prison places to a level where there is no overcrowding would be an even more ambitious enterprise; and even if that could be realized, a large part of the prison population would still have to be housed in antiquated and unsuitable buildings'.[54]

Finally, can the expansion of the prison system be justified in terms of benefit to society, in the way, perhaps, that schools and hospitals can be justified? Putting up huge, grim-looking secure edifices around the country may symbolize a commitment to law and order, but does it do any good? On the contrary, no benefits come to society from having a high prison population. Consider for instance the position of a low-prison-using country like Holland compared with a place of equivalent population with a high use of prison, the state of Texas. The population of both is about 15 million. The number of crimes known to the police is about the same, around 1 million. The prison population of Holland in 1985 was 4,600. In Texas it was 50,000. Few would claim that Texas is safer than Holland or gains in any other measurable way from locking up 50,000 of its people. A high prison population consisting of relatively minor offenders against property brings no benefits to a society, but has costs, the costs of imprisonment, of disruption to people's lives, of after-care and social work services, and a crippling financial commitment tying up resources that could be used for more socially useful purposes, such as preventing crime.

The building programme and the expansion have other deleterious effects by absorbing the resources that are really needed to improve the system as it is now. The postponement

[handwritten margin note: what abt type of crimes?]

of refurbishment at Wandsworth was due to the demands of expansion. The sudden surge of the population in the summer of 1985 led to the purchase of an old RAF station at Lindholme in South Yorkshire at a cost of £17.5 million for the site, building work and running costs for the rest of the financial year. The consequence was that a circular went out to all governors telling them that for the remainder of the year 'it is necessary for us to be certain that money is spent in a way which enables the Service to concentrate on the immediate and pressing priority of dealing with the increased levels of population'.[55] This meant postponement of maintenance and refurbishment and cuts in training for staff.

Against this background, the attempts of the prison service to get to grips with the industrial relations problems, poor financial control, inadequate management and difficulties of controlling long-term prisoners are to be admired. It is hard though to believe that attempts to improve matters which concentrate so entirely on budgetary and financial control can be successful. The Chief Inspector says that 'in 1987 many Governors still perceived the Department to be concerned above all with economies of cash and manpower, at the expense of regime, development and other caring initiatives'.[56] What is lacking is a basic premise of what a decent prison service looks like, what the service should be aiming at, what staff are supposed to do to do a good job, how that can be developed and then measured. The central premise was put in a way which cannot be bettered by the Home Office's own Control Review Committee: 'Prisons cannot be run by coercion: ... Nothing can be allowed to qualify the need for staff to be in control at all times, but we are sure that the very great majority will agree with us this is best achieved by the unobtrusive use of their professional skill at involvement with prisoners.'

One must conclude that the prison system has embarked on the wrong course and has the wrong priorities. The capital and future revenue costs of the expansion are, relatively, enormous. The expansion will increase the revenue costs by a half – if no improvements are made in provision as it is now. In 1981 the Home Affairs Committee of the House of Commons recommended a different priority. Their first recommendation was:

'Priority within the prison building and maintenance programme should be given to substantial redevelopment and refurbishing of the existing local prisons, including the provision of integral sanitation.[57]

This recommendation is echoed by Rod Morgan in his 1982 Noel Buxton lecture where he said:

The whole of the capital programme should be devoted to the modernization or replacement of those prisons already in the system and which will meet its future needs best. The local prisons are in the right places and the future depends on them. If this Government, and future Governments, allow the prison population to rise – for ultimately it will be a political decision – it would be better to open emergency camps, whatever their short-term costs, than mortgage the future with prisons of no long-term value.[58]

To do both, that is, improve the existing prisons and build new ones, would cost more than anyone imagines could be made available. The expansion also drains money away from dealing with the really pressing problem of the service, that is, deciding what it should be doing with prisoners and then working out how to provide that with existing staff and in spite of existing buildings.

Such a reversal of priorities, away from expansion to refurbishment, with a target of giving all prisoners access to integral sanitation, and away from sterile budgetary control to development of humane and constructive prison regimes, can only be achieved if the major obstacle to progress is removed – the burgeoning prison population. Ways have to be found to reduce the use of prison. But how? The next chapter considers this dilemma.

10   A Structural Problem

Reducing the use of prison

> Soon after the Working Party had been set up and our terms
> of reference announced, Lord Devlin in an address to the
> Annual General Meeting of the Howard League for Penal
> Reform expressed the 'alarm' which the words 'judicial train-
> ing' occasioned him. In the course of his address he said of
> the judge's role:
>
> 'He sits as the man who speaks for the ordinary citizen.
> Once you start training him in anything, whether it be pen-
> ology or anything else – and if there is a case for training him
> in anything it is obviously penology first, anyway – but once
> you start training him in anything, then he loses the essen-
> tial character of the English Judge. He no longer speaks and
> reacts as the ordinary man, he sits on the bench as what
> can never be more or better than a half-trained expert.'
>
> Though understandable this reaction to our appointment
> seems to us to result from misconceptions . . .
>
> From the *Consultative Working Paper of the Working Party on
> Judicial Training and Information.*[1]

At the centre of the problems of the prison service is its lack
of control over the number of its customers. The prison service
cannot put up House Full signs nor is it allowed to set up
waiting-lists, as hospitals do. Its workload is entirely at the mercy
of a group of people, magistrates and judges, who themselves
have no structural involvement in running the prison system
and no responsibility for allocating the resources to it. The law,

as represented by magistrates and judges, not only has no connection with running prisons, it also has no involvement in prison conditions. In the United States judges are involved in hearing cases brought against bad conditions and overcrowding in prisons. They can make judgments on what prison conditions are acceptable and what are unacceptable. In Canada the prisons are the administrative responsibility of the Solicitor-General, a law officer in the Canadian government. In Holland prisons come under the same Ministry as the courts, prosecutors and judges, that is, the Ministry of Justice. In this country there seem to be no rules about the physical conditions of imprisonment which, at the moment at least, are legally enforceable and would require the courts to get involved in considering the conditions in which prisoners are held.

Therefore the structural and practical separation is great between those in the courts who daily make decisions about how many people are to be held in prison (which ultimately become decisions about what conditions they are held in) and those who provide the places to hold them in, the regimes they undergo, the quality of justice and fairness they experience inside.

Strangely, this great gulf between those who provide the resources, that is, the Home Office, and those who consume them, that is the judges and magistrates, is regarded as a good thing. The Home Office, responsible for providing and running prisons, and the Lord Chancellor's Department, responsible for the judiciary, do talk to each other but there is an element of regarding this as a rather daring and dangerous activity. For the Home Office to talk directly to the judges is regarded with even more suspicion. It is rumoured the Home Office started giving little buffet suppers for selected judges, just to get to know them, but they were stopped after the second one, presumably because someone regarded it as unconstitutional. Whoever it was, it was certainly not Judge Pickles, who, in an interview with the *Guardian*, said:

The trouble is that we never get together with the Home Office to discuss these things. The only forum we have is the Council of Her Majesty's Circuit judges which is a body almost exclusively involved with expenses and salaries and pensions for judges. If you got up and spoke about, say, delays they would say, 'My dear child, what are you on about? For goodness sake!'[2]

It was noted in Chapter 3 how tentative and apologetic the Home Office Introduction to their sentencing handbook is. The judiciary also has its sensitivities, illustrated best perhaps by the tale of the Working Party set up in 1975 by the Home Secretary, the Lord Chancellor and the Lord Chief Justice to consider improving the way judges were informed of latest developments in criminal justice and trained for their sentencing task. The extract at the beginning of the chapter shows that the idea of 'training' for judges provoked quite a hostile reaction. The Working Party, made up of judges, civil servants, academics and other legal people issued a consultative paper setting out some ideas for how judicial training and the giving of information to judges might be organized. They clearly felt the need to answer Lord Devlin's objections, which they did by asserting how far 'training' was from an encroachment on the independence of the judges: 'It is axiomatic and fundamental that any programme of judicial training must avoid encroaching in any way . . . on the independence of the judiciary.' But, they go on, the danger is largely imaginary. As they point out: 'Sentencing is far from being an exact science . . . there could be no question of any training programme seeking to impart a particular philosophy of sentencing in this highly controversial field.'[3] They have no intention of trying to turn judges into 'half-trained experts'. However, people who work with offenders in fields other than the law do have useful knowledge to pass on and they go on: 'We find it hard to understand why the attempt to enable the judge to profit from this illumination need in any way impair his capacity "to speak and react as an ordinary man".'[4]

They also attack the 'fundamental' misconception that a judge needs no more than a background of experience in court and the capacity that goes with being an ordinary man (there are very few women judges), to fully carry out his sentencing responsibilities. At the very least, they say, 'a judge who is quite unfamiliar with the day-to-day conditions under which a prisoner serves his term of imprisonment can hardly be considered well-qualified to determine the length of a prison sentence'.[5]

By the time the Working Party produced its final report however, the confidence of its counter-attack had been greatly dented. Clearly Lord Devlin was not the only eminent judicial person to object to the idea of being trained. In its final report, the Working Party had to admit that they had faced 'a widely felt and strongly voiced objection to the use of the phrase "judicial training" '. The objection, they said, goes like this:

... 'training' implies that there are 'trainers' who can train people to be judges, and so long as this concept is capable of influencing the thought of those concerned with the provision of 'judicial training' this must . . . represent a threat to judicial independence; that those of the stature and experience to fit them for appointment as judges will resent the implications that they need to be 'trained'; and moreover that the public image of the judge must be impaired if the public are told that he is required to undergo a period of 'training' on appointment.[6]

The Working Party caved in before this onslaught, but not without showing some signs of impatience. They now had, they said, a fresh difficulty, that of finding a word that meant 'the procedures which it is appropriate that judges should experience on or after appointment in order to enhance their judicial capacity and more specifically their capacity to perform the functions of sentencers in the Crown Court' that is, what everyone else would call training, without saying 'training'. Though they found it 'inelegant' they had to be content with the phrase 'judicial studies', and they went on to recommend a Judicial Studies Board and judicial studies programmes.

The same sort of feeling, that judges are in some way different and should not be involved in the practices and disciplines that are taken for granted in other professions, no doubt lay behind the decision of the Lord Chief Justice in 1981 when he refused to give his permission for research into how sentencing is done in the Crown Court. This decision, as Andrew Ashworth who was to carry out the work says, had the effect of 'not only depriving members of society of knowledge with which to evaluate the sentencing practice of the judges but also depriving policy-makers of the necessary empirical basis for formulating penal policy'.[7]

As Andrew Ashworth points out, if we know so little about what goes through the judge's mind when deciding on a particular sentence those who have to formulate penal policy have to work in the dark.

Attempts to bridge the separation between those trying to devise a penal policy and those deciding on its input have not been well received. Policies do of course emerge from the judiciary, though one suspects that 'policy' might be a word regarded as unfavourably as 'training'. The preferred description would perhaps be 'guidance'. Guidance on sentencing certainly comes from time to time from the Court of Appeal. As we have seen in Chapter 8 in 1980 the Lord Chief Justice pointed out that: 'Sentencing judges should appreciate that overcrowding in many of the penal establishments in this country is such that a prison sentence, however short, is a very unpleasant experience indeed for the inmates.'[8] And he went on to comment that short sentences should be passed when possible.

In 1986 the Lord Chief Justice laid down some guidelines for courts to follow when deciding on sentences for rape. He said on this occasion that sentences for rape were too low and went on to suggest that for rape committed by an adult without any aggravating or mitigating features a sentence of five years should be taken as the starting point in a contested case.[9]

The way the Court of Appeal tries to impose some coherence on the decisions of the many hundreds of sentencers, all of whom have a great deal of discretion, has been criticized. Andrew Ashworth identifies some weaknesses as 'a dearth of guidance on the question of whether to impose a custodial sentence or not' and very little guidance at all on how and when to impose non-custodial sentences and what to do about the lower end of offences.[10] He also points out that on some issues the Court of Appeal produces contradictory guidance and fails to refer to its own previous decisions.[11] In the pilot research study carried out as a preliminary to the major piece of research that the Lord Chief Justice declined to agree to Andrew Ashworth found that: 'Some judges interviewed . . .

expressed a scepticism towards Court of Appeal judgments which bordered on contempt.'[12] Their main complaint was that the court had too little experience of the sort of run-of-the-mill cases that the courts deal with every day to say anything very useful about them.

So this is the peculiar structural position from within which most Home Secretaries since 1964 have tried to reduce the use of prison by the courts. For the first ten years of this effort they could have felt reasonably optimistic. In 1967, for instance, the proportion of men over twenty-one sentenced for indictable offences who went to prison was nearly a quarter. By 1974 the figure had fallen to fifteen out of every hundred. This was not to be an enduring trend however. 1974 was the turning-point and since then it has been creeping up, to reach twenty-one out of every hundred in 1987. This is in spite of valiant efforts that have been made, backed up by a steady stream of official and unofficial reports and research findings from the Home Office's own research unit and outside. These efforts fall into three distinct categories – creating new ways for the courts to deal with offenders and hoping they will use them instead of prison, changing the rules on when and how prisoners can be let out, and making the courts jump through various hoops before they are allowed to impose a prison sentence.

To deal with each of these in turn, Chapter 4 showed how creating new alternatives and then hoping they are used instead of custody has not exactly been a success. Suspended sentences were introduced in good faith in 1967 by Roy Jenkins as a measure to reduce the prison population. We have seen how the view now is that they have not reduced, and may have increased, it. The Criminal Justice Act of 1972 saw the introduction of community service orders, and the possibility of day training centres and detoxification centres for drunken offenders. Community service orders were introduced with a lack of clarity about their place in sentencing which has caused problems ever since. Are they meant to be 'alternatives to custody' as suspended sentences were meant to be? If so, why did the Act not say so? The confusion about their use, and the disagreements between benches of magistrates who have decided community service orders should be used as alternatives and those who feel they should be used more widely, have dogged them since introduction. As Ken Pease pointed out in his study of community service orders: 'differences between areas mean that sentencing policy can depend on which side of the road an offender lives'.[13]

The Home Office handbook *The Sentence of the Court* cites the view of the Court of Appeal that a community service order might 'effectively serve the same punitive purpose'[14] as a sentence of some months' imprisonment. Undoubtedly this has happened in many cases. Yet those who thought up and introduced the community service order must be disappointed at its failure to make real inroads into the number of short prison sentences passed every year. Neither did day training centres and detoxification centres, designed presumably to remove from prison persistent petty offenders with a range of social problems, make the mark intended by the progenitors. Four day training centres were set up by the probation service. The 1982 Criminal Justice Act gave the courts the power to require someone to spend up to sixty days at a probation centre as a condition of a probation order, but this measure has not had a significant impact either. Detoxification centres on the lines proposed in the 1972 Act never really got off the ground at all. Three were set up but faced great difficulties getting funding.

The next foray into supposed alternatives to custody was the introduction of partly suspended prison sentences. Partly suspended sentences had been made possible by the Criminal Law Act of 1977 but not been implemented largely because of doubts in the Home Office about their possible effect. In 1981 the Home Office said of the measure:

That section has not been activated because of fears that the new sentence would be used to give a 'taste of imprisonment' in cases where at present the courts would impose a fully suspended sentence or non-custodial sentence. Inevitably too, in a proportion of cases the suspended part of the sentence would be subsequently activated. Thus there can be no certainty that implementing Section 47 would achieve any reduction in numbers in custody.[15]

In his address to the Annual General Meeting of N A C R O on 10 November 1981, William Whitelaw nevertheless stated that the time may have come to bring in the partly suspended sentence, neither the first nor the last example of the Home Office having to change its mind. The measure was brought in in amended form in January 1983. It is clear from the Criminal Statistics that, as expected, it has replaced some of the fully suspended sentences previously given and has had scarcely any impact on the overall use of prison.

So no substantial progress has been made by devising alternatives and then hoping there will be a large-scale switch from custody to community penalties. Varying the rules about when people can be released has been more successful, as one would expect, as it is the method which depends, not on the courts, but on the Home Office or agencies it sets up. There are three methods of arranging matters so that the sentence actually served is less than the nominal period imposed by the court – remission, parole and executive release. Remission is available to all prisoners serving more than five days and allows a prisoner to be released automatically after serving two thirds of the sentence unless any of the remission has been lost through bad behaviour. Remission, for most categories of prisoner, has stood at one third since the early 1940s when it was brought in as a wartime expedient. However, the one-third is not immutable. It can be changed quite easily by a simple parliamentary procedure, a device resorted to during the population crisis of July 1987 when Douglas Hurd brought in, to the great displeasure of some Conservative backbenchers and some Conservative leaderwriters, half remission for prisoners serving a year or less. Northern Ireland has a different system. Parole does not operate there because of political difficulties. In 1976, during the time of Merlyn Rees as Northern Ireland Secretary, a system of conditional release was brought in. For prisoners serving sentences of one year or less the release is unconditional. For longer-term prisoners, if they are convicted of an imprisonable offence during the remitted part of their sentence, they are liable to serve the balance of their sentence plus the penalty for the new offence. In the debate on the 1986 prison disturbances, Merlyn Rees was moved to reminisce about his efforts to bring in a similar system in England and Wales:

There had to be a radical cut in the size of the prison population. That was easier to implement in Northern Ireland than elsewhere. The judges in Northern Ireland know what is going on. There is no establishment – with a small 'e' – to say, 'Oh, no, this will upset people.' Therefore, the Labour Government introduced the 50-per-cent remission system.

Why did I not do that here? The rest of the United Kingdom is a different place. My Hon. Friend, the Member for Knowsley North (Mr Kilroy-Silk) put it to me firmly that it would look daft. Others also put it firmly that, in the run-up to the general election, we would be crucified on law and order.

It was made clear to me that the judiciary would not support what I was doing. If I had introduced the scheme, the tariff would have gone up to match the 50 per cent.[16]

Such a scheme was recommended by the All-Party Penal Affairs Group, chaired by Robert Kilroy-Silk, in 1980, but has never been adopted.

Parole was introduced in 1967, at the same time as suspended sentences, as part of Roy Jenkins's measures to reduce the prison population. The difference between remission and parole is that remission is given automatically to everyone with no conditions attached unless it is lost for misbehaviour. Parole is granted through a complex machinery of committees, can be given with conditions, for example to live at a certain address, and involves supervision by a probation officer and recall to prison if the parole goes wrong.

It was in 1964 that the case for a parole system was clearly made in the Labour Party Report *Crime: A Challenge to Us All*. The Report said:

We doubt the value of keeping men in prison after they have learnt their lesson; at this point the cost of continuing to keep them in prison is no longer justified. Parliament has provided that borstal sentences shall not be for more than two years, but that the Prison Department can release any borstal trainee under supervision after he has served at least a quarter of this period. We recommended that the Home Secretary should appoint a Parole Board, with one or more representatives of the judiciary upon it; with similar powers in relation to any sentence of imprisonment.[17]

The Home Secretary did as he was advised and parole was

introduced in the Criminal Justice Act of 1967. The first parolees were released on 1 April 1968. Although the hidden agenda was to reduce the prison population, high claims were being made at the time that parole would be 'effective' in some way, and play its part in helping prisoners to keep out of trouble. As a former Parole Board member, Elizabeth Barnard, wrote in 1976:

> The official objective was clearly rehabilitative: after some decades of optimism about the potential of training and therapy in the custodial setting, it was thought that further progress could be achieved by some flexibility on discharge dates and by supervison during the difficult period of transition to ordinary life. It was alleged that prisoners reached 'a recognizable peak' in their potential for good post-custody adjustment, and that if they were detained for longer, they may deteriorate.[18]

Parole started gradually. When the first prisoners were released on licence in April 1968 there was great disappointment on the part of prisoners accompanied by an outcry in the press because fewer than one in ten actually got parole. Since 1968 however the rate has risen substantially. In 1976 54 per cent of those eligible for parole received it. In 1987 the figure was 71 per cent. Parole can well be regarded as a success if judged by the small number of parolees who are recalled either because they commit another offence or because they break the conditions of their licence, as it is called, or give cause for alarm in some way or other. The percentage of those who fail in these ways hovers around one in ten. In 1987 it was 5 per cent.

Since it was established in 1968 the parole system has not stood still. In 1975 Roy Jenkins was again at the Home Office. While there he broadened the scope of the parole system by drawing a distinction between prisoners guilty of grave crime and less serious offenders and encouraging more parole for the latter. In 1983, as we saw in Chapter 8, Leon Brittan made some changes in the parole system. He broadened the system at one end by lowering to ten and a half months the minimum sentence which qualifies a prisoner for parole and narrowed it at the other by refusing parole to those serving more than five years for an offence involving violence or drugs, unless circumstances were exceptional or just a few months on supervision would be very beneficial.

Parole is quite controversial and has become more so as ideas about rights and justice for prisoners have developed. In this country parole is a purely administrative procedure carried out in private, with no rights for the prisoner to be heard, to put her or his case, or to know the reason why the application for parole was turned down. In 1983 a prisoner called Gunnell took the Home Secretary to court arguing that he had had his parole revoked and had been put back in prison without being heard before the Parole Board, without written reasons, and without him or his legal representative being allowed to see the documents on which the decision to lock him up again was based. The Divisional Court decided that the Parole Board was not a judicial body so the rules of natural justice would not apply. In 1984 four of the prisoners affected by the parole changes introduced by Leon Brittan in 1983, and likely to stay in prison longer than they had expected, took the Home Secretary to court to challenge the new policy. In the Divisional Court one of the judges supported the Home Secretary and the other did not. The case then went to the Court of Appeal where two judges backed the Home Secretary and one backed the prisoners. Finally the case went to the House of Lords where the Law Lords backed the Home Secretary unanimously and declared the policy lawful.

The fact that such cases are being brought is indicative of a change of attitude. Opinion is moving more towards proper judicial processes whenever deprivation of liberty is at stake. An example of this is the Prior Committee recommendation that a properly constituted independent tribunal should be established to deal with prisoners' disciplinary offences. By this criterion the parole system looks rather old-fashioned, even if the formulation of the way it works given by a former chairman, Sir Louis Petch, is a little too simplistic. He told the House of Commons Expenditure Committee in 1978: 'The panel of the Parole Board which looks at a case just soaks in the factual information about the man and makes up its own mind what it wants to do about him without at the moment having to justify what they want to do to anybody else and without at the moment having to give the man himself any reasons.'[19]

A move to give prisoners reasons for not granting parole failed. The question first appeared when the Parole Board Report of 1973 noted that the Board was talking to the Home Office about giving prisoners reasons; but it was 'by no means simple to resolve'.[20] By 1975 seven paragraphs of the Report are devoted to the problem. It says:

> One argument for the giving of reasons for the refusal of parole is that 'natural justice' requires it. Those who wish to see parole as a judicial process with the 'rights' of the prisoner determined by due process of law take this stand. We have not adopted a judicial model for our parole system, but this does not dispose of the argument for giving reasons. Even in a paternalistic system, it can be urged that anyone who is refused a privilege should in fairness be told why . . .[21]

No decision on giving reasons had as yet been reached. In 1977 it is reported that an experiment is in progress to see how feasible it would be to give reasons. In 1979, six years after the discussion began, the Board's conclusion is reported. Giving reasons is not feasible.

Not only old-fashioned, the parole system is also inherently unfair, in the sense that the good risks, people with stable homes and families to go to, and fewer previous convictions, are more likely to be granted parole than those without. Lord Hunt, the first person to chair the Parole Board, faced up to these points in a debate in the House of Lords in 1979. When parole began in 1967 its official value was rehabilitative. Now it seems to be solely a measure to reduce the prison population. He says: 'Seen in this perspective, parole could be dubbed a mere palliative for an expensive, largely negative penal policy in regard to the use of imprisonment and the length of prison sentences in our criminal law.' There is, he said, no doubt that it is a resentencing process conducted without judicial safe-guards, which is wrong. Prisoners should have certain rights within the process, namely, the right to a hearing before a review committee, and the right to be given reasons for refusal of parole. 'There has been,' he concluded 'a failure to fulfil a matter of natural justice for too long.'[22]

Another problem that has arisen now that parole applies to shorter-sentence prisoners is that the differentials between sentence lengths at the lower end are being eroded. Defendants sentenced to nine months, twelve months, fifteen months and eighteen months could all possibly come out on the same day, after serving six months. Prisoners who spend a long time in custody on remand get the worst deal, because the time spent on remand counts towards their sentence, but does not count towards the minimum for parole. The Parole Board is aware of this defect in the operation of the system. It points out in its latest report how under the present arrangements 'parole can have the effect of eliminating differentials in the length of sentences of imprisonment of up to two years particularly in the cases of associates'.[23] The judges do not find such an outcome at all satisfactory.

Reacting to these concerns, the Home Secretary set up a committee under Lord Carlisle in 1987 to review parole. The Carlisle Committee, as it is called, must have come up very quickly against the dilemma posed by parole, that is, if it were being devised in 1988 it would undoubtedly be very different. Parole as we know it is out of tune with current thinking; but the alternative, to abolish it, is unthinkable because of the effect on the numbers in prison. Parole may not accord with current needs but without it many more people would be in prison. So parole is likely to carry on – unless there is a radical restructuring of the sentencing system which makes it unnecessary, or the Carlisle Committee recommends a radical change such as a supervised release scheme applicable across the board to everyone or to all prisoners serving below a certain limit. It is a strong argument for such a scheme that all the research suggests that the supervision that goes with parole is quite effective in keeping ex-prisoners out of trouble.[24]

One more method exists of reducing the prison population after sentence – that is executive release. We saw in Chapter 8 how at the height of the prison officers' dispute in 1980, Parliament gave William Whitelaw powers to release certain prisoners early if there was a real crisis in the prison system. These powers, which allow the Home Secretary to release certain prisoners up to six months early if 'he is satisfied that it is necessary to do so in order to make the best use of the places available for detention',[25] became a permanent part of the law in the Criminal Justice Act of 1982. At the time of the 1986 prison officers' dispute there was talk of using these powers to release non-violent prisoners in the last six months of their sentence, but in the event they were not used – so far they never have been. They are there, though, as a safety-valve, the Home Office's last resort.

In addition to providing measures intended as alternatives to custody and finding ways of releasing prisoners early there is a third method of reducing the use of prison – that is to put obstacles in the way of the courts' use of it. An outstanding example of this approach is the Bail Act of 1976 which requires a court to grant bail unless there are very good reasons not to. The Act put in statutory form practices recommended in a Home Office circular of 1975. Following the circular and the Act the number of untried and unsentenced prisoners kept in prison went down from over 68,000 in 1975 to 52,000 in 1978. The reduction was short-lived and by 1986 the figure was up again to well over 63,000. However, without the Bail Act it would certainly be much higher.

The number of children and young people, that is those aged under seventeen, kept in prison before their trial has been reduced by restricting the circumstances in which courts can issue unruly certificates before they remand a young person to prison. In 1977 the Certificate of Unruly Character (Conditions) Order allowed courts to remand under-seventeen-year-olds to prison only when they are charged with a very serious offence, or a violent offence, or have a past conviction for violence or have kept running away from or caused havoc in a community home (a children's home). Girls can no longer be remanded to prison at all, nor can fourteen-year-old boys.

A measure in the Criminal Law Act of 1977 cut the time that could be imposed on someone for not paying a fine. This cut the average daily population of fine defaulters in prison from 1,037 in 1972 to 775 in 1978.

Also over the years it has become statutory for courts to conform to certain requirements before passing a prison sentence. Defendants under twenty-one and those who have not served a prison sentence before must be given an opportunity to be legally represented before they can be sentenced to custody and the court must normally consider a report from a probation officer, a social inquiry report.

All these measures represent real reforms which have had some impact but they have made little impression on the practice of those who sentence nor reversed the slow but steady upward rise in the proportionate use of custody. More far-reaching attempts to intervene have not been so successful. When the suspended sentence was first introduced in 1967 it was mandatory for the courts to suspend prison sentences of six months or less except when they were imposed on those convicted of violence and those who had been to prison before. The Conservative Opposition was strongly against mandatory suspension and repealed it as soon as their chance came in 1972. The requirements that no sentence of between six months and three years could be passed on a young offender – the gap to be automatically filled by borstal training the length of which was determined by the prison authorities – was always unpopular with the judiciary and its repeal in 1982 was greeted with satisfaction. The latest and most radical of attempts to structure the way courts reach their decision about prison or not prison is Section 1(4) of the 1982 Criminal Justice Act as amended by the Criminal Justice Act 1988. Before sending an offender under twenty-one to custody the court has to decide that he or she qualifies for a custodial sentence. There are three ways to qualify. First, the offender can have 'a history of failure to respond to non-custodial penalites' and be 'unable or unwilling to respond to them'. Alternatively, 'only a custodial sentence would be adequate to protect the public from serious harm from him'. Or finally, 'the offence of which he has been convicted or found guilty was so serious that a non-custodial sentence for it cannot be justified'.[26]

Further conditions apply to magistrates courts. Before sending someone to prison for the first time they must get a social inquiry report unless there are special reasons not to. They must state in open court why they feel that only custody will do and must write down their reasons in the court register and the warrant of commitment. This new set of requirements is an amplification of a provision that has been in the law since 1948, which required courts not to pass a custodial sentence on someone under twenty-one unless no other method was appropriate. Whether these devices work is hotly debated. When the tighter criteria were brought in in 1983 they were often treated as of little importance or even ignored by some courts.[27] However, as time has gone on they have been used more widely by lawyers as a basis to argue appeals against a sentence. Also they may well have prevented the large increase in custodial sentencing which critics of the Criminal Justice Act feared would come from the new, short detention centre order.

Nevertheless, looking back over all these efforts one is forced to conclude that the answer has yet to be found. There seem to be two main reasons why all these attempts have met such a conspicious lack of success. One is the need to clarify who can make penal policy (which includes ways of controlling how many people get into the system) and how it can be made. Penal policy covers more than sentencing policy of course. Decisions about how many people come to court and who should be prosecuted are important. Who, for instance, decides that 'spiky-haired Katherine' should be prosecuted for stealing a pint of milk worth seventeen pence rather than be told off and sent on her way? All these decisions are important. The introduction in 1986 of a new prosecution system, and official encouragement to the police to caution more people rather than bring a case against them, should help to keep the most trivial matters out of court. Even so, without some reconsideration of sentencing policy all other efforts can only make improvements at the margins and anyone proposing a reconsideration of sentencing policy comes up against the argument about the independence of the judiciary. The usual reaction is to shy away. When the Home Affairs Committee in 1980–81 got to this point in its deliberations it found itself on shifting sands. William Waldegrave, MP, tried very hard to get it on the agenda. In questioning witnesses from NACRO he asked:

If the Government were to spend over the next years the money necessary to bring the British Prison system up to a not very high standard but up to an acceptable standard we would be talking about spending ... about £1,400 million, but it is inconceivable that that kind of expenditure is going to be forthcoming and, therefore, there is really going to be a crisis quite soon. Would you therefore say that it is urgent now to tackle the quite deep constitutional problems of the relationship between judiciary and Parliament in terms of the statutory limitation of prison sentences.[28]

The NACRO witness assented.

He became even bolder later on when he said to the Lord Chancellor of the time, Lord Hailsham:

Your primary role is to protect the Judiciary, but when the Judiciary have taken their judicial decisions and come to consider sentencing they become part of society pre-empting resources from the taxpayer for expenditure on the particular person. The difficulty seems to me to be that the considerations which they apply to that bear no relationship to the availability of the resources.[29]

His boldness extended to putting a very pointed question to the Home Secretary, William Whitelaw: 'Do you feel the institutional framework of this country is such that you can really have a penal policy?'[30] Mr Whitelaw, rather less boldly, replied: 'Yes, I think it is, but of course it inevitably means by agreement between a lot of people who have different interests which have to be reconciled, but that after all, is a feature of any country's life ...'[31]

The argument about the independence of the judiciary is not likely to be easily resolved. Perhaps the view of Andrew Ashworth on the nature of the constitutional issue is the clearest currently available:

... is it constitutionally appropriate that the judges should possess such great power to shape sentencing policy? The answer is that in principle the formulation of general policy should be for the legislature and its implementation and individuation for the judiciary. However, there is no constitutional inappropriateness in the legislature delegating its policy-making function to the judicary: what is inappropriate is any assumption that this function is by right that of the judiciary, for there is no constitutional bar to legislation on any aspect of sentencing policy.[32]

The political problem of the need to clarify who can make

penal policy has dogged all efforts to grasp the nettle of the rising prison population. The other problem has been a practical one, that those who try to develop and implement a penal policy have no tools to do it with. A good example of this gap is the Criminal Justice Act of 1982 which brought in a whole new sentencing system for the under twenty-ones with scant resources for induction and preparation for the magistrates who were to operate it. Two one-day conferences were held and a few articles appeared in the Magistrates Association magazine. Then the 28,000 magistrates, all lay people with other occupations, were expected, with the help of their court clerks who organized some local training, to be ready to do all their sentencing of young offenders differently. It did not work out quite according to plan. Magistrates seemed not to want to send young people to detention centres but to prefer youth custody. Since youth custody could only be given to those serving over four months, sentences of four months and a day began to appear. The Home Secretary then had to find an opportunity to make a speech saying this would not do – in his words 'it would be difficult to justify varying the sentence length appropriate in a particular case solely in order to enable it to be served in one kind of institution rather than the other'.[33]

Over the years recommendations on how to reduce the use of prison have been numerous and repetitive. They can be divided up under five headings: remand prisoners, 'those who should not be there', fine defaulters, removing imprisonment altogether from certain groups and rationing the intake.

The remand population continues to grow in spite of wide agreement about what a bad thing it is to have such a large remand population – although it is fair to say that this is one area where we do better than those in Europe; our remand population forms a smaller proportion of the total than it does in other Council of Europe countries. The remand population comes about through the interaction of two factors: remanding people to prison before their trial and the length of time they stay there. Measures to reduce the remand population have to address both.

First more people should be given bail, bearing in mind that when they come to court over a third of those kept in prison before trial do not get a prison sentence. A major problem is that there are great differences between areas in granting bail. Douglas Hurd told the East Midlands Area Conservative Women that he was 'looking at the reasons for the wide disparities in custody rates in different parts of the country – which vary from significantly less than 10 per cent of those remanded in some areas to well over 30 per cent in others.' Certainly some court decisions seem strange. A brief experiment carried out by the Inner London Probation Service in Wormwood Scrubs, aimed at increasing the numbers getting bail, unearthed many examples of what could be described as 'inappropriate remands in custody'. They found 'trivial offenders – the theft of two bottles of whisky; foreigners with language problems – a Bengali who could not speak English and was unable to understand what was happening; ... a black student from Essex University whose address in a hall of residence and regular attendance at classes seemed to be ignored without any attempt at verification; defendants who appeared to be mentally ill and needed medical help'.[34] Measures must be taken to even out these discrepancies and ensure that the Bail Act is consistently and properly used.

Courts are likely to be influenced when deciding on bail by information about defendants' jobs, homes and families. In 1975 a pilot scheme, run by the Inner London Probation Service and the Vera Institute of Justice, was set up at Camberwell Green Magistrates Court. It involved volunteers finding out as much as possible about the community ties of defendants held over-night in police custody and presenting the information to the court the following day. It was generally agreed that the project was useful, but, as so often in matters to do with the penal system, the pilot remained a pilot, to be admired, written about in papers and reports, but not extended. In 1987 another pilot scheme was established, run by the Association of Chief Probation Officers and the Vera Institute of Justice. It involved providing the Crown Prosecution Service with as much verified information as possible about defendants which was relevant to the decision to oppose bail. During the pilot year it is estimated that the scheme's work was successful in getting bail which would otherwise have been refused in three out of ten cases. In May 1988 the Home Secretary said he was 'urgently considering' how the experience of the pilot schemes can be built on.[35] In November 1988 an extension of the scheme was announced.

One reason for people being kept in prison unnecessarily is that they have nowhere to live. Bail hostels are a solution to this problem. People with no fixed address can get bail on condition they live in such a hostel. In 1988 there were sixteen hostels with room for 248 bailees as well as access to beds in eighty-five probation hostels. By 1990 nine more hostels are to open providing 200 places. However, the number of hostel places is still too small.

The restriction placed on the Bail Act of 1976 by the decisions in the Nottingham Justices case of 1980 and the Slough Justices case in 1982 are also a barrier to more use of bail. In the case of the Nottingham Justices, the decision was that they would not hear arguments in support of a bail application after a custodial remand unless circumstances had changed considerably. In the case of the Slough Justices the High Court upheld their ruling that committal for trial did not constitute a change of circumstances.

The Home Affairs Committee concluded that these decisions 'have had an unfortunate effect in creating a degree of rigidity in the treatment of bail applications which was never envisaged in the Act'. They went on: 'We feel that a defendant's right to seek a review of a bail decision ought not to be circumscribed in this way.'[36] The modification of the Nottingham Justices' decison made in the Criminal Justice Act of 1988, which allows a second hearing, is in no way adequate in removing the barrier to more bail that this decision creates.

Shortening the time people have to wait for their trial is also an important way of reducing the numbers held in prison, and also of reducing injustice. Putting limits on the amount of time someone can be held has been discussed for many years. In Scotland, for instance, there is a rule that no one should be detained for more than 110 days without the trial commencing. Applications can be made to extend the time, but only if the delay is the fault of, or at the request of, the defence. If it is the fault of the prosecution an extension is not allowed and the remand prisoner is set free. Importing this idea into England and Wales has been discussed many times. It was recommended by the Home Affairs Committee in 1981 and firmly rejected by the Government: 'The Government ... does not believe that to introduce the 110-day rule into England and Wales would help to reduce pressure on the prison system or make for speedier justice.'[37] Then they changed their minds. In 1985 the Home Secretary was given powers to impose time limits. In 1987 they were imposed in Avon, Somerset, Kent and the West Midlands. In 1988 another ten areas were included.

Women suffer particularly from the injustices of the remand system. Whereas one third of men remanded in prison subsequently get a non-prison sentence, over half of women do. Some people looking at these figures argue the opposite, that women are getting a better deal and avoiding prison when men in the same position would be imprisoned. This argument is not very convincing. One reason for the high number is because the courts are remanding women to prison for reports, often medical reports, but sometimes reports about social circumstances. In 1979 Dr Bull, then governor of Holloway, told the Expenditure Committee:

We have a very large proportion of women remanded for medical reports and a high proportion are negative in the sense that there is no medical recommendation, and I think sometimes this is simply a device to put a woman in prison for three weeks with the supposition that a medical report might do something, or perhaps just as a punitive way, because a very high proportion are negative.[38]

Such reports could be prepared on bail. The Home Office circular of 1975 which preceded the Bail Act suggested that court clerks should compile lists of doctors and psychiatrists prepared to do court work. In 1981 the Home Affairs Committee noted that the Home Office was trying to find out if this had been done and recommended that once they had found out they should encourage courts to get on with it.[39]

There is wide agreement that the remand population should be cut down. The proposals set out here would help to reduce it. Wide agreement also exists about 'those who should not be there' and has done for many years. Unfortunately most of the ideas have not come to fruition and most of 'those who should not be there' are still there. The most obvious group are the mentally disordered. Every report of the last fifteen years has highlighted how wrong it is that people who need help for mental illness are instead being punished in prison. The latest of this line of reports, that of the Social Services Committee, said:

... people who are mentally ill and severely mentally impaired as defined by the Mental Health Act should be in hospital and not in prison ... At Bedford prison we were told that a severely disturbed prisoner had recently spent almost eight months naked in a stripped cell. During our visit there, we saw a prisoner lying in a catatonic stupor with only a sheet for covering in an empty cell smeared with filth. This is wholly unacceptable.[40]

Many recommendations have been made over the years suggesting how alternative, more humane arrangements can be made for mentally disturbed people and some proper functioning relationship set up between the Home Office, which is responsible for prisons, and the Department of Health, which is responsible for health. After years of protest, the number of prisoners who satisfy the criteria under the Mental Health Acts for transfer to a mental hospital but are still kept in prison has dropped. In 1977 there were 769. In 1987 there were 344, 156 sentenced prisoners and 188 on remand.[41] This is an improvement but leaves untouched the wider question of those who do not satisfy the criteria. Similar concerns have been expressed regularly about drug addicts and alcoholics in prison and it has often been recommended that there should be enough centres and clinics outside where they can go in conjunction with some order of the court, such as a probation order. Also under this heading come people classed as 'petty persistent offenders' or, less kindly, as 'inadequates' who have a range of social problems, are often homeless and have no community ties, and spend much of their lives going in and out of institutions – mainly prisons and psychiatric hospitals. Lord Hailsham told the Home Affairs Committee of 'one awful fact which experience has led me to believe, that society tends to send to prison those whom it does not know what else to do with. The prisons are very full of inadequate people, for instance, and they get there and they do not quite know how and when they get out they go back again.'[42]

The Parliamentary All-Party Penal Affairs Group recommended in 1980 that people in prison whom it is agreed should not be there might be released and sent instead to a place where they could get treatment. The Group recommended that prison governors should be able to go to a local magistrates court and apply for 'a variation of a custodial sentence'[43] so that the prisoner could go to a place in a hostel or another place offering treatment in conjunction with some other non-custodial sentence.

Another group whom it is widely felt 'should not be there' are fine defaulters who represent more than one-fifth of all sentenced offenders entering prison, although only 1.4 per cent of the average population because the time they serve is generally short. The law requires that people should only end up in prison for not paying a fine if the failure to pay is because of 'wilful refusal or culpable neglect', not simply if they cannot pay. It is quite strongly felt, however, that many of the 19,000 people who end up in prison every year for not paying their fines are there because they cannot pay. A major recommendation aimed at reducing these numbers is the proposal to establish a 'day-fine' or 'means-related' fining system which would link the amount of the fine very closely to the income of the fined person. The principle is a simple one. For example, X and Y are convicted of speeding and, other things being equal, both are given fifty day fines. X earns twice as much as Y so while X's day fine is calculated at £2, Y's day fine is £1. X pays £100 in all, while Y pays £50. Systems based on this principle operate successfully in Sweden, Austria and West Germany. Its relevance in this country becomes more pressing because more and more people coming before the courts live entirely on state benefits – and the use of the fine has dropped steadily since 1979 – a period which has coincided with a steep rise in unemployment. The Government has made encouraging noises about moving in the direction of the 'day fine' – the Home Secretary talked about day fines as 'successful' and said in a speech in Leeds in early 1986 that they were being 'considered' – but so far nothing more has come of it than the inevitable pilot projects. Two are being run, one in Basingstoke and one in Bradford. After they have been set up, taken place, evaluated, the evaluation considered, proposals prepared and comments received on the proposals, change may come, but it may take ten years.

Much campaigning energy and commitment and many, many pages of reports, official and otherwise, have been devoted to arguing the case for removing from prison the sick, the mentally ill, the addicted, the homeless and rootless people who might find a shared cell in Pentonville rather cosy in a bad winter. Some small steps have been taken but basically they are still there. Their numbers are not great, not so great that their removal would reduce the prison population significantly. But their removal would end one of the major scandals of the prison system – the subjecting to punishment of many people who need, and are entitled to, medical treatment or social care. Similarly with fine defaulters. Many recommendations have been made, but still people go to prison for not having enough money.

A further way of reducing the use of prison is to remove its availability. After years of argument the 1982 Criminal Justice Act removed prison as a punishment for soliciting. Prostitutes still go to prison for not paying the fines that are imposed on them, but not for soliciting itself. The 1982 Act also removed the availability of prison for sleeping rough and begging.

Another group that it is often argued should be removed from prison are children and young persons under seventeen. In 1987, 3,885 fourteen-, fifteen- and sixteen-year-olds went into some prison establishment. On 30 June 1987 (the day the statistical snapshot is taken of the prison population), there were 798 fourteen–sixteen-year-olds inside.

In 1969 an act was passed, the Children and Young Persons Act, which had sections saying that putting the under-seventeens in prison establishments would be phased out, and they would go instead to places run by the local authorities. Nothing happened and as the years went by more and more convicted under-seventeens went into Prison Department custody. In 1982 the unimplemented clause was repealed, thus ending the reform that never was. This country is unusual in using the prison system to deal with its young teenage delinquents. In Holland, for instance, the minimum age for going to prison is effectively eighteen. Although a judge can reclassify a mature sixteen- or seventeen-year-old as old enough for youth prison the numbers are very small, about 150 a year. Stopping the under-seventeens going to prison establishments would not reduce the prison population much – but it would end a particularly uncivilized and ineffective way of responding to the criminality of the young.

Finally, the prison population could be reduced by rationing the intake by, for example, deferring the serving of the sentence until accommodation is available. Such a system was set up in Holland in 1974. The system affects people who have not been kept in prison up to their trial and have turned up in court on the due date. If they are then given a prison sentence it is not served immediately. They go home and wait to be called. The call-up time varies according to pressures on the prisons. In 1988 there were 535 places in prisons for 'self-reporters'. In 1988 the call-up time was around four to six months. 'Self-reporters' serve their sentence in what the Dutch call 'semi-open' and what in this country would be called open conditions. On average, out of ten of those called to prison four fail to deliver themselves up without a good excuse. They are generally found by the police and have then forfeited their chance to serve their sentence in an open prison.

Such arrangements have attracted some support in this country, but have never progressed beyond the stage of recommendation. The Home Affairs Committee in 1981 said:

> Giving a moderate amount of discretion to the prison authorities as to when an offender might be summoned to begin his sentence could also be a useful means of spreading the prison population to maximize administrative convenience and resources, without resorting to devices as haphazard in their operation as quotas or a place-finding system. *We recommend that the Home Secretary should introduce such a call-up system on an experimental basis for certain selected categories of offenders.*[44]

The Government reply to this recommendation was decidedly cool: 'The government does not dismiss the idea for the longer term ... but ... believes that in present circumstances an arrangement for calling in offenders to prison could make no real contribution to solving the current problems of the prison system.'[45] Maybe, as on the 110-day rule, they will change their minds on this too in due course.

All these ideas are admirable and worth implementing: but a major reduction in the use of prison will require more than this. It will require a change of heart and a move away from traditional views about what prison is for, what it contributes to protecting the public and reducing crime, and how much of it should be used at any one time for any particular offender. It will take considerable time to bring about this change of heart and will require action on many fronts at once. If there is to be any progress at all, machinery needs to be established to make things happen and develop, to find a way through the current log-jams, lack of political will and fear of hostile public or media reactions. Some structural change, a formal statutory mechanism, is needed to bring the various parts of the criminal justice process into a working relationship where they have to listen to each other, understand each other's problems and solve problems jointly. This is not a new idea. Andrew Ashworth has proposed that sentencing policy should be reshaped by a Sentencing Council which would consider sentencing practice, commission research which would 'provide systematic knowledge about the reasoning of judges and magistrates' and then 'reformulate sentencing policy so that it is no longer excessively reliant on custodial measures'. The Council would be chaired by the Lord Chief Justice and would draw on 'persons with considerable experience of the penal system, from magistrates to a circuit judge sitting in second-tier and third-tier centres, to a probation officer, a prison governor, a Home Office official and an academic'. It would be a requirement that wider experience than that of a few senior judges should be drawn on, that no one group 'cocksure' of what public opinion expects should hold sway, and that 'it should be capable of developing realistic guidance for sentencing at all levels with the element of co-ordination and overall planning which is now absent'.[46]

The mind of the Home Affairs Committee moved in a similar direction. In its 1981 Report it analysed in some detail why the system worked so badly, why much-needed and agreed-upon reforms were not implemented. They pointed out how interdependent the system is – what the police do affects the courts, which in turn affects the probation and prison services.

They highlight how difficult it is for the system to respond, citing as examples 'the apparently unavailing exhortations of successive Ministers on sentencing, and the lengthy delays which continue to impede proper secure provision for mentally disturbed offenders'.[47] They list all the current methods that government departments have for keeping in touch with each other and find them wanting. They conclude that crime rates will continue at a high level, no hope exists at present for discovering penal methods that will really deter or reform, and the allocation of much greater resources to the penal system is unlikely. Therefore, they declare: 'Coming to terms with a significant level of crime and social disorders without excessive repression on the part of the State, and at the same time maintaining public confidence and participation in the maintenance of order, is in our view one of the challenges central to the continued existence of free societies.'[48] They end up proposing a structural means of 'filling the lacunae in English criminal policy-making'. They recommend a National Criminal Policy Committee to allow criminal policy to be planned. It would be at the highest level and served by expert staff. Its function would be 'to construct a comprehensive criminal policy in the light of the most modern administrative knowledge and research findings'.[49]

The proposal did not get a warm reception from the Government. In fact the Government's reply poured a bucket a cold water over the whole idea: it doubted the effectiveness of such bodies; if Ministers want advice on a specific subject they set up a body on that; a single unifying Committee would not simplify the process of policy formation or improve the product; the Home Office has a lot of contacts already; but they will keep the idea under review.[50] The response, which does not even admit there is a problem, looks quite odd when set against the evidence given by the Home Secretary and his officials to the

Committee about the problems they faced in the prisons and the need for radical solutions.

The Sentencing Council and the National Criminal Policy Committee leave the current system as it is and try and pull it together. A more radical suggestion would shake the whole system up and put it together differently. This is the proposal for a restructuring of central government to produce a Ministry of Justice. Such a ministry would put under one roof many of the Home Office's current responsibilities: prisons, probation, magistrates courts and those of the Lord Chancellor's Department, that is the judiciary and the higher courts, together with the law officers and the Director of Public Prosecutions, now head of the Crown Prosecution Service.

In the current position it would seem that the first idea, for a Sentencing Council, is too narrow on its own and the last, for a Ministry of Justice, is too fundamental to happen quickly, even if it were thought to be the right direction to go in. The middle proposal, for a National Criminal Policy Committee, seems to combine the least upheaval with the most breadth and scope for practical achievements. Work on setting it up should start at once. It should have resources and staff and set about imposing some coherence on the criminal justice system, looking at the resources available, how they can best be used and devising policies that can command widespread support. Membership will have to include all the participants in the criminal justice process, as well as those departments whose actions have a bearing on what happens in criminal justice, such as the Department of Health. The Committee will need to establish sub-committees, of which one could have the functions of the Sentencing Council proposed by Andrew Ashworth. Another sub-committee, on crime prevention, would be a useful balance, ensuring that the arguments for resources to go directly to reducing crime are heard.

The agenda for the first year's work of the new Committee will be a crowded one. Its priority among all the pressing issues it faces should be measures to reduce the use of prison. It could immediately set up a task group or Working Party to review community service orders, to look at their use so far, to draw up guidelines as to how the confusions surrounding the use of community service orders can be resolved. Is it an alternative to prison? How many hours community service equal roughly how much prison? Should someone get another community service order for a further offence if they have in the past completed community service successfully? The task group should bear in mind the view of David Thomas, one of the country's leading writers on sentencing, who said:

... among the attractions of the tariff for judges are undoubtedly the reasonably clear principles on which sentences are calculated and the unambiguous nature of the statement which a sentence of imprisonment conveys. If something of the same order can be imposed on non-custodial measures, and clear symbolic meanings attached to those measures ... some of the remaining judicial reluctance to use non-custodial measures may be eroded.[51]

The task group should review the way community service is provided. At present the number of places is limited to what the probation service can provide out of budgets allocated at the beginning of a financial year. Community service could become as demand-led as prison. If more orders were made more staff could be taken on to provide them – just as, at the moment, another body and then another is crammed into a local prison. Its use as the standard replacement for a short prison sentence should become the basis of a major training programme for sentencers.

The second area the Committee could develop in its initial programme of work is the promotion of local action to provide for the courts the services they need to keep less serious offenders out of prison. There is a model for this. The Department of Health, with a relatively small injection of money, has mobilized local organizations to set up projects to serve as alternatives to custody for the under-seventeens and to make sure the courts know about them and understand them. By working alongside the magistrates in this way and establishing constructive projects, significant reductions have been made in the numbers sent to custody in the areas concerned.[52] Such a process could work equally well for those over seventeen. Finally, in its first year the Committee might like to establish a crash programme of training on the effectiveness of sentencing, based on the precepts in Chapter 3 of *The Sentence of the Court*, namely that sentencing, within the realistic range of choice, has little effect on crime levels, that long sentences are no more effective than short ones, the deterrent effect of particular sentences is minimal, prison has the most serious side-effects of all penalties available to the courts and that the Court of Appeal's principle, that prison should only be imposed if truly necessary and then be as short as possible, is a good one to follow. There are many candidates for the Committee's second year of work, but what to do about the declining use of the fine would be high on the list.

The establishment of such a committee, and such a programme of work pursued with energy and commitment, could turn round the over-use of prison in this country and start a downward trend. Such a change is essential if the prison system is to be brought up to the standards that those who work in it hanker after and that society ought to expect. What to do to change the prison system is the subject of the next chapter.

11 One Bath a Week

Steps towards a better prison system

> I can illustrate the point by describing the occasion I was
> asked by a prisoner who was on Rule 43 Good Order and
> Discipline to read a paragraph in a folded booklet he had in
> his hand. He pointed to the paragraph and asked me to read
> it. I asked him to read it to me but he pressed me to read it. I
> could not quite read the typescript, put on my reading glasses
> ... and still could not see the print. I asked for the lights to
> be put on. The prisoner protested that I should read it with-
> out the light. Still unable to read, the light was switched on
> and I read:
>
> > In all places where prisoners are required to live and work
> > (a) the windows shall be large enough to enable the prisoners
> > to read or work by natural light, and shall be so constructed
> > that they can allow the entrance of fresh air whether or not
> > there is artificial ventilation.
>
> On closing the booklet I saw it was of course the *Standard
> Minimum Rules for the Treatment of Prisoners* adopted at the
> first United Nations Congress on the Prevention of Crime
> and Treatment of Offenders, 30 August 1955.
>
> Ian Dunbar, when governor of HM Prison Wormwood
> Scrubs, giving one of the 1982–3 Noel Buxton lecturers.[1]

The Prisons Act of 1865 required the authorities to make
sure that there were the same numbers of cells as there were
prisoners.[2] The regulations said that every prisoner should
sleep in a cell alone unless there were special circumstances. In

1949 the new Prison Rules specified that each prisoner should occupy a cell alone unless, again, there were special reasons. In 1952 we took a great leap backwards. The 1952 Prison Act had no such requirements. All it asked was that the Home Secretary should 'satisfy himself from time to time that in every prison sufficient accommodation is available for all prisoners'. The 1964 Prison Rules went even further in the wrong direction. They only said that sleeping accommodation should be certified for a specific number and once it was certified the Home Secretary had to give permission for it to be overcrowded.

There is no shortage of clear-sighted reformers among prison service staff and Home Office civil servants. But the lack of any rules or standards in the prison system that have to be kept to leaves them with few weapons in the battle for reform. Society has been content to leave it to the prison service to get by as best it can with a certain amount of money, an unpredictable supply of prisoners, a vague hope that nothing really bad or scandalous will go on behind the walls and a strong desire not to have to think about prisoners or, worse, see them. The prison service has never been given a clear idea of what it should be aiming at, or what is the minimum level of, for example, quality of accommodation, amount of activity, or respect for individuality – the level below which it would be wrong to fall. Conditions have often been described as inhumane, scandalous, an affront to civilized society or human dignity but no authority has ever existed for someone to say, 'Not only is it an affront, a scandal and a disgrace – but it has got to stop.' Without such authority to say 'it has got to stop', the prison service has had no way of arguing back at politicians who expect them to cram in another few hundred prisoners, and then just another few hundred, and, to save money, to lock up the prisoners just a little earlier every night and then just a little earlier still.

If there were rules – prisoners have to have so many square metres of space each, prisoners have to spend at least so many hours a day out of their cells, prisoners have to have enough light to read by, prisoners have to have specific opportunities to make arrangements for their release – then the prison system

would take a different path. In the last few years these arguments have crystallized around the idea of a code of minimum
standards.

Rules exist already. The prison system in England and Wales
is governed by the Prison Rules, last revised completely in
1964 and now generally agreed to be out of date and in need
of a complete rewrite. The Home Office is committed to rewrit-
ing the rules but at the moment argues that it has not got the
time. In any case the rules do not specify detailed minimum
standards of imprisonment that are enforceable by the courts.

In 1955 the United Nations produced its *Standard Minimum
Rules for the Treatment of Prisoners*. In 1968 the Council of
Europe decided to adapt the UN rules to a European context
and in 1973 the Council of Europe's version of the rules was
adopted by the Committee of Ministers of the Council of Europe.
The rules were revised and adopted as the European Prison
Rules, by the Committee of Ministers, in February 1987. The
Rules set out high standards for imprisonment, for instance:

The sanitary installations and arrangements for access shall be
adequate to enable every prisoner to comply with the needs of nature
when necessary and in clean and decent conditions.[3]
... every prisoner may be enabled and required to have a bath or
shower ... at least once a week.[4]
The regimes of the institutions [should] minimize the detrimental
effects of imprisonment and the differences between prison life and life
at liberty which tend to diminish the self-respect or sense of personal
responsibility of prisoners.[5]

Unfortunately they also allow lower standards to continue.
For instance Rule 14(1) requires that prisoners should
normally sleep in individual cells, but goes on to add the words
'except in cases where it is considered that there are advantages
in sharing accommodation with other prisoners'.[6] Also, the
European Prison Rules are only guidelines to be brought in
'progressively'.[7] Member governments have to report regularly
to the Council of Europe on the progress they are making on
implementing the rules. The British government does not seem
to have taken the rules very seriously. It sent a note to prison
governors with their copy of the original European Rules noting

that our prison rules were broadly consistent with the European ones, and where we fell down, that is on standards of accommodation and opportunities for work, lack of resources prevented Britain from reaching the European standard.[8] In fact, in the opinion of the prison governors themselves: 'In plain language ... these *Standard Minimum Rules* are neither standard nor minimum nor even rules as far as our adherence to them is concerned.'[9]

Prison governors have played a key role in the movement towards a code of minimum standards. This is understandable. It is governors who have to preside, daily, over worsening conditions in local prisons. It is governors who have no chance to protest publicly as they have to take in more and more prisoners, and it is among governors that many of those most committed to reform of the prisons are to be found. In December 1981 the governors, acting through their trade union, the Society of Civil and Public Servants, met the Home Secretary, William Whitelaw, to make the case for a set of standards 'which would be applicable to all our prisons'. The aim was 'to reduce overcrowding and assist in the process of eliminating the deplorable conditions that exist in many of our establishments'.[10] It was a very successful meeting. The Home Secretary was interested. In April 1982 he wrote to the Chairman of the Prison Governors Branch to say that he had decided to draw up a draft code. The promise was repeated in the House of Lords in June when Lord Elton responded to an amendment tabled by members of the Parliamentary All-Party Penal Affairs Group by announcing that the Prison Department would produce a draft code to be published in 1983. In July 1982 the responsible Home Office official told a conference that the code would cover size and design of cells, arrangements for sharing and access to sanitation. Being realistic, he said, it would take several years before such a code would apply to the whole system and 'still longer before we should welcome its enforcement through the courts'.[11] However, it was still important for three reasons. It would give the prison system a very clear idea of what it had to do to reach the standards and what its priorities should be. It would help the Government to be absolutely clear how much a decent prison system was going to cost if used at the present rate. Also it would give those concerned with measuring the success or otherwise of the system some tools to measure it with.

The Chief Inspector, one of those most concerned with measuring the state of the prisons, pointed out in his first report, published in 1982: 'We regret that there are few specific binding standards of entitlement which have been approved by Parliament concerning such matters as the size of the cell to which an inmate is entitled, or the hours he must spend outside it and which would serve as guidelines for us.'[12]

As 1983 wore on and the draft code did not appear, the prison governors became restless and produced their own. It was strongly worded. They called for no compulsory cell-sharing, an absolute ban on three people sharing a cell, privacy curtains round beds in dormitories, as there are in hospitals, access to lavatories at all times for prisoners, one bath or shower a day, at least two changes of underwear a week with a third set held by the prisoner, at least ten hours a day out of cell and at least thirty-five hours' work a week for each prisoner.[13] In April 1983 a House of Commons Select Committee, the Education, Science and Arts Committee, applied the idea to prison education. What was needed, they said, was 'a clear statement of principle to give direction, with a binding set of standard minimum rules as reference points'.[14] This should be enshrined in a new Prison Regimes Act covering the whole of the prison regime.

In June 1983 William Whitelaw was replaced at the Home Office by Leon Brittan. Then the blow fell. In December 1983 Lord Elton gave an oblique reply in the House of Lords to a direct question on when the code would appear. In January 1984 the extent of the retreat from the earlier commitment became clear. Something would be published – but it would only be an account of the physical standards used in building new establishments. The code had been abandoned.

The idea has been kept alive, however. In 1984 NACRO published its own draft code of minimum standards covering accommodation, hygiene, food, exercise/recreation and safety. The Chief Inspector in his 1983 Report noted the NACRO publication and promised to consider further the question of

Code A1 Space/Occupancy

STANDARDS

1   Every prisoner shall be entitled to spend a minimum of 10 hours in every 24 hours outside the confines of his/her cell. For the purposes of calculating time spent out of cell, time spent for access to sanitary conveniences when these are not integral, and a minimum exercise/recreation period of one hour daily shall not count as time spent out of cell.

2   New establishments shall provide a minimum of 60 sq ft of floor space, with at least 7ft between walls, and ceilings not lower than 8ft, for each prisoner in single or shared accommodation.

3   In new establishments accommodation not exceeding the minimum space requirements shall not be used to confine prisoners for periods in excess of 13 hours per 24 hours.

4   In existing establishments accommodation providing the equivalent of the minimum space requirement per prisoner for new establishments shall not be used to confine prisoners for periods in excess of 13 hours per 24 hours.

5   In existing establishments accommodation providing less than the minimum space requirements shall not be used to confine prisoners for periods in excess of 10 hours per 24 hours.

6   In existing establishments accommodation providing less than the minimum space requirements shall be phased out as part of a modification plan over the course of a period not exceeding 15 years. Timetables for reconstruction programmes shall be established on an individual establishment basis and shall be subject to independent monitoring. Tripling in cells shall be phased out within the next two years; at the expiration of that period a prisoner shall be allowed to choose whether or not to live in single cell accommodation.

Silvia Casale, *Minimum Standards for Prison Establishments*, NACRO, 1984.

minimum standards for penal establishments. In an interesting development the Inspectorate now provides at the back of its reports on individual prisons a series of appendices saying how many baths a prisoner gets in a week, how many changes of clothes, the number of hours of work available over a typical period, and the number of education classes. In its evidence to the Prior Committee, the Prison Officers Association gave its support to enforceable rules about minimum physical standards in prisons.[15] In his evidence to the Social Services Committee, Dr Cooper of the Prison Medical Association said: 'the problem is there are no minimum standards that we can refer to. They always say, "Well it was worse five years ago." You see, there are no minimum standards laid down in prisons as regards overcrowding, the number of toilets, the amount of living space, the quality of medical care or anything, so we are really working against a background which is elastic and can be manipulated according to the number of people you have in the system.'[16] In May 1986 the TUC, in a policy statement backed by seven trade unions involved in the prison service, called for a code of minimum standards for prisons.[17] A resolution supporting the statement went through the Congress in September. In October 1986 members of prison Boards of Visitors passed a resolution at their Annual Conference calling for such a code.

Adopting a code of minimum standards for the prison system is an essential first step in any determined effort to improve the prisons. The Home Secretary prepared to take such a plunge was William Whitelaw but he was not in the job long enough to see it through. Without a code of minimum standards, it is easy to imagine the head of the Home Office being called before Parliament in 2009 to be asked when this disgusting two-centuries-old practice of slopping out is to be brought to an end and having to answer, 'I do not know.'

A code of minimum standards would give the prison service a clear idea of what its priorities were. It would also give an entirely new impetus to the discussion about objectives. In Chapter 5 the objectives of the prison system were looked at from the point of view of sentencers. Traditionally these have been described as retribution, deterrence, containment and

ANNEX B

PRISONS BOARD STATEMENT OF THE FUNCTIONS OF PRISON DEPARTMENT ESTABLISHMENTS

Custody of Unsentenced Prisoners

1   To receive and keep in custody prisoners awaiting trial or sentence, civil prisoners and any other persons lawfully committed to their custody.

2   To release such prisoners from custody on the directions of the court or other lawful authority, or when the conditions of bail have been met.

The Court Commitment

3   To ensure that prisoners are produced at court as required.

4   To provide the requisite reports and documentation.

5   To provide staff required at the Crown Court and Court of Appeal (Criminal Division) and keep prisoners there in custody.

Custody of Sentenced Prisoners

6   To receive sentenced prisoners and keep them in custody.

7   To calculate and implement release dates.

8   To assess prisoners for the purpose of determining or recommending (a) an appropriate level of security and (b) an appropriate allocation.

9   To keep each prisoner's security category and allocation under regular review. In the case of life sentence prisoners, to maintain regular formal Review Board procedures.

10   To give effect to the provisions relating to parole and release on life licence.

Security, Safety and Control

11   To maintain a level of security appropriate to the prisoners who are or may be held at the establishment.

12   To maintain good order in the interests of the operation of the prison, and take such steps as are necessary for the safety of its staff and inmates.

Services and Facilities for Prisoners

13 To provide in accordance with the statutory provisions and Departmental instructions: (a) accommodation (b) meals (c) facilities for personal hygiene and sanitation (d) clothing (e) opportunities for exercise and (f) access to privileges.

14 To provide a service for the diagnosis, treatment and prevention of physical and mental disorders and the promotion of health.

15 To provide help and advice with personal problems.

16 To enable prisoners to practise their religion.

17 To provide, with a view to occupying prisoners as fully as possible throughout the whole week, a balanced and integrated regime, which may include work, education, physical education, access to libraries and individual and collective leisure activities.

18 To enable prisoners to spend the maximum possible time out of their cells.

Community Links and Preparation for Release

19 To enable prisoners to maintain contact with the outside world, and in particular to communicate with their families, friends and legal representatives.

20 To operate the home leave scheme.

21 To assist prisoners to prepare for release, which may include (a) providing such opportunities as are practicable for them to go out into the community on temporary release (b) providing pre-release courses and (c) putting prisoners in touch with the probation service and other external agencies.

22 To make arrangements as required for prisoners' after-care.

From *Report on the Work of the Prison Department 1984–5*, HMSO, pp. 137–8.

rehabilitation. The limitations of prison's deterrent role were argued, as was its now generally accepted failure to reform. Prison Rule 1, to prepare prisoners for 'a good and useful life', still stands but everyone knows it means very little. The official view is that prisoners go to prison *as* punishment not *for* punishment, but any attempt to be more specific comes up against a yawning gap. There has been much work done on the functions of the prison service. In 1983 the prison service published in the Annual Report its new formulation of the functions of the service. The tone of that formulation gives a clear indication of what the priorities are. First, not wasting money: 'To use with maximum efficiency the resources of manpower, money, buildings and plant made available to it by Parliament . . .'[18] Then, to do the most mechanical parts of imprisonment, namely, to keep all types of prisoners inside when they are meant to be inside, and to get them to court on time when appropriate. Then, to provide prisoners with the basics of life and some activities. Finally, to allow prisoners to keep links with the community and 'where possible' to prepare them to return to it.

These functions have been amplified in a further statement, published in the following year's Annual Report[19] (and reproduced on pp. 208–9). This statement also starts off with a list of the mechanical tasks required: keeping people in (functions 1, 5, 6, 11), letting people out (functions 2, 7, 10), getting them to court on time (function 3), allocating them and doing all necessary reports on them at the right time (functions 4, 8, 9, 10), keeping everyone under control (function 12), making sure everyone has the basics of life, for example, food, exercise and medical care (functions 13, 14). Then, towards the end, come the sections that reveal that the system is dealing with human beings, that a prison is an institution with a social purpose, not just a human warehouse. Function 15 provides for help and advice with problems. Prisoners should be enabled to practise their religion (function 16). Activities like work and education are to be provided (function 17) and the maximum possible time is to be spent out of the cell (function 18). Finally the recognition that prisoners go back to the outside world and prison is for most a brief sojourn comes in the last four functions which are about keeping links with the community. Prisoners' rights are not mentioned.

Individual prisons now also have their own lists of functions, some scant to the point of reticence. For example, Rudgate prison's list of functions, numbered a–g, covers receiving prisoners, keeping them secure, maintaining prescribed standards (prescribed by whom is not clear) in relation to accommodation, food, religious observance, work and so on, releasing prisoners on the right day, caring for staff, keeping the building in good condition and maintaining 'continuous monitoring of expenditure'.[20] Pentonville on the other hand has an eight-page document with several accompanying schedules and uses the opportunity to make some points. It is a function of the establishment to maintain Category B level security. However the document also lists fifteen constraining factors, including 'limited security fence ... window bars are in the main not tungsten steel ... access and egress of coaches and large vehicles requires both gates to be open simultaneously ... ability of the public to park vehicles along the outside wall'.[21]

Something is missing in all these statements. Somehow they do not fill the 'moral vacuum' which the May Committee identified and which they feared would lead to the 'routine brutalization of all the participants'.[22] Prison staff still do not really know what all these functions are for. They know they are supposed to save money. If that was not already clear it certainly became so after the traumatic events of April and May 1986. They know they are supposed to do their work more efficiently. They know they have to feed and clothe and allow baths to 50,000 men and women and get them to the right place at the appointed time. But no one is saying what they are supposed to be doing for, or with, or about those 50,000 people. Are they meant to be helping them or punishing them? Should they ignore them most of the time or make relationships with them? They have been told about the means, but not about the ends. Such a moral vacuum soon fills up with cynicism and defeatism.

It is not easy to find a formulation that would fill the moral vacuum, which is maybe why the Home Office in its pronouncements shies away from it and concentrates on messages that everyone can understand – efficiency, spending less than was spent last year, management objectives. The Education Select Committee noted the lack of a 'governing piece of philosophical prose ... to give a general direction to the prison regime'.[23] They went on to propose: 'The purpose of the detention of convicted prisoners shall be to keep them in custody which is as secure as is necessary and yet positively promotes their self-respect, social responsibility and all possible progress towards rehabilitation.'[24]

In response to pressure for a 'mission statement', one emerged from Prison Department Headquarters at the very end of 1988. It reads:

Her Majesty's Prison Service serves the public by keeping in custody those committed by the courts. Our duty is to look after them with humanity and to help them lead law-abiding and useful lives in custody and after release.[25]

Maybe a little more inspiring is the formulation from Dennis Trevelyan, Director-General of the prison service from 1978 to 1983, in a speech given in 1982. He said that imprisonment should be set in a new framework which places the emphasis on three realistic objectives: 'First to implement the sentence of the court in accordance with public policy and within the appropriate level of security; second, consistent with the first objective, to preserve prisoners' individuality, humanity and dignity; and third, so far as possible, to prepare prisoners for release.'[26]

If the Prison Department's formulation of its functions started not with 'to use with maximum efficiency the resources of manpower, money, buildings and plant'[27] but with 'to provide a prison system which aims to preserve prisoners' individuality, humanity and dignity', it might not make much difference to daily life on every landing in every prison. But it might set a different tone. It might enable those responsible for communicating to staff what their task is to start from a clear view of what is acceptable and what is not, based on principles of humanity and decency. It might establish a framework in which discussions of how the prison system should be run could take place.

Starting from such a premise – to preserve prisoners' individuality, humanity and dignity – almost every aspect of daily life in most prisons could be examined and found wanting. To start with basic conditions, it is not conducive to human dignity to be dirty, to smell and to live for months in a small smelly room. Sanitary and washing facilities and clean clothes

are therefore fundamental. To deprive people of the opportunity
to keep themselves clean, to make them perform their natural
functions in front of two others, to make men wear the same
pair of socks or underpants for between three and seven days,
does not preserve anyone's dignity.

Individuality and humanity are also affronted by giving
people no chance to express themselves through activity. To
impose weeks or months of total boredom is to deaden their
minds and diminish their ability to function. The effect of being
locked in cells for many hours is, according to the Chief Inspector, 'a dispiriting experience which deadens intellect, para-
lyses initiative and promotes bitterness and depression. All
but the strongest willed find that unemployment accelerates
descent into institutionalization and dependency.'[28]

Having the objective of preserving individuality, humanity
and dignity would also call into question many other aspects of
prison life. How does taking away male prisoners' clothes and
putting them into a prison uniform assist in maintaining their
individuality? How does calling them by a number followed by
their surname help to preserve their dignity? How does reading
prisoners' letters to their husbands or wives help them to retain
their humanity?

Filling the moral vacuum is essential if the prison service is
to put itself on the path to reform. A clear formulation of
objectives on the lines of preserving individuality, humanity
and dignity would also give a useful sense of direction to the
long-running debate about security and control. Although often
lumped together, security and control are two different problems. Security is the need to keep prisoners inside, to stop
them from escaping, to stop anything, such as firearms, being
smuggled in that could be used in an escape. Its importance
varies throughout the system. In open prisons it is not a problem because there is little security. Prisoners are sent to open
prisons because it is believed they will not run away. If they do
there will be no danger to the public. They will soon either give
themselves up or be picked up by the police; and their punishment for escaping will be a return to a closed prison and a loss
of some remission. Even if a dozen teenage burglars escape
every year from a youth custody centre the consequences are

not likely to impinge on public safety. Security is really important for the prisoners in the higher categories, especially prisoners deemed to be Category A.

Control is something different. Control means ensuring that
prisons run peacefully, people are not assaulted, bullied or
victimized, and the establishment is not vandalized or torn
down. The two are often confused. The Chief Inspector said in
his 1984 Report:

> Security and control are central core functions of all prison establish-
> ments and their separate demands inevitably affect all regimes. This
> being so it is vitally important in our view that the two functions are
> carefully distinguished . . . This simple distinction is in our experience
> often blurred. Thus we have found in the course of our inspections
> that security considerations are sometimes advanced as a reason for
> restricting regimes, for example, by closing workshops and stopping
> association – measures which are not in our view necessary on secur-
> ity grounds, although they may be justified on control grounds.[29]

On neither security nor control could the system at present
be said to have got it right. It is agreed that there is too much
security. On the other hand there seems to be too little control.
Ever since the security scares of the mid-sixties and the Mountbatten report security has been weighed against other considerations and has won. Security is measurable. So many of
the other goals of the system have not been made measurable
in the same way. Chapter 7 showed how expensive high security
is and how much high security is devoted to prisoners who
do not need it, so that the few Category A prisoners can be
'dispersed' among them. The Home Office's own Control
Review Committee questioned the wisdom of the dispersal
system which had been recommended by the Radzinowicz Committee in 1968. Radzinowicz feared that the Mountbatten proposals of concentrating maximum-security prisoners in one or
two prisons, if implemented, would lead, as a prison governor
wrote, to 'difficulties of establishing a satisfactory regime in a
prison containing the worst prisoners. The fear was that the
atmosphere would become predominantly custodial with excessive staff strain and prisoner discontent.'[30]

What actually happened was that instead of these difficulties arising in the one or two prisons where the top-security prisoners were, they arose in all the eight to which the top-security prisoners were dispersed. Roy King and Rod Morgan describe very vividly how the high hopes of dealing with the top-security prisoners by dispersing them went terribly wrong. As they say, nobody escaped, but soon the most serious riots broke out: 'As the problems of control mounted, so the relaxed and civilized regime was whittled away.'

High security moved inwards from the outside wall to the internal buildings, the cells, the workshops and the segregation units. Movement between bits of the prison was cut down and covered by closed-circuit television surveillance. Time spent by prisoners with other prisoners was cut down and a limit put on how many prisoners could be together at any one time. Dining rooms were abandoned and meals eaten in cells. And, King and Morgan conclude: 'All of this was additional to the double security fences, barbed wire, geophonic alarms, high-mast flood-lighting, perimeter defence forces, dog patrols, V H F radio systems, emergency control rooms, and links with local police forces and so on, which comprised the normal security barriers at such establishments.'[31]

'Dispersal' started off in 1968, meaning simply 'spreading around', or 'diluting'. It is an indication of the unhappy history of the dispersal idea that the word now carries negative connotations of trouble, tension and riot. In spite of this manifest lack of success the dispersal system continues. One brand-new dispersal prison, Frankland, near Durham, costing £15 million to build, opened as a dispersal prison in 1982. The Chief Inspector inspected it in 1984 and concluded that Frankland was 'a high-cost, staff-intensive prison with a regime which keeps many prisoners comparatively idle in conditions of security which many of them do not need'.[32] Another dispersal prison at Full Sutton in Yorkshire, costing £29 million, opened in August 1987.

The Control Review Committee hoped that the way out of the costly mistakes of the dispersal system would be through architecture. The Americans had been building, they said, prisons to a new design which would overcome the objections to concentrating top-security prisoners in one place. Such prisons, called 'new generation' prisons, could be built in the UK and two of them would do for all the top-security prisoners, say 300–400 of them.[33] The trouble with a solution dependent on architecture is that it is very long-term and very costly. At the moment there are no plans to build top-security 'new generation' prisons. In the meantime no substantial scaling down of the unnecessarily high level of security is envisaged. To improve the system and reduce the pressures small units are being set up – not, it has been energetically and frequently said by the Home Office, like the discredited control units of the early seventies but therapeutic and sensitive to individual needs. C wing at Parkhurst on the Isle of Wight is one of these, where it seems determined efforts are being made to provide a therapeutic atmosphere for disturbed prisoners. Other small units have been opened at Lincoln and Hull prisons.

Finding better ways of controlling prisoners is not so difficult. The Control Review Committee provided some clues to the basic principles of how to run peaceful and humane institutions:

> Prisons cannot be run by coercion.[34]
> ... it is most important that both staff and inmates should feel that they are getting a fair deal, and that all who live and work in a prison should have a stake in preserving its orderly management ... prisons function on humane personal relations between staff and inmates.[35]

A former top-security prison governor observed: 'What is more frustrating to those wishing to develop a more effective prison system, is the knowledge that the more control authority imposes, the more control it will need to maintain its grip. Imposed control for its own, exclusive purpose is self-defeating.'[36]

The Prior Committee, putting its inquiry into prison discipline into the context of how prisons are run, looked at how control is maintained in prisons. They concluded that control derives from three elements. First is the quality of relationships between prisoners and staff. The Committee noted that in one training prison they visited, on the day of the visit there were no adjudications to be held on prisoners for breaking the rules and no prisoner was undergoing punishment. They say: 'The governor attributed this partly to the good facilities but mainly to the professionalism of his staff, who knew how to "manage out" a great deal of misdemeanour and did not over-react to situations.'[37] The second element was a full programme of purposeful and worthwhile activities. They noted: 'We are persuaded that the Chief Officer who said to us on one of our visits that they have few disciplinary problems in his prison because the prisoners had so much to do was making a good if simple point.'[38] The third element is fairness. Prisoners have to see that the system is fair otherwise 'a sense of injustice will fester and spread'. The Committee noted that many prisoners feel that nothing that goes on in prisons can be fair. But, they noted, 'in our visits and in the evidence submitted to us by serving prisoners, how many expressed a strong sense of justice. Many made a clear distinction between procedures which were fair, even though the outcome might be unfavourable to the prisoner, and those which were not.'[39] A similar point comes from a small study of the Dutch prison system carried out by an Australian academic in 1985. He noted the comment of one prison governor, which echoed comments made to him by many others: 'It is the close involvement with prisoners in a full range of activities that gives the officers a good measure of safety.'[40]

The recommendations made by the retiring Deputy Director-General of the Prison Service, Gordon Lakes, in his report on the 1988 riots at Haverigg and Lindholme distil the lessons of many years of controlling prison institutions. Some of the recommendations he makes are about security. Most of them are not. They range over every aspect of prison management. Activity is important. He recommends that the programme of evening and weekend activities should be expanded to 'provide a better and fuller life for prisoners, to reduce boredom and to provide more opportunities for the development of constructive staff/inmate relationships'.[41] Prisoners should be properly and fairly treated. He recommends that 'arrangements should be made to enable prisoners to be consulted about the conditions and regime of the prison'.[42] A pre-release programme should be established for all prisoners. An information booklet should be produced for prisoners. Notice boards should be put up in the 'billets' for the display of up-to-date information. Relationships between staff and prisoners are important. He recommends that staff should talk to prisoners about matters that concern them rather than leaving notes for them on their beds. Staff training should be set up 'to underpin the measures to be taken to improve staff/inmate relationships'.[43] Little things also matter. He recommends that boilers should be installed so that prisoners can make hot drinks. The governor should find some volunteers to run a refreshment bar in the visiting room and improve the facilities for mothers with young babies visiting the prison.

It is greatly to be hoped that these recommendations, rather than proposals about locks, bars, closed circuit TV cameras and electronic double gates, prevail. Indeed the Home Office is not closed to considering new approaches to controlling prisons. The glossy publication on the American 'new generation' prisons makes that clear. The publication comes from another Home Office Working Party, also consisting of experienced prison administrators and staff, who visited a number of new prisons in the United States. The most interesting points to come out of the report are about how to manage prisons. The Working Party were clearly very impressed with what they saw in these new prisons. They praised 'the relaxed atmosphere', 'the clear sense of purpose and commitment', the 'feeling of personal safety' of both staff and prisoners, the reduction in the 'stresses and tensions of imprisonment'. They tried to pin down the reasons for this and identified the system of dividing prisoners up into small individually managed groups, the elimination of corridors, the colourful and attractive furnishings, the unbarred large windows, the high ceilings and wide circulation areas, the telephones for prisoners to make outgoing calls, long hours out of cell, proper wages for working and generous visiting arrangements.[44]

They also noted that the provision of attractive buildings was only half the story. The other half was a new system of organization, the Unit Management System. Each of the units is managed by a team of five or six people made up of a unit manager, a case manager, one or two counsellors, one secretary and one 'shift correctional officer'. Such a team would be made up of men and women and would incorporate all the functions that in a prison in England and Wales are divided among prison officers, probation officers and assistant governors. All the staff are trained in what in Britain would be called prison officer duties, that is, security and control, as well as in working constructively with prisoners. They are all discipline staff first, and all start at the bottom of the career ladder with the same professional training. The aim is to build up relationships of trust. The unit management team has its office on the unit.

Andrew Rutherford, from Southampton University, who has also studied prisons in the United States, found that 'new generation' prisons could be as repressive and brutal as 'old generation' prisons, and questions whether buildings can ever be 'a solution': 'The American experience emphatically concludes that no such architectural solution exists. It identifies management as the key component to secure and decent containment.'[45]

Indeed, the idea that good architecture alone will produce a good prison is a total and dangerous illusion. The contrary assumption, that reasonably humane prisons cannot exist in bad old buildings, is also misguided. A humane and decent prison system will not emerge inevitably from sorting out old bad management and industrial relations practices or from building modern new establishments with brightly coloured curtains and telephone booths. The Australian professor, Tony Vinson, who researched the Dutch system found this out. He wrote:

If the physical environment in some of the older prisons was sometimes disappointing, the social environment was strikingly different to that to which I am accustomed. In the wings, the workshops, and recreational and communal areas there was a notable lack of tension. A number of physical and social factors contributed to this impression: the fact that the prisoners and detainees wore ordinary clothing, and the subdued styling of the officers' 'uniform', the use of standard fittings and furnishings in buildings that in Australia would bristle with locks, bars and hardened glass, the intermingling of staff and inmates were some of the factors involved.

He was even more surprised at the 'naturalness of the interactions' between staff and between staff and prisoners. This does not mean that they were always happy with each other. That would have been unnatural; but when prisoners were angry their anger was about something specific and when staff responded they did not question the prisoner's right to be angry. He goes on: 'the social environment was generally friendly, robust and, as far as I could judge, devoid of the point-scoring that tends to characterize staff/inmate relations in Australian prisons'.[46]

His conclusion is helpful, though it must be seen in the Dutch context of only having one person per cell and not permitting overcrowding to exist. He says:

I have long agreed with the view that plumbing and physical amenities should not be the major concerns of those engaged in improving prisons. The major focus of reform should be those very matters that are at the heart of Dutch penal policy, such as the just and humane treatment of offenders and the development of an improved social environment in the institutions.[47]

As a footnote to Professor Vinson's mention of the unobtrusive uniform, it is worth noting that the Dutch prison officers' casual uniform of grey trousers and navy blazer with a Ministry of Justice badge is to be replaced: they will be supplied with civilian clothes, all in the same colour but completely non-institutional.

One feature is central to these systems that are regarded as successful. Prisoners have something to do most of the time. In England and Wales this is not the case. Enough has already been said about lack of activity to show that enforced idleness is a central and urgent problem. The need for a radical new approach to what prisoners do all day is clear. Hours of work available have been dropping year by year (see Chapter 7). What work there is is not necessarily useful or constructive. Education is being squeezed, from 3.55 per cent of the prison's budget in 1984–5 to 3.08 per cent in 1987–8. The Prison Department's Director of Regimes and Services told the Education Select Committee in March 1986 that he accepted that 'there has been some reduction' and went on to attribute this to the need to pay for new prisons and more prison officers.[48] Large numbers of prison workshops are to be closed. In March 1986 the Home Secretary announced the closure of fifty-four workshops, twenty-five of them to close immediately (they were probably already effectively closed) and a further twenty-nine to close when the prisoners working in them had been reallocated to other work, or education and training. Thirty-one would stay open but only if they could do better than they were doing currently. It is unfortunate that this decision seems to have been taken on financial grounds rather than because there is a need to occupy prisoners constructively. Announcing the closures, the Home Secretary referred to the conclusion that 'prison industries in their present form do not provide value for money', and went on: 'The Prisons Board will shortly be getting firm financial and other management targets for prison industries. It is also essential that they be managed with the right blend of commercial skills and business acumen.'[49]

The Chief Inspector, writing in 1988, took rather a different view. He said 'we accept the general proposition that the Prison Service needs to be managed with greater efficiency. We also accept . . . that over-provision and under-use of workshop facilities are costly and wasteful. However, the consequences of further reductions in the availability of work for inmates seem likely to be more costly in the long run.'[50]

The Control Review Committee was as bold as it could be in questioning the long-held view that what prisoners should do all day is manual work, that this is what society expects and it is good for prisoners. Even if it is but a pale imitation of real work in the outside world, produces nothing useful and teaches the prisoner no useful skills, it is the right thing to do. The primacy of work in the ethos of the prison service may account for this failure to come to terms with the unemployment discharged prisoners will face in the outside world. Fantasies about becoming a commercially viable enterprise using a workforce paid around £3 a week led to the emphasis on equipping new prisons with expensive machinery and building magnificent workshops that are never used.

The Control Review Committee listed the following defects in the industry-based system. The supply of work is unpredictable.

Prisoners know that their chances of a job outside are very low so they cannot see the point. Prisoners often are required to eke out the work to make it last so they get bored and frustrated. And, as a result, the workshops are a source of friction between staff and prisoners. Also, prison industries are very expensive to run. The Committee concludes: 'an *industry-centred* regime may now be impracticable'.[51] What they wanted to see was a move towards individual programmes for prisoners, more varied than at present and related much more to what the prisoner wants to do, or learn, or occupy time with.[52]

From all these developments, and the experience of other countries, emerges a fairly clear view of the direction the prison system should move in, and what it should move away from. It needs to leave behind the impersonality of the big institution, loud with the banging of cell doors, the clanking of keys and the echoing shouts of B12748 Smith or 35916 Jones, where officers and prisoners barely know each other and the aim is to get through the day having fulfilled the minimum functions of a prison. It needs a different approach to the value and contributions of a prison officer, and an appreciation of what happens to people's self-image and morale when all the interesting parts of their jobs are gradually hived off to people with longer training who do not have to do the mundane bits of the job.

It is not necessary to tear down all the existing buildings and put up modern prisons built on the small unit concept before incorporating the spirit of those ideas. The aims should be clear. Prisons should be organized in small units or in small groups. Prison staff should be allocated to the small groups and their job should be to run the groups according to agreed principles but with scope for imagination and experiment. They should be responsible for ensuring that activities are available and that prisoners have a programme of activities that reflects choice, variety and a chance to progress and develop. All prison staff should have a chance to attend training courses that will equip them to provide a constructive living environment, for example counselling, working with small groups, providing activities, making contact with outside organizations, various sports, and art and craft. The training for prison staff should be progressively upgraded and the opportunity given to them to get qualifications that are acceptable outside the prison service. The Prison Department should talk to the training bodies about trying to establish transferable qualifications so that prison staff could move in and out of the prison service.

Prison staff are still predominantly male. The virtual absence of women prison officers working in male prisons in the UK is a strange left-over from another age. In the United States and Canada women form a substantial minority of the staff of men's prisons. The Prior Committee found that in North America opinion was generally in favour of a mixed staff. The presence of women had, it appeared, had a 'civilizing influence' and had eased tension and produced less aggressive responses. The employment of women had led to 'an overall improvement in control and discipline'.

Prison Department headquarters needs to adjust, similarly. At present, its structure perpetuates the separation of functions, the division and hiving off that ends up with security and control taking the centre of the stage and the other functions of the prison taking up positions on the periphery. A strong central department needs to be established at headquarters responsible for what prisoners do all day and how staff are to be trained to ensure that it happens. The Control Review Committee noted this glaring gap, that for some years, no part of the Prison Department had had the overall responsibility for regime policy, that is, for what actually went on all day.[53]

Nothing less than such a radical restructuring of approach will ensure a prison system that most of those working in it would like to see. How the prison service organizes itself is only part of the story, though. How the prisons relate to the world outside is the other part. To this we now turn.

I2   The Closed World

The prison and the community

> It's very frustrating being in prison. I think it's more so for women than for men. The majority of women have children, homes, financial commitments ... I lost my flat and practically all my belongings. Everyone's worried ... Are they going to take my flat away from me? Am I going to have to live on the street when I get out? What's happening to my little girl? She's growing up and I'm not there ...

> Sharon, an ex-prisoner, talking to Una Padel and Prue Stevenson for their book *Insiders: Women's Experience of Prison*.[1]

If the new approach proposed in Chapter II was put into practice a number of benefits would result. Prison staff would have more satisfying jobs. Prisons would be more peaceful and prison management would not have to lurch from crisis to crisis. But prisons are not there for prison staff and prison management. They have a wider social duty, if not to improve the people that are sent to them, at least to minimize the damage that enforced removal from the community into what a prisoner called 'a further education college of crime' can do. It is in the community's interest that the prison system should be just, open and accountable. The fairer and more open a system is, the less likely it is to turn out embittered and cynical ex-prisoners. The prison is expected to contain, not to brutalize.

At the moment, as the result of history, we have the opposite of a community-oriented system. The system is self-contained and looks inwards. The people who work in it normally give themselves to it for life. They grow old in the system, moving, if they are governors, round and up the system, into the Home Office for a spell and then out again – finally, for the very few, to end up on the Prisons Board. The very fact of moving round and not being able to put down roots pushes them inwards to the company of other prison people. Their reputations precede them in this closed, gossipy world where everyone has long memories. Albany in 1972, Gartree in 1978, Wormwood Scrubs in 1979 pass into myth and legend. Everyone who works in it is subject to the Official Secrets Act, so technically it is an offence to tell anyone how many footballs there are at Gartree or who the new governor of Holloway is. In fact the secrecy of the prison system has diminished considerably over recent years, but the aura of the obsessively secretive past still lingers.

The system does not feel any need for the outside world. It has its own teachers, doctors, welfare workers and ministers of religion. It could manage quite well on its own. For those who work in it the prison service is their world. For the prisoners it is different. When they come to prison they have left their world behind and the main impact of imprisonment is that of deprivation. Never mind the grim surroundings, the overcrowding, the institutional food, the boredom. These are undoubtedly uncomfortable – but the real pain of imprisonment is the loss of family and friends, of jobs and homes, the fear of being forgotten, the anxiety that you might not fit in when you eventually come out. For prison staff prison is their world. For prisoners the outside world is their world which they have temporarily lost.

The way the prison system is currently organized accentuates the removal of prisoners from their world. The prison system has its own priorities. It has to cram too many bodies into too few spaces. It has to divide up people according to its security categories. The needs of the system to 'tactically manage', as it is called, its accommodation and maintain security come before the needs of the people in it. Many prison buildings are in sites chosen specially for their remoteness from towns and cities and thus their remoteness from the public objections that nearly always come from a neighbourhood when any institution for disadvantaged or cast-out people is proposed. The system also requires that remand prisoners and short-termers take up the places in the big city prisons. Thus the long-termers who have the greatest need to keep in touch with the outside world are sent on to the training prisons, usually deep in the countryside.

This system places tremendous obstacles in the way of developing a new community approach to prisons. The community in the rural area where the prison is to be found is very different from the inner-city, ethnically mixed communities from which most prisoners come. The services that can help the prisoners when they come out are not based on the Isle of Wight or the wilds of Northumberland but in, for example, Manchester, Birmingham and London. The most generous visiting allowance, for example, one visit a week instead of one a month, is not much use to a family from many miles away, living on state benefits, who can only get financial help for one visit a month. A prisoner said: 'I went to see probation . . . to see if I could get more visits, and they said they were going to go around to see her . . . They did send her a letter to say how to get to the prison, but she could only come once a month and that wasn't enough to sort your marriage problems out.'[2]

A major change of approach is needed. The case has been argued (Chapter 9) that no more prisons should be built in remote rural areas. The money should be used to improve the existing prisons on the sites where they are needed. Ideally, small neighbourhood prisons on the lines of the Swedish system would be a better solution.

In 1969 the White Paper *People in Prison* said confidently: 'The Government sees no reason to expect any considerable increase in the number of women and girls in custody in the foreseeable future.'[3] In 1968 the average figure was 805, a figure that had not changed much for thirty years. Today it is more than double the 1968 figure. Yet the women's prison system is still an afterthought, an adjunct. It is significant that the Holloway Board of Visitors, concerned that no judge had visited Holloway for the last six years, invited judges to visit. The reply was that applicants for positions as Recorders usually visited Wandsworth but they would include Holloway.[4] What works badly for men, when applied automatically to women, is much worse. If small neighbourhood prisons are desirable for short-term male prisoners, they are even more so for the small numbers of women who have to be in prison. Certainly another solution than the present system has to be found. The idea of mixed prisons has been floated by the Howard League for Penal Reform although the disadvantages were also recognized. In the provincial system run by the state of Ontario in Canada male prisons have small, totally separate women's wings attached to them. Women in the women's prison in Kingston, Ontario, can join some of the training courses run in the men's prison, such as micrographics and telecommunications, and men come into the women's prison to use the word-processing training centre. In Sweden the neighbourhood prisons have accommodation for women as well as men and both can make use of the facilities.[5]

All these solutions are worth exploring. The exploration should be soon. For many years, calls have been made for an inquiry into the women's prison system. The Holloway Project Committee were of the same mind. They recommended a full review of the female prison population so that provision could be made to meet its needs.[6] The Prison Medical Association has called for a new approach to the problems of women in prison.[7] There is wide agreement, as reported in the Howard League study, that action should be taken on women's imprisonment.

Geography cannot be changed overnight. Prisons in remote rural areas cannot be picked up and put somewhere else. Until at least the middle of the next century many of Britain's prisons will be well away from the main centres of population, including some not yet built.[8] The major challenge to the prison system for some time to come must therefore be to overcome this fundamental defect. Much could be done. Important improvements in both men and women prisoners' ability to keep in touch with family, friends and community could be made immediately. The cost would be minimal; the benefits great. Prisoners could be allowed to write and receive as many letters as they liked. For all but Category A prisoners they could be opened to check for contraband but not read by staff. It might also be a small but welcome reform if all prisoners could write letters on whatever notepaper they chose instead of on the instantly recognizable prison-issue lined notepaper. Telephones are available in many comparable prison systems and neither security nor control have suffered. In fact the opposite has happened. Visits could come up the priority list and get more of the time available, the staff resources and the accommodation. Home leave allowances are much less generous in Britain than in comparable systems and should be increased. These things should be done for their own sake. They will also have the consequence of creating a more peaceful and manageable system. The daily pressures and frustrations of life inside, where every molehill looks like a mountain and the tiniest incident can spark off an outburst, can be much eased by contact with the outside world and by having something to look forward to and plan for.

Letters, visits, telephones and home leave help to keep individual prisoners in contact with their bit of the outside world. Larger questions about the prison and its relationship with the outside world are also important. Should it be such an 'administrative, social and cultural, as well as a physical, enclave'?[9] Should there be a medical service specially for prisoners separate from the National Health Service which is for everyone else? Should there be a prison chaplaincy service with a chaplain-general who is a civil servant with an office and staff at Prison Department headquarters, and prison chaplains who work not in the local church structure but in the structure of the Home Office?

Much opinion over a long period has argued that the answer to these questions is no. Services to prisoners should be provided by the normal services that are given to the rest of the community. Particularly contentious is the Prison Medical Service.

It has long been accepted by prison reformers that the Home Office should not be the employer of the prison doctors. Two thirds of the medical workload is already carried by GPs, consultants and other specialists from the NHS who come in to service the prisons by arrangement with the prison medical officer. Either a separate authority or some form of integration with the National Health Service is the usual recommended solution. It is often argued in reply that prisoners would suffer because they would come at the bottom of the NHS list of priorities. This outcome could be avoided if the solution put forward by NACRO to the Select Committee were followed. NACRO representatives suggested that the Home Office should buy in a medical service from the NHS, following the same model that exists already for education. The Home Office pays local education authorities for the services of education officers and teachers who work in the prisons but are employed by the local education authorities. Certainly whatever the detailed arrangement, the Prison Medical Service should no longer be under the managerial control of the Home Office.

The question of the chaplains is not as controversial – perhaps because religion is less immediately important to most people in prison than medicine. However, the same principles apply. If chaplaincy services were provided by the local churches then benefits could be great. The local church community would have an impetus to get involved in the prison. More local ministers of religion would acquire a first-hand knowledge of the prison system.

Providing such services by outsiders would certainly bring the prison service nearer to the spirit of European Prison Rule 65, which requires that activities for prisoners 'are organized, so far as possible, to increase contacts with and opportunities within the outside community so as to enhance the prospects for social resettlement after release'.[10]

The logic of looking outwards towards the community rather than inwards to the prison must also be applied to how prisons use prisoners' time. A much higher priority should be given to preparation for release in the thinking and activity of each establishment. Every year 90,000 prisoners are released from prison. The majority of prisoners are serving short sentences. Within months many prisoners will have left the prison behind them and will be trying to make a go of it out in the world. Preparing prisoners for this should be the focus of what goes on in prisons. Dennis Trevelyan said in 1982, in his Italian speech referred to in Chapter 11:

. . . if there is no counter to the necessary institutional and coercive apparatus of a prison establishment, [the prisoner's] capacity to return to society with what I described as his individuality, humanity and dignity intact is seriously undermined. Prison management must make conscious attempts to open up prisons to contact with the outside world and to develop regimes which as far as possible replicate social norms and activities outside the prison environment.[11]

The problem with prison as it is now is that it does the opposite of preparing prisoners for release. It de-prepares them for the outside world because it takes away all their responsiblilty and power to make decisions. Male prisoners do not need to worry about what clothes to wear. They wear the clothes they are given. Prisoners do not have to make choices about how to spend their time. Their choice of relationships is limited to those inescapably around them. They do not have to worry about paying the rent, buying and cooking food, saving enough to pay the electricity bill. They can worry about their families outside but the worry cannot lead to any action. If they work, the conditions and pressures are quite different from work outside. If they have no work the opportunities and temptations are quite different from unemployment outside.

Then, suddenly, they have to leave and face all the problems of being a discharged prisoner. A study was carried out in a men's prison in 1981 to ask the prisoners what they thought their problems would be when they were released. Nearly all of them said finding a job or finding somewhere to live. More than nine out of ten said keeping out of trouble would be a problem, as would be managing personal relationships. Over half mentioned alcohol, drugs, reactions to prisons, relations with police and probation officers and being an ex-prisoner.[12]

Some prisoners interviewed in a NACRO survey knew exactly what was wrong and what they needed:

The problem I experienced on leaving prison was finding employment and getting back into friendships.

There should be some organization when someone comes out of prison to find accommodation.

Well, there should be a few people there who you could actually have a talk to without them saying, 'Look, I've got five minutes. Be quick.' Because really you don't get any chance to talk. They're too busy running about.

It doesn't have to be sympathetic, just somebody who you can get some sense out of, get a bit of information out of them.

Sometimes they give you these leaflets, you read them, you're no wiser.

We definitely, while we're inside, need some kind of education. They ought to sort something out – tell you what to do, how to go about looking for a job, how to go about sorting your money out, find you somewhere to live. They ought to tell you that while you're still inside.[13]

Preparation for release is all too often on the edges of prison activity, a luxury which falls all too easily off the bottom of the list of things that have to be done. Moving it to the centre of the stage would bring many benefits. If time were given from the beginning of the sentence to looking at prisoners' practical problems and how they could be solved, prisoners' morale would be raised and the prison would become a much easier place to live and work in. A systematic programme for each prisoner would require all prisoners to be treated as individuals and require staff to form relationships with them. Second, it would involve a whole range of community groups in coming into the prison to work with individual prisoners and participate in courses. The prison would need to call on housing advisers, law centres, citizens advice bureaux, ethnic minority organizations, employment schemes, and any other community organization that had something to offer. In the Ontario provincial prison system in Canada, with 3,000 prisoners, there are 2,500 volunteers – individuals and members of organizations – coming into the prisons to work with prisoners on what they call 'programs'. Two projects run by NACRO have shown the possibilities. One which brought qualified housing advisers into Midlands prisons to sort out prisoners' housing problems managed to reverse the usual decline in prisoners' housing position that results from a prison sentence.[14] The other, the Women Prisoners Resource Centre, has found a substantial demand for help with plans for release from prisoners in all the women's prisons.[15] The Apex Trust has run very successful schemes bringing outsiders in to help prisoners prepare to find employment in a hostile and difficult environment.

A third great advantage of shifting the emphasis of imprisonment towards preparation for release is the effect it would have on prison officers' jobs. Their work would be much more interesting as they would need to be out and about in the community, making contacts, visiting projects, finding people to invite in. Spending some time working in a community project, or in an advice-giving organization learning the basics, would be useful and would help break down the myths and stereotypes that outside people have about prison officers and that prison officers have about organizations that 'do good'. The attractions of sitting in court all day would surely fade when compared with the variety and purposefulness of such a programme.

Another benefit would be better working relationships inside. Prison officers would need to work alongside education officers and probation officers as part of an integrated team. The barriers between the specialists and the main grade officers might begin to disappear, and the myths and stereotypes that prevail here too might begin to fade. Finally, preparing prisoners properly for release might really stop some of them coming back. It would be unwise to expect too much – but it seems that having a place to live and something to do all day can help to keep people out of prison.

In its report *The Resettlement of Ex-Offenders: Towards a New Approach*, NACRO made two major proposals. Each prison, especially those in cities, should set up a consultative group of the community organizations that could help the prison with its preparation for release. Nationally the Prison Department should also set up a consultative committee where other government departments and the main voluntary organizations could meet the Prison Department and the probation service to ensure that they were doing all they could to help prisoners, pre-release and after release.

If the prison system is to look outwards however, there must be something out there for it to look towards. Rather regrettable therefore is the direction taken by the Government's Statement of National Objectives and Priorities for the probation service, which has a welcome emphasis on keeping people out of prison but gives a much lower priority to prisoners' after-care.

Even more regrettable – positively short-sighted in fact – is the Government's parsimony when allocating resources to hostels and housing schemes for homeless ex-prisoners. All new developments were stopped in March 1985 and only resumed in 1988. There are about 4,000 places currently in such hostels and projects. Their cost to the Home Office is around £6 million a year. That is what it cost to run Leicester prison, for around 400 people a year.

Proper preparation for release will certainly cost money, albeit very much less than new prisons cost. It will also require changes of attitude.

Outward-looking moves will not necessarily come easily to a service that has traditionally looked inwards, but the benefits to prisons would be considerable. However, a new openness on working with prisoners is only half the story. The prison service needs another kind of openness as well, an openness whereby it accounts to the community for what it does in the name of the community. All closed institutions are vulnerable to abuses of power. People are also suspicious of what goes on inside them and assume the worst, sometimes rightly, sometimes not. The outside world, and those that run the prison service, need to have ways of satisfying themselves that power is being used properly and within limits. Neither the Home Secretary, nor the Director-General, nor even the governor of a prison, can be sure that what goes on is what ought to go on. Therefore, mechanisms for accountability must exist. They do already, of course, but are widely felt to be inadequate.

Two particular aspects of the prison system currently cause particular anxiety. The first is what is happening to black prisoners. We know what can happen to black people in other parts of life. Racism in the Metropolitan Police Force was documented in detail in the Policy Studies Institute Report *Police and People in London*, published in 1983, and by Lord Scarman in his 1981 Report. In the closed world of prisons the dangers of racist practices are even more acute, especially while black people are over-represented among the prisoners but barely represented at all among the staff. The Prison Department cannot be accused of ignoring the danger it faces. A circular went out in 1981 saying: 'The potential sensitivity however of race relations problems adds a new dimension to the professionalism required of the Prison Service . . .'[16] The circular went on to advocate that prisons should make links with local community relations councils and ethnic minority organizations, race relations liaison officers should be appointed in prisons, and staff should be trained in race matters. The circular was updated in 1983 and took the statement further, arguing for race relations liaison officers to be senior staff in the prison and pointing out that jobs and training courses for prisoners must be allocated without discrimination and the allocation monitored. Further measures were reported in 1984 including the jettisoning of staff selection tests which had been in use for twenty-three years – and were found to contain 'some cultural bias'.[17] In November 1986 a new circular contained for the first time a public declaration of commitment to racial equality to be posted widely around all prisons.

Since there are so few black people in any positions of power or influence in the prison system the need for vigilance is all the greater. Navnit Dholakia, a member of the Board of Visitors at Lewes prison, wrote in the Association's journal: 'It remains a source of deep concern to all of us connected with the prison service that black staff account for only 1 per cent of the total . . . the prison service has made efforts to increase recruitment from the minority communities but . . . these have proved abysmally unsuccessful.'[18]

Black people are slowly becoming involved in prisons through membership of Boards of Visitors. The number of black Board members has risen from 34 out of around 1,500 in 1981 to 160 in September 1988, still a very small proportion. Boards have an important role in monitoring race matters in prisons. Governors should report regularly to them on what is happening to black prisoners, and provide an ethnic breakdown of allocation to work and training courses, disciplinary hearings and punishments, parole granted and numbers in segregation. The Wandsworth Board of Visitors leads the way on this. Its Annual Report has a section on race relations. In its Report for 1987 it says that it 'has taken a keen interest in monitoring figures which are produced regularly and has looked particularly closely at work allocation and provision of facilities for worship, both of which give cause for concern'.[19]

The second major controversial area is the use of informal punishments – putting prisoners in segregation for reasons 'of good order and discipline' without reasons and with no appeal, transferring them without reasons and with no notice (called 'ghosting'), and shunting them round the system to spend a month in a different prison and then be moved on under Circular 10/74. All these procedures are carried out far away from the public gaze, with no explanation called for and no published account of their use and the reasons. This cannot be good for prisoners or the prison system. It gives rise to suspicions and questions that cannot be answered because there is no mechanism for asking or answering them. The Chief Inspector is not happy with the use of Rule 43 segregation. In 1985 he recommended more elaborate safeguards for such prisoners often held 'for weeks and even months in inferior conditions at the prison governor's discretion'.[20] No safeguards have been introduced.

It is in the interests of the Home Office to do away with this secret use of absolute power. It may buy some short-term control but in the longer term that major element of a just and humane prison system, fairness, is missing. A sense of injustice is fostered by such measures that leads in the end to loss of control. A proper recording system for decisions should be used; the information should be published and such decisions should be authorized by an independent body.

The involvement of independent bodies in the prison system is another tricky problem. The Howard League looked at the organization of the prison system as part of its study of women in the penal system and concluded: 'The Home Office control is virtually total.' It controls policy, administration, the appointment of staff. It appoints the Boards of Visitors. The Howard League Report concludes that while this total control makes it easier for the Home Office to deal with things quickly, it does also 'limit the extent to which the system is exposed to outside ideas and criticism'. It allows 'the Home Office to act as its own judge and jury'.[21]

Boards of Visitors are the Home Office's answer to accountability to the community. With distinguished exceptions neither their image nor their record have given much cause for confidence. Their job is two-fold, to act as a watchdog, a sort of amateur inspector and representative of the public conscience on the one hand, on the other to constitute a tribunal to try cases against prisoners accused of breaking the disciplinary rules. The combination of these two roles has long been felt to be improper and the Prior Committee, set up to look at the disciplinary system, recommended a separation of the two roles. A truly independent tribunal was needed to hear cases against prisoners – not controlled by the Home Office but by a judge. Boards of Visitors could then devote themselves entirely to their watchdog role. The Home Office study commissioned to see how Boards carried out this role did not make encouraging reading. Boards, it said, 'are largely composed of middle-class, middle-aged people, steeped in a strong tradition of public service'.[22]

The visits Boards are supposed to make to see how the institution was functioning were often as superficial as a Cooks tour. They often had a very limited knowledge of how prisons were supposed to work and relied very heavily on the governor to tell them. They were deficient in the systems they adopted for hearing prisoners' complaints; they 'were generally either unable or unwilling to exercise their critical faculties to any substantial degree when they were dealing with the governor'.[23] They felt that although they had to sign an authorization for a prisoner to be held in segregation this was just a 'token gesture of involvement'.[24] They were not highly regarded by the prison community. Prisoners 'do not place a great deal of faith in the value of Boards as "watchdogs"'.[25] Prison staff regard them as rather out-of-touch and superficial.

The publication of this rather damning report and the recommendations of the Prior Committee seemed to inject new life into Boards of Visitors. There were moves to strengthen their collective organization, improve their training, and draw up some guidelines so they knew what they should be looking for when they 'inspected'. Wandsworth and Holloway Boards showed the way by publishing detailed Annual Reports telling some of the truths that need to be told about their establishments. Others are now following suit and a composite Annual Report is now produced by the Boards' Co-ordinating Committee. However, a close look at how Boards could be more representative, more independent of the Home Office and local prison-management, and more effective, is urgently needed. It is often proposed that local authorities would take more interest in the prisons in their area if they had representatives on the Boards.

Boards are the amateur inspectors. The Chief Inspector of Prisons is the professional. Much of the information that we have about prisons, as this book shows, comes from Reports from the Chief Inspector – not from the Prison Service. The work of the new Prisons Inspectorate, since it was set up in 1980 following a recommendation by the May Committee, has made an enormous difference to public knowledge and understanding about prisons. Without the Inspector's Reports public knowledge of the prison system would be not much greater than what can be gleaned from the Prison Service's own Annual Reports, that is, painfully little. Since 1982 the Chief Inspector has been a statutory Crown officer and as such independent of, although part of, the Home Office. However, Inspectorate Reports go to the Prison Department for consideration before they are published. The staff of the Inspectorate, apart from the Chief Inspector who is an outsider, come from the Prison Service and go back there. They are therefore in some difficulty if they see a conflict between their duty to the Inspectorate and their future career in the prison service.

The Inspectorate is certainly not perfect, but it is a great step forward. To become more effective it needs more staff. The total cost of the Inspectorate in February 1987 was £730,000, less than 0.1 per cent of the prison budget. The Inspectorate also needs more specialist advice. It should certainly take on a consultant in race relations, should ensure that the inspection teams are made up of men and women, and should feel freer to draw in all sorts of different experts from time to time. It also needs to consider how to fill the gap created by the prison system's immunity from prosecution under the public health and safety legislation. Ideally, of course, such crown immunity should be done away with.

The Chief Inspector, however, cannot deal with individual complaints from prisoners – which is where the machinery for accountability is fundamentally defective. We saw in Chapter 6 the long and fruitless path a prisoner's complaint can travel to arrive nowhere – at least nowhere that satisfies the prisoner. The Board of Visitors is not an effective channel for an individual prisoner because 'it has virtually no executive powers and can only rarely provide redress'[26] as Professor Graham Zellick puts it. Most advocates of a fairer system have advocated the establishment of a prison ombudsman with direct access to prisoners. Graham Zellick sees a prison ombudsman as 'the single most important step that could be taken to ensure the proper treatment of prisoners and subject the extensive and largely unchecked discretion of the prison authorities to scrutiny and control'.[27]

The ombudsman would have to be completely independent of the Home Office and be able to receive complaints direct from prisoners, examine decisions for fairness and quality, launch investigations and make recommendations based on experience of individual cases.

Many things are wrong with the prison system – stretching from day-to-day problems about the management of people and plant to fundamental issues of justice and fairness. The delicate question must be asked, is there something basically wrong with the machinery? Is the Home Office the right place to put the running of prisons? Two separate issues prompt this question, both crucial to the condition of the prisons. First, can a complex machine employing 30,000 people to look after another 50,000 ever be run satisfactorily by a centralized machine directly accountable on a day-to-day basis to ministers? On the one hand it is highly desirable that there should be more uniformity. All prisoners should be certain of getting the same minimum standard of life. The differentials currently are much too great. On the other it has to be recognized that running a decent establishment centres on creating and nurturing good relationships, a task which needs confidence, flexibility and imagination. It will be hard to produce in a system run from Whitehall by Circular Instructions. The challenge is whether within a framework of minimum standards of life for all prisoners, prison governors can take on a more creative management role and become much more involved in a decentralized decision-making process. Some advocate that we should go even further. In a Tawney Society pamphlet Sean McConville and Eryl Hall Williams argue for a dual prison system on the Canadian and United States model. They would like to see long-term prisoners (say those serving five years or more) dealt with in a national system and short-termers placed in prisons run by local management boards to national standards with an inspection system. It has also been suggested that local authorities might run their local prisons. The Prison Reform Trust has called for the prison service to be hived off and run as an agency at one remove from Government.

The second reason for considering critically the current location of prison administration is the desirability of more judicial involvement. The Home Office, because of its responsibilities, is more concerned with law enforcement than with individual liberty. It is noticeable how little involvement there is from the judiciary in running the prison system. Apart from some judges on the Parole Board judicial involvement is non-existent. This is very different from some other prison systems, where the judiciary is much closer to the prisons and how they are run. A case could well be made for saying that the political process has failed to deliver a decent prison system. It reacts to a crisis but once it is over is happy to turn its attention quickly to other things. If the political process really cannot do any better, then perhaps the time has come to build in a different type of accountability, for example, an accountability to the law and the judiciary through minimum standards and enforceable rules. If really radical change was on the agenda a possible model would be an appointed body working to minimum standards of imprisonment laid down by Parliament, accountable financially to a central government department and operationally to the courts and with strong community and judicial involvement at local level.

Certainly, whatever direction is taken, the prison service needs to move towards an entirely different way of relating to the public and enlisting public support for its work and the changes that it knows must be made. The prison service suffers greatly from a structure which prevents it having at its head an identifiable public figure – a stark contrast to the police.

Many people could name the head of the Metropolitan Police. He is regularly seen on the television. How many people could name the person who runs the prisons? The debate on the police and how they should account to the public is open and vociferous. The public debate on prisons and how they should account to the public is non-existent. Indeed it is almost impossible to get such a debate going. The professionals in the prison system are not allowed to get involved. Police representatives from all levels of the police service appear regularly on the media. Television programmes on prisons show prisoners sometimes, and staff speaking as trade unionists sometimes, and nearly always end with a measured and unchallenged statement by the responsible minister at the Home Office, whose job is not to open up debate but close it. The comparison is not a perfect one, but there are enough parallels for the onus to be on the prison service to look again at its level of participation in public life.

No one benefits from the inwardness, the secrecy, the lack of accountability, the untrammelled discretion of prison governors – not the prisoners, not the system, and certainly not society. The prison system can only benefit from turning away from its inward-looking habits and facing the outside world. More than ever it needs public knowledge, public understanding and public sympathy. To call this forth, it must open itself up from headquarters downwards to interested outsiders, to community groups, to discussion, debate, controversy even. The present structure was set up in 1963 when the Home Office took over from the Prison Commissioners. Twenty-six years later the time has come to look again at the structure. It was changed in 1963. It could well be time for it to be changed again.

13 Conclusion

As a stranger, coming from outside the prison system and going on a tour of Britain's prisons, you would see much to ponder. You would walk round the grey landings of Wandsworth and Strangeways, and look out through small barred windows at hundreds of men in badly fitting grey and blue clothes walking round and round a yard. You could visit the dungeon-like segregation blocks with their cardboard furniture where battles of will are fought out with those prisoners who have decided that survival depends on fighting back – and both sides struggle on knowing neither can win. You can see boys of fourteen – not yet old enough to shave – subjected to strict discipline in an effort to shock them out of their criminality, and young women convicted of petty crimes lying on their beds all day in modern yet claustrophobic, overcrowded cells. You would see 19,000 people, devoting considerable time and energy to imposing security and control on another lot of people who will soon be back in the outside world, with no security, controlling themselves.

You might well ask yourself, what is all this for? Why are we doing this and why are we planning to do more and more of it? Why, when spending on education in real terms is only 8 per cent higher in 1988 than in 1983 and investment in housing is down by 27 per cent,[1] has expenditure on prison building gone up by 117 per cent in real terms since 1979?[2] One answer is clear. The system is protecting society from people who would otherwise cause great damage to it – but they are a small proportion. What about the rest? Well, comes the answer, it is because we have got a lot of crime and so obviously we have to have a lot of people in prison.

So what is the necessary connection between a lot of crime, protecting the public and having a big and expanding prison population? As we have seen, there is no necessary connection. The relationship between the great mass of minor criminal activity that goes on and some people who do it ending up in prison is very tenuous. Crime is a very widespread activity. Only a small proportion, maybe a fifth, of all crimes come to the attention of the police. It has been estimated that only five of every hundred offenders even reach the sentencing stage;[3] of these, sixteen out of a hundred go to prison. Even that decision, given the differences in sentencing patterns between courts, is haphazard.

The comparison between Holland and Texas shows that the crime rate is not what determines the size of the prison population. So what does? It has been suggested that one reason for a rising population is a high rate of unemployment. Research carried out in the United States, Canada and the UK has been able to show that prison populations increase roughly in line with rises in the unemployment rate.[4] These increases are not connected with rises in crime but seem to stem from a greater likelihood of unemployed people going to prison, maybe because the court sees them as less good bets, or because they have no money to pay the size of fine the court would want to impose. However other studies have not shown the same connection. Andrew Rutherford, for instance, points out that in England in the thirties unemployment was very high and the prison population was dropping.[5]

Another suggestion is that there is a direct connection between how many people are in mental hospitals and how many are in prison. It is argued that prisons and mental hospitals provide different ways for society to respond to the same behaviour. Some societies will put more of the people who commit offences and are mentally disturbed in prison while others will treat them in hospital.[6]

While these explanations may account for some of the people in prison being there, they do not explain why our prison population is the size it is, and growing all the time. The answer is not the crime rate, because prison is no solution to the crime rate. As Andrew Rutherford says, 'prison populations are not delivered by a providential stork'.[7] The Norwegian sociologist Thomas Mathieson puts it thus: '. . . criminal policy and the use of imprisonment is dependent on political inclination and choice on the part of political and legal authorities'.[8]

Prison populations are the result of choice. Rising rates of recorded crime do not mean you automatically have to have a rising number of people in prison. The size of the prison population is the result of choices, choices made at all stages of the process by people who are operating in what they regard as the right way, according to the policies they are trained to operate. Choices are made at all points in the system. A fifteen year old is picked up for shoplifting and admits it. There is a choice. Either the police can call in the parents and administer a caution, that is a stiff telling-off; or they can put the fifteen year old through the Juvenile Court and start another young person on to the first step of a criminal career.

A young woman is picked up for stealing a bottle of milk. Either she can be sent on her way with a lecture about sorting herself out or she can be charged and end up spending thirteen days in Holloway waiting for a report to be written on her. A young man, a small-time burglar with a string of minor offences, can come up in court yet again. One Bench will decide that all small-time burglars have to go to prison and this one has had more chances than is good for him. The Bench in the next town will decide that what he needs is a community service order. An alcoholic who persistently shoplifts appears in the Crown Court for two offences of theft of small value, and is also in breach of a probation order for similar offences. The judge could decide that the probation service should try again and that a place in a hostel for alcoholics should be found for him; or he could send him to prison for one month, three months, six months, or, as was eventually decided on appeal, thirty months.[9] A bank clerk who steals a small sum of money from her employer and through going to court loses her job, her reputation and the chance of ever working in a bank again can be sent to prison for one month, three months, six months, a year, longer, or not at all.

These are all choices. When the choices have been made the end product is a prison population that has to be accommodated, given the basics of life, protected from others, and prepared for release. What is the connection of all this with crime? First, it has to be said that rising prison populations may well increase crime. Prison weakens the elements in people's lives that keep them out of crime – family, chance of job, stability. That is why great efforts are made to keep young people out of custody by most of those involved in the system. The Department of Health puts money into alternatives to custody for juveniles. The Home Office sends out a circular to encourage the police to caution more young people rather than bringing them to court. The reason is that everyone knows locking up young people can so easily start them off on a life of crime. In our system these approaches tail off after the young person's seventeenth birthday – for no good reason, except that that is the system.

Ian Dunbar, at that time governor of Wormwood Scrubs prison, said in 1983, 'we have to accept the proposition that in spite of our hopes and aspirations prisons may train people to be bad. People are sent to prison to prevent and reduce crime. If it does neither we have to think seriously about it.'[10]

Secondly, imprisoning so many minor offenders is of no help at all to those suffering daily from crime. The new interest in crime prevention has not come about by chance. While prison does not protect the public from minor crime, crime prevention measures can. It is not much consolation to the residents of a vandalized crime-ridden housing estate to know that 50,000 people are in prison. Their crime problems will only be solved on their own estate – by better lighting, home security, more activities going on, something for the young people to do, attention to the needs of the elderly. To put half a dozen young vandals or burglars from the estate into youth custody may give a temporary respite – for which the residents may be grateful – but how much worse off they will be when the six come back, fully fledged professionals now, tougher and with even less to lose. That community would do much better if the six were put on community service and at the same time an attempt was made to get them something to do in the longer term that they would see as worthwhile.

In fact, if the aim is to tackle levels of crime in society, the whole process of police, courts, prisons, probation, is not the place to start. As a former head of the Home Office, Sir Brian Cubbon, put it: 'The massive incidence of crime represents an inherent feature of society and human behaviour which calls for something more than the necessarily reactive approach of the criminal justice system.'[11] Douglas Hurd, in an act of some courage, gave the same message to the 1988 Conservative Party Conference. He told them 'if we doubled the police, doubled the penalties, doubled the prisons – say until all three reached American levels – we might still find ourselves with American levels of crime and violence – much greater than our own. The police can catch criminals, the courts can punish them, the prisons can lock them up, but it is the *community* which creates the climate in which they flourish or decline.'[12] Crime rates do not come ultimately from what happens or does not happen to criminals. They come from what is going on in society more generally, from housing policies, the state of the labour market, education, the level of affluence, the social and moral climate.

We have a very high prison population from choice. The time has come to make a different choice and to reduce it. No good purpose is served by keeping it so high. Resources are needed, desperately, to implement crime-prevention measures, to reduce levels of crime and to tackle the fear of crime which stops so many people from living as full a life as they should. To increase prison capacity to more than 60,000 in such circumstances is irresponsible and indefensible. Our failure to develop the right priorities in dealing with crime is well put by the Archbishop of Canterbury:

We treat crime both too seriously and not seriously enough. Too seriously, in that we often impose conditions of imprisonment that are, by most people's reckoning, too harsh, and out of proportion for the pathetic character of some of those who undergo them. Not seriously enough, in that policies to 'deal with' the problems caused by crime are too often piecemeal and provisional.[13]

The way ahead should be quite clear. New machinery must be created to bring together all the elements that contribute to penal policy. Through this machinery measures must be set in train to reduce the prison population. A high-level body must be established to look at the structural and constitutional position of the prison system. The building of brand new prisons in out-of-the-way places must be halted. Capital investments must be switched to refurbishing the old city prisons. A target date for giving all prisoners access to sanitation must be fixed and a plan devised to meet it. A code of minimum standards must be drawn up in consultation with all interested parties. Prison officers must get an entirely new deal, and get training in how to work in a different way. The Prison Rules must be revised and become a legally enforceable package giving prisoners certain rights. The women's prison system should be reviewed in consultation with all interested outside organizations. There must be a concerted drive to recruit more black staff especially in the governor grades and more black members of committees. A prisons' ombudsman should be appointed and independent machinery should be established to hear disciplinary cases against prisoners. Children and young people under seventeen should no longer be sent to prison at all but should be dealt with by local authorities. The ideas behind the neighbourhood borstal scheme must be dusted off to become the basis of how prisons relate to the community. Preparation for release should become the focus of prison activity. Staff must be given enough freedom to experiment. The prison authorities must take every opportunity to involve lay people in the system, and through them stimulate a public debate on imprisonment and what it is for. The more that people are involved, the more they know about crime and punishment, about prison and its effects, the easier it will be to turn the prison system round to face the community and the more support there will be for a big reduction in the prison population. The public is not just a homogeneous mass waiting to give a thumbs down to any politician soft on prisoners. It also consists of employers, who can decide to give ex-prisoners a chance or 'not to touch them with a barge-pole'. It consists of careers officers, housing managers, teachers and lecturers, members of voluntary organizations – all of whom can contribute to the resettlement of ex-prisoners. It also consists of the residents of the most crime-ridden housing estates, who can either shrug their shoulders and hope the young burglars go down and never come back, or who can organize themselves into providing youth facilities and working to make their estate a better and safer place. Involving the public in debate about crime, as well as in campaigns to prevent crime and reduce the fear of crime, can only help the prison system.

The history of Britain's prisons since 1945 has not been a happy one. It is a story of many dedicated people trying to make things better, and continually trapped by what can only be called 'the system' – the system in which the sentencers produce a steadily rising prison population; the system that fears political embarrassment and revelations in newspapers about prisoners enjoying themselves watching colour videos more than it fears revelations about prisoners locked up for twenty-three hours a day and having no access to sanitation; the system where the processes, procedures, rules, Standing Orders and Circular Instructions take on a life of their own, and gradually blot out the consciousness that it is people not numbers being locked up.

Very few people can be proud of our prison system. Why then does it continue the way it is? As we have seen, there are many reasons – structural, political, managerial, organizational – and also human ones. David Wickham, a young assistant governor, wrote of his experiences during the industrial action in 1980 when he worked in a temporary prison staffed mainly by people from the army. What struck him was the quality of what he called 'staff-inmate relationships' which were better than he had seen elsewhere in his career. The reason for this was neither difficult nor expensive. It was, he says, very simple. The military staff dealing with the prisoners addressed them as 'Mister'.[14]

Are the prisons going to get better? They can, but only if the politicians and Parliament begin to take their responsibilities seriously. At their door must be much of the blame for the failure over the years. But they have not been helped by the inertia and apathy of those in society who believe that it is their duty to leave the world a little better than they found it.

Members of civil rights and civil liberties groups, churches, decent and humane people everywhere, have acquiesced in the wish of the system to be closed and secret. They have not asked loudly enough, what is going on behind the walls? They have not bothered to find out what happens to the nearly 100,000 people every year who leave society to enter that closed world. If they do know what goes on, they have not protested enough. They have not convinced the politicians that anyone out there really cares about what happens to prisoners. The administrators know that the system they run is indefensible, an 'affront to a civilized society'. But how civilized are we then, all of us who just let it carry on?

Notes

1 An Affront to a Civilized Society

1 *Report of HM Chief Inspector of Prisons for England and Wales 1981*, HMSO, 1982, para. 3.07.
2 Home Office press release, 'Threatened Prison Officers' Dispute', Prime Minister's letter to prison governors, 18 April 1986.
3 Peter Paterson, 'Disgrace of the men who run our prisons', *Daily Mail*, 2 May 1986, p. 6.
4 Reported in *Gatelodge*, the prison officers' magazine, May 1986, p. 300.
5 'Curb on Jail-Protest Doctor', *The Times*, 7 November 1983.
6 *Minutes of Evidence taken before the Social Services Committee, Session 1985–6*, 27 November 1985, HMSO, 1985, Q. 105.
7 *Minutes of Evidence taken before the Committee of Public Accounts, Session 1985–6*, 17 February 1986, HMSO, 1986, Q. 1,332.
8 Foreword to Adrian Speller's *Breaking Out: A Christian Critique of Criminal Justice*, Hodder & Stoughton, 1986, p. 7.
9 POA, *Financial Management Initiatives*, 1985, p. 11.
10 *Report of the Inquiry into Prison Escapes and Security by Admiral of the Fleet, the Earl Mountbatten of Burma*, HMSO, 1966, para. 207.
11 *Seventh Report from the Select Committee on Estimates, Session 1951–2, Prisons*, HMSO, 1952, para. 28.
12 ibid., para. 11.
13 ibid., para. 11.
14 *Report from the Departmental Committee on Prisons* (the Gladstone Report), HMSO, 1895, para. 104.
15 *Report of HM Chief Inspector of Prisons 1983*, HMSO, 1984, para. 2.06.

2 People in Prison

1 James Campbell, *Gate Fever*, Weidenfeld & Nicolson, 1986, p. 25.
2 Section 5 of the Penitentiary Act (19 Geo III, c. 74) quoted in Harding, Hines, Ireland and Rawlings, *Imprisonment in England and Wales*, Croom Helm, 1985, p. 117.
3 Charles Dickens, *Great Expectations*, Penguin, 1965, p. 36.
4 ibid., p. 46.

5 ibid., p. 71.

6 Figure for June 1988.

7 Figures for Scotland are the average daily population in prison establishments in 1986 and for Northern Ireland 1986–7.

8 See *Prison Information Bulletin*, December 1987, Council of Europe, Strasbourg, p. 28.

9 *Report on the work of the Prison Department 1981*, HMSO, 1982, para. 139.

10 'The Ethnic Origins of Prisoners: The Prison Population on 30 June 1985, and Persons Received July 1984–March 1985', *Home Office Statistical Bulletin*, issue no. 17/86, June 1986.

11 ibid.

12 John C. Baldock, 'Why the Prison Population Has Grown Larger and Younger', *Howard Journal*, vol. XIX 3, 1980, pp. 142–55.

13 Roger Shaw, *Children of Imprisoned Fathers*, Hodder & Stoughton, 1987, p. 71.

14 *Adult Prisons and Prisoners in England and Wales*, Home Office, HMSO, 1985, pp. 18–20.

15 *First Report from the Education, Science and Arts Committee, Session 1982–3, Prison Education*, HMSO, 1983, para. 63.

16 *Minutes of Evidence taken before the Social Services Committee, Session 1985–6*, 27 November 1985, HMSO, 1985, para. 6.5.

17 ibid., *Minutes of Evidence*, 20 November 1985, para. 5.

18 Richard Smith, *Prison Health Care*, BMA, 1984, p. 47.

19 *Minutes of Evidence taken before the Social Services Committee, Session 1985–6*, 27 November 1985, op. cit., p. 36.

20 *Observer*, 23 March 1986.

21 Baroness Seear and Elaine Player, *Women in the Penal System*, Howard League for Penal Reform, January 1986, p. 9.

22 *Holloway Project Committee Report*, Home Office, 1985, para. 7.10.

23 ibid., para 7.27.

24 *Official Report*, House of Lords, 13 December 1985, cols. 465–6.

25 *Official Report*, House of Lords, 20 January 1986, col. 6.

26 *Official Report*, House of Commons, 1 July 1982, col. 1,132.

27 Statement by the Home Secretary on *Report by HM Chief Inspector of Prisons for England and Wales on HM Prison Birmingham*, Home Office, 1982.

28 *Report on the Administration of the Prison Service 1986–7*, HMSO, 1987, para. 2.1.

29 *Official Report*, House of Commons, 17 April 1986, col. 467.

30 *Report on the Administration of the Prison Service 1986/7*, op. cit., para. 2.4.

31 *Report on the Work of the Prison Service, April 1987 – March 1988*, HMSO, 1988, p. 78.

32 ibid., p. 79.

33 *Adult Prisons and Prisoners in England and Wales*, op. cit., p. 17.

34 *Fourth Report from the Home Affairs Committee, Session 1980–81, The Prison Service*, vol. I, HMSO, 1981, para. 54.

35 *Report by HM Chief Inspector of Prisons on HM Remand Centre, Risley*, Home Office, 1988, para. 4.30.

3 Too Many Prisoners

1 David Thomas (ed.), *Encyclopaedia of Current Sentencing Practice*, Sweet & Maxwell, 1984, pp. 3,024–5.
2 *Seventh Report from the Select Committee on Estimates, Session 1951–2, Prisons*, HMSO, 1952, p. viii.
3 *Report of the Inquiry into Prison Escapes and Security by Admiral of the Fleet, the Earl Mountbatten of Burma*, HMSO, 1966, para. 207.
4 Unpublished speech to the AGM of NACRO, 21 July 1975.
5 *Report by HM Chief Inspector of Prisons on Brockhill Remand Centre*, Home Office, 1988, para. 4.6.
6 *Report on the work of the Prison Department 1966*, HMSO, 1967, para. 6.
7 *Report of HM Chief Inspector of Prisons for England and Wales 1981*, HMSO, 1982, para. 3.03.
8 *Hussey, Schneider et al v. The Attorney-General of Ontario et al*, information supplied by Professor Sean McConville of the University of Illinois at Chicago.
9 *Report on the Administration of the Prison Service 1986/7*, HMSO, 1987, para. 1.2.
10 *Report on the Work of the Prison Department 1966*, op. cit., para. 9.
11 ibid., para. 10.
12 *Prison Service Journal*, January 1986, p. 18.
13 For example, see *Official Report*, House of Commons, 12 May 1988, col. 485.
14 *The Bail Lottery*, Prison Reform Trust, 1986.
15 Unpublished speech to the AGM of NACRO, op. cit.
16 Home Office Working Paper, *A Review of Criminal Justice Policy 1976*, HMSO, 1977.
17 See *Probation Statistics, England and Wales, 1986*, Home Office, 1987, p. 137.
18 *Non-Custodial and Semi-Custodial Penalties*, HMSO, 1970, para. 151.
19 *Fifteenth Report from the Expenditure Committee, Session 1977–8, The Reduction of Pressure on the Prison System*, vol. 1, HMSO, 1978, paras, 218–26.
20 *Annual Report of the Magistrates Association 1981*, appendix XII, para. 2.
21 *Report on the work of the Prison Department 1970*, HMSO, 1971, para. 12.
22 *Sentences of Imprisonment: A Review of Maximum Penalties*, HMSO, 1978, para. 265.
23 *Criminal Justice, Plans for Legislation*, HMSO, 1986, para. 12.
24 *Punishment, Custody and the Community*, HMSO, 1988, para. 1.6.
25 Andrew Ashworth, *Sentencing and Penal Policy*, Weidenfeld & Nicolson, 1983, p. 59.
26 *The Sentence of the Court*, HMSO, 1986.
27 David Moxon (ed.), 'Sentencing of Adults and Juveniles in Magistrates Courts', *Managing Criminal Justice*, HMSO, 1985.

4 A Good and Useful Life

1 *The Prison Rules 1964*, Home Office, 1983.
2 *Fourth Report from the Home Affairs Committee, Session 1980–81, The Prison Service*, vol. II, HMSO, 1981, Q. 1,025.
3 Speech to Conservative Party Conference, 11 October 1983.

4 *Report from the Departmental Committee on Prisons* (the Gladstone Report), HMSO, 1895, para. 25.
5 ibid., para. 38.
6 ibid., para. 73.
7 *Penal Practice in a Changing Society: Aspects of Future Development* (*England and Wales*), Home Office, HMSO, 1959, para. 44.
8 *People in Prison* (*England and Wales*), Home Office, HMSO, 1969, para. 8.
9 ibid., para. 13.
10 Quoted in *Holloway Project Committee Report*, Home Office, 1985, para. 1.2.
11 Alison Morris, *Women, Crime and Criminal Justice*, Blackwell, 1987, p. 109.
12 See 'Criminal Careers of Those Born in 1953, 1958, and 1963', *Home Office Statistical Bulletin*, issue no. 7/85, 3 April 1985.
13 The Gladstone Report, op. cit., para. 25.
14 *Report of the Committee of Inquiry into the United Kingdom Prison Services*, HMSO, 1979, para. 4.24.
15 ibid., para. 4.28.
16 *Report on the Work of the Prison Department 1983*, HMSO, 1984, para 7.
17 *The Sentence of the Court*, HMSO, 1986, para. 3.2.
18 See Iain Crow, *The Detention Centre Experiment*, NACRO, 1979.
19 Address to Conservative Party Conference, October 1979.
20 Prison Department Note of Guidance to Staff, para. 1.
21 *Tougher Regimes in Detention Centres*, HMSO, 1984, para. 8.4.
22 ibid., para. 8.18.
23 ibid., para. 8.21.
24 *Official Report*, House of Commons, 24 July 1984, col. 580.
25 Quoted in J. J. Tobias, *Nineteenth-Century Crime: Prevention and Punishment*, David & Charles, 1972, p. 150.
26 Geoff Tucker, 'The Workforce We Need', *Idle Hands, Report of a Consultation held on 28 June 1985, Apex, BIC and NACRO*, 1985, pp. 11–12.
27 Tobias, op. cit., pp. 165–6.
28 A. Keith Bottomley, *Criminology in Focus*, Martin Robertson, 1979, p. 135.
29 R. Baxter and C. Nuttall, 'Severe Sentences: No Deterrent to Crime?', *New Society*, January 1975, pp. 11–13.
30 L. Radzinowicz and J. King, *The Growth of Crime*, Hamish Hamilton, 1977, p. 131.
31 Philip Cook, 'Research in Criminal Deterrence', *Crime and Justice*, vol. II, Chicago and London, 1980, p. 218.
32 ibid., p. 262.
33 *Taking Offenders out of Circulation*, HMSO, 1980.
34 *The Sentence of the Court*, op. cit., para. 3.2.
35 ibid., para. 3.3.
36 ibid., para. 3.4.
37 ibid., para. 3.5.

5 The Custodians

1 *Official Report*, House of Commons, 25 July 1988, col. 45.
2 See *Prison Service News*, June 1988, p. 6.
3 *Briefing No. 2*, September 1988, Home Office.
4 *Daily Mirror*, 8 November 1988.

5 POA Magazine, June 1985, p. 307.
6 Phil Hornsby, *Our Undermanned Prisons*, Police Review, 27 November 1987, p. 2,366.
7 *Gatelodge*, June 1988, p. 38.
8 *Staff Attitudes in the Prison Service*, HMSO, 1985, p. 100.
9 *Submission by the Prison Officers' Association to the Inquiry into the United Kingdom Prison Services*, POA, undated, p. 171.
10 *Report of the Committee of Inquiry into the United Kingdom Prison Services*, HMSO, 1979, para. 5.8.
11 ibid., para. 5.4.
12 ibid., para. 10.22.
13 *Staff Attitudes in the Prison Service*, op. cit., p. 22.
14 ibid., p. 50.
15 ibid., p. 57.
16 ibid., p. 95.
17 ibid., p. 56.
18 *Gatelodge*, February 1988, p. 11.
19 *Gatelodge*, June 1988, p. 40.
20 *Gatelodge*, February 1988, p. 26.
21 *Gatelodge*, April 1988, p. 21.
22 *Gatelodge*, August 1988, p. 18.
23 *TUC Report, Brighton, 1980*, TUC, 1980, p. 408.
24 *Official Report*, House of Commons, 27 March 1986, col. 545.
25 *Report by HM Chief Inspector of Prisons on HM Prison Liverpool*, Home Office, 1988, para. 5.07
26 *Report by HM Chief Inspector of Prisons on HM Youth Custody Centre Northallerton*, Home Office, 1988, para. 5.09.
27 *Report by Chief HM Inspector of Prisons on HM Prison Ford*, Home Office, 1988, para 3.12.
28 *Report by HM Chief Inspector of Prisons on HM Youth Custody Centre, East Sutton Park*, Home Office 1988, para 5.08.
29 *Report on the Work of the Prison Department 1969*, HMSO, 1970, para. 14.
30 *Report on the Work of the Prison Department 1972*, HMSO, 1973, paras. 1 and 2.
31 ibid., para. 147.
32 'Whitelaw's Whitewash', the *Abolitionist*, no. 2, 1982, p. 5.
33 *Official Report*, House of Commons, 22 October 1979, col. 8.
34 *Home Office statement on the background circumstances and action subsequently taken relative to the disturbance in D wing at HM Prison Wormwood Scrubs on 31 August 1979, together with the Report of an Inquiry by the Regional Director of the South-East Region of the Prison Department*, HMSO, 1982, p. 3.
35 ibid., para. 86.
36 ibid., para. 92.
37 *Report on the Work of the Prison Department 1983*, HMSO, 1984, para. 127.
38 *Report on the Work of the Prison Department 1984–5*, HMSO, 1985, para. 157.
39 *Report of the Committee on the Prison Disciplinary System*, vol. I, HMSO, 1985, para. 2.11.
40 *Report by HM Chief Inspector of Prisons on HM Prison Liverpool*, op. cit., para. 3.04.

41 *Report by HM Chief Inspector of Prisons on HM Prison Ford*, op. cit., para 2.35.
42 *POA* magazine, May 1985, p. 261.
43 *Our Undermanned Prisons*, op. cit., p. 2,366.
44 *Gatelodge*, June 1988, p. 33.
45 *Staff Attitudes in the Prison Service*, op. cit., p. 53.
46 Roger Shaw, 'Shared Social Work in a Local Prison: A Matter of Trust', *Prison Service Journal*, July 1984, p. 6.
47 'Prisons Outwards: Some New Developments in Holland', address by Dr Hans Tulkens, 1 October 1984, unpublished.

6 Doing Time

1 David Downes, *Contrasts in Tolerance: Post-War Penal Policy in the Netherlands*, and *England and Wales*, OUP, 1988, p. 163.
2 Audrey Peckham, *A Woman in Custody*, Fontana, 1985, p. 167.
3 *Report of HM Chief Inspector of Prisons 1984*, HMSO, 1985, para. 5.04.
4 *Aspects of Life in Local Prisons*, NACRO briefing, NACRO, 1988.
5 *HM Prison Wandsworth Board of Visitors Annual Report 1987*, p. 7.
6 ibid.
7 *Financial Times*, 10 May 1986.
8 PDG/80/228/1/1.
9 *Alexander* v. *Home Office*, notes of a judgment handed down by Judge Whiteley at the Southampton County Court on 1 May 1987, p. 5.
10 ibid., p. 6.
11 Law Report, *The Times*, 22 February 1988.
12 Philip Wheatley, 'Riots and Serious Mass Disorder', *Prison Service Journal*, October 1981, pp. 1–4.
13 ibid., p. 3.
14 Standing Order 4, Home Office, May 1985, para. A8d.
15 ibid., para. A8c.
16 ibid., para A9.
17 Standing Order 5, Home Office, June 1981, Section 5.
18 *Report of the Inquiry into Prison Escapes and Security by Admiral of the Fleet, the Earl Mountbatten of Burma*, HMSO, 1966, para. 212.
19 *The Regime for Long-term Prisoners in Conditions of Maximum Security*, HMSO, 1968, para. 19.
20 *The Abolitionist*, no. 23, 1987, p. 15.
21 *Official Report*, House of Commons, 14 June 1988, col. 96.
22 *Report of HM Chief Inspector of Prisons 1983*, HMSO, 1984, para. 3.03.
23 Standing Order 5, op. cit., para. B34, 1, iii.
24 *Prisons in Scotland*, Report for 1984, HMSO, 1985, para. 10.
25 *Minutes of Evidence taken before the Expenditure Committee, Session 1978–9*, 14 February 1979, HMSO, 1979, Q. 795.
26 *Prison Leave*, Council of Europe, Strasbourg, 1983.
27 *Managing the Long-term Prison System, Report of the Control Review Committee*, HMSO, 1984, para. 104.
28 *Report on the Administration of the Prison Service 1986/7*, HMSO, 1987, para. 1.13.
29 See Richard Smith, *Prison Health Care*, BMA, 1984, p. 1.
30 See *Minutes of Evidence taken before the Social Services Committee, Session 1985–6*, 27 November 1985, HMSO, 1985, p. 24.

31 *Prison Health Care*, op. cit., p. 1.
32 *Minutes of Evidence taken before the Expenditure Committee*, op. cit., Q. 133.
33 ibid., p. 34.
34 ibid., Q. 174.
35 ibid., p. 36.
36 Benjamin Lee, 'On Standing Up and Being Counted', *Lancet*, 4 June 1983, p. 1,268.
37 ibid., p. 1,269.
38 *Minutes of Evidence taken before the Expenditure Committee*, op. cit., p. 38.
39 ibid., Q. 151.
40 *AIDS/HIV : Statement of Current Prison Department Policy*, Prison Department, Home Office, 1987, p. 4.
41 *Managing the Long-term Prison System, Report of the Control Review Committee*, op. cit., para. 108.
42 *Becker v. Home Office* (1972) 2QB407.
43 (1979) QB425 quoted in *Report of the Committee on the Prison Disciplinary System*, vol. II, HMSO, 1985, p. 129.
44 *Raymond v. Honey* (1982) I AC I.
45 *Report on the Work of the Prison Service April 1987–March 1988*, HMSO, 1988, para. 63.
46 Home Office Evidence to the Committee on the Prison Disciplinary System, published in *Report of the Committee on the Prison Disciplinary System*, op. cit., p. 32.
47 *Report of the Committee on the Prison Disciplinary System*, op. cit., p. 65.
48 *Report of HM Chief Inspector of Prisons 1983*, HMSO, 1984, para. 2.14.
49 See 'Inspection', Discussion Paper by the Home Office, in *Inquiry into the United Kingdom Prison Services*, vol. II, Evidence by HM Treasury, the Civil Service Department and the Central Policy Review Staff, HMSO, 1979, pp. 237–42.
50 See *Report on the Work of the Prison Department 1981*, HMSO, 1982, paras. 241–52.
51 *Report of HM Chief Inspector of Prisons 1987*, HMSO, 1988 para. 2.35.
52 *Silver and Others v. United Kingdom, Report of the European Commission of Human Rights*, Strasbourg, 1980, p. 61.
53 ibid., p. 61.
54 ibid., p. 72.
55 ibid., p. 78.
56 ibid., p. 79.
57 Joyce Plotnikoff, *Prison Rules: A Working Guide*, Prison Reform Trust, 1988, p. 20.
58 *Raymond v. Honey* (1983) I AC I.
59 *R. v. Secretary of State for the Home Department ex parte Anderson* (1984) I QB 778.
60 See Genevra Richardson, 'Judicial Intervention in Prison Life', *Accountability and Prisons*, Maguire, Vagg and Morgan (eds.), Tavistock Publications, 1985, p. 50.
61 ibid., p. 57.
62 Law Report, *The Independent*, 27 October 1988.
63 *The Prison Rules 1964 as amended by the Prison [Amendment] Rules of 1968, 1971, 1972, 1974, 1976, 1981, 1982, 1983*, p. 15.
64 *The Prison Disciplinary System*, Prison Officers Association, 1984, pp. 6–7.
65 *Report of HM Chief Inspector of Prisons 1984*, HMSO, 1985, para. 5.15.

66 Mike Maguire and Jon Vagg, *The 'Watchdog' Role of Boards of Visitors*, Home Office, 1984, p. 141.

67 *HM Prison Wandsworth Board of Visitors Annual Report 1985*, p. 12.

68 *Managing the Long-term Prison System, Report of the Control Review Committee*, op. cit., para. 46.

69 *Report of the Committee on the Prison Disciplinary System*, op. cit., p. 14.

70 *HM Prison Wandsworth Board of Visitors Annual Report 1987*, pp. 18–19.

71 Maguire and Vagg, op. cit., p. 211.

72 *Report of HM Chief Inspector of Prisons 1984*, op. cit., para. 5.16.

73 *Official Report*, House of Lords, 28 July 1988, col. 485.

74 *Report of the Committee on the Prison Disciplinary System*, vol. I, op. cit., para. 2.27.

75 See *Report by the Parliamentary Commissioner for Administration to Mr R. Kilroy-Silk, MP, of the results of his investigation into a complaint made by Mr Scott Stevens*, C37/84, para. 22.

76 *The Prison Rules*, Rule 47 (12), p. 16.

77 *Report of the Committee on the Prison Disciplinary System*, vol. I, op. cit., para. 7.51.

78 *A Review of Prisoners' Complaints*, Report by HM Chief Inspector of Prisons, Home Office, 1987, para. 8.13.

79 *Boards of Visitors Coordinating Committee Response to HMCIP Review of Prisoners' Requests and Complaints Procedures*, 1988, p. 4.

80 *Justice in Prison*, Justice, 1983, pp. 3–4.

7 Two Hundred and Seventy-five Pounds a Week

1 *Report on the Work of the Prison Department 1981*, HMSO, 1982, para. 16.

2 *Official Report*, House of Commons, 19 December 1988, col. 148.

3 *Prisons in Scotland, Report for 1986*, HMSO, 1987, p. 28.

4 *Report on the Administration of the Prison Service 1986/7*, HMSO, 1987, p. 23.

5 *Official Report*, House of Commons, 21 December 1988, col. 282.

6 *Report on the Work of the Prison Department 1984–5*, HMSO 1985, para. 96.

7 *Official Report*, House of Commons, 5 February 1987, col. 785.

8 *Report of the Committee of Inquiry into the United Kingdom Prison Services*, HMSO, 1979, para. 6.22.

9 ibid., para. 6.26.

10 F. B. O'Friel, 'Strangeways Makes a Fresh Start', *Prison Service Journal*, July 1988, p. 16.

11 *Study of Prison Officers' Complementing and Shift Systems*, vol. I, HM Prison Service and PA, 1986, para. 2.5.

12 ibid., para. 2.6.

13 ibid., para. 2.9.

14 ibid., paras. 2.19–20.

15 *Report on the Work of the Prison Service 1986/87*, HMSO 1987, paras. 54–56.

16 *Report of HM Chief Inspector of Prisons on HM Prison Dorchester*, Home Office, 1986, para. 4.05.

17 *Report of HM Chief Inspector of Prisons on HM Remand Centre Risley*, Home Office, 1988, para. 5.39.

18 *Report of HM Chief Inspector of Prisons on HM Prison Pentonville*, Home Office, 1988, para. 4.10.
19 *Official Report*, House of Commons, 22 June 1988, col. 564.
20 *Report of the Committee of Inquiry into the United Kingdom Prison Services*, op. cit., para. 6.9.
21 *Fourth Report from the Home Affairs Committee, Session 1980–81, The Prison Service*, vol. II, HMSO, 1981, Q. 127.
22 *Official Report*, House of Commons, 12 March 1987, col. 253.
23 *Fourth Report from the Home Affairs Committee, Session 1980–81, The Prison Service*, vol. II, op. cit., Q. 75.
24 *Report by HM Chief Inspector of Prisons on HM Prison Birmingham*, Home Office, 1982, para. 1.04.
25 *Report of the Committee on the Prison Disciplinary System*, vol. I, HMSO, para. 2.7.
26 *Report of HM Chief Inspector of Prisons, 1983*, HMSO, 1984, para. 2.06.
27 *Report of HM Chief Inspector of Prisons on HM Prison Liverpool*, Home Office, 1988, p. 77.
28 *Fifteenth Report from the Expenditure Committee, Session 1977–8, The Reduction of Pressure on the Prison System*, vol. I, HMSO, 1978, para. 170.
29 *Observations on the Fifteenth Report from the Expenditure Committee, The Reduction of Pressure on the Prison System*, Home Office, HMSO, 1980, para. 84.
30 *Inquiry into the United Kingdom Prison Services*, vol. III, op. cit., p. 15.
31 *The Regime for Long-term Prisoners in Conditions of Maximum Security*, HMSO, 1968, p. v.
32 *Inquiry into the United Kingdom Prison Services*, op. cit., para. 6.70.
33 *Report on the Work of the Prison Department 1966*, HMSO, 1967, para. 7.
34 *Prison Categorization Procedures, Report by HM Chief Inspector of Prisons*, Home Office, 1984, para. 3.26.
35 *Official Report*, House of Commons, 27 June 1985, col. 237.
36 *Report of HM Chief Inspector of Prisons 1987*, HMSO, 1988, para. 2.17.
37 *Report by the Comptroller and Auditor-General, Home Office and Property Services Agency: Programme for the Provision of Prison Places*, National Audit Office, HMSO, 1985, para. 4.5.
38 ibid., p. 26.
39 *Minutes of Evidence taken before the Committee of Public Accounts, Session 1987–88*, 22 February 1988, HMSO, 1988, para. 2,268.
40 *Report of HM Chief Inspector of Prisons on HM Prison Acklington*, Home Office, 1988, p. 2.
41 *Report of HM Chief Inspector of Prisons on HM Prison Liverpool*, op. cit., para. 4.29.
42 *Report on the Work of the Prison Department, 1984–5*, op. cit., para. 1.84.
43 *Minutes of Evidence taken before the Committee of Public Accounts, Session 1985–6*, 15 January 1986, HMSO, 1986, para. 714.
44 ibid., para. 723.
45 *Minutes of Evidence taken before the Committee of Public Accounts, Session 1987–88*, 22 February 1988, HMSO, 1988, para. 2,268.
46 Stephen Shaw, *Paying the Penalty: An Analysis of the Cost of Penal Sanctions*, NACRO, 1980.
47 *The Price of Prisons Compared*, Ministry of Justice, The Hague, 1984, p. 82 (conversion from guilders to sterling at 3.9 guilders to the pound).

8 No Votes in Prisons

1 Hansard, *Parliamentary Debates*, New Series, vol. II, cols. 491–3, 496, quoted in J. J. Tobias, *Nineteenth-Century Crime: Prevention and Punishment*, David & Charles, 1972, p. 137.

2 Geoffrey Pearson, *Hooligan*, Macmillan, 1983, p. 127–8.

3 Stephen Shaw, *The People's Justice*, Prison Reform Trust, 1982.

4 *Mail on Sunday*, 27 October 1985.

5 Mike Maguire, *Burglary in a Dwelling*, Heinemann, 1982, p. 139.

6 *The British Crime Survey, First Report*, Home Office, HMSO, 1983, p. 28.

7 *Taking Account of Crime: Key Findings from the 1984 British Crime Survey*, Home Office, HMSO, 1985, p. 43.

8 'Dealing with Offenders: Popular Opinion and the Views of Victims, Findings from The British Crime Survey', Mike Hough and David Moxon in the *Howard Journal of Criminal Justice*, vol. 24, no. 3, August 1985, p. 171.

9 'Once a Thief', London Weekend Television, 1986, p. 9.

10 *The Times Guide to the House of Commons 1966*, 1966, p. 281.

11 ibid., p.291.

12 *A Better Tomorrow: Conservative Manifesto 1970* p. 26. (I am grateful to Tim Goddard for pointing out the error about this in the first edition.)

13 'Now Britain's strong let's make it safe to live in', Labour Party manifesto for the 1970 General Election, 1970, p. 24.

14 *The Times Guide to the House of Commons, May 1979*, 1979, p. 289.

15 ibid., p. 304.

16 ibid., p. 314.

17 *The Times Guide to the House of Commons, June 1983*, 1983, p. 324.

18 ibid., p. 298.

19 *Imprisonment in the Eighties*, Tory Reform Group, September 1983.

20 *Justice Policy*, Adam Smith Institute Omega Report, 1984, p. 64.

21 ibid., p. 66.

22 Peter Young, *The Prison Cell*, Adam Smith Institute, 1987, p. 2.

23 David Downes, *Law and Order: Theft of an Issue*, Fabian Society, 1983, p. 22.

24 Stephen Shaw, *Conviction Politics: A plan for penal policy*, Fabian Society, 1987, p. 23.

25 *Inquiry into the United Kingdom Prison Services*, Evidence by the Home Office, etc., vol. II, HMSO, 1979, p. 203.

26 *Magistrate*, 1976, p. 188.

27 *Non-Custodial and Semi-Custodial Penalties*, HMSO, 1976, para. 9.

28 Home Office Working Paper, *Review of Criminal Justice Policy 1976*, HMSO, 1977, para. 3.

29 *The Length of Prison Sentences, Interim Report of the Advisory Council on the Penal System*, HMSO, 1977, para. 3.

30 *Fifteenth Report from the Expenditure Committee, Session 1977–8, The Reduction of Pressure on the Prison System*, vol. I, HMSO, 1978, para. 48.

31 *Fourth Report from the Home Affairs Committee, Session 1980–81, The Prison Service*, vol. I, HMSO, 1981, para. 38.

32 *Report of the Committee of Inquiry into the United Kingdom Prison Services*, HMSO, 1979, para. 3.69.

33 ibid., para. 3.7.

34 *Observations on the Fifteenth Report from the Expenditure Committee, The Reduction of Pressure on the Prison System*, HMSO, 1980, paras. 7–9.

35 *Fourth Report from the Home Affairs Committee*, vol. II, op. cit., Q. 191.
36 ibid., Q. 917.
37 ibid., Q. 917.
38 *Report on the Work of the Prison Department, 1980*, HMSO, 1981, para. 14.
39 *Review of Parole in England and Wales*, Home Office, HMSO, 1981.
40 *The Times*, 27 November 1981.
41 *Official Report*, House of Lords, 24 March 1982, col. 988.
42 *The Times*, 19 November 1981.
43 *Daily Telegraph*, 30 November 1981.
44 Home Secretary's speech to Conservative Party Conference, 11 October 1983.
45 Home Secretary's speech to the Police Superintendents Association Annual Conference, 27 September 1983.
46 Home Secretary's speech to the Prison Officers Association National Conference, 21 May 1985.

9 Mortgaging the Future

1 *Minutes of Evidence taken before the Committee of Public Accounts, Session 1985–6*, 17 February 1986, HMSO, 1986, Q. 1,285–9.
2 *Seventh Report from the Select Committee on Estimates, Session 1951–2, Prisons*, HMSO, 1952, p. viii.
3 ibid., Q. 19–21.
4 ibid., p. x.
5 ibid., p. xii.
6 *Holloway Project Committee Report*, Home Office, 1985, para. 4.3.
7 *Seventh Report from the Select Committee on Estimates, Session 1951–2, Prisons*, op. cit., p. xv.
8 ibid., p. xxiii.
9 ibid., p. xvii.
10 *Report of HM Chief Inspector of Prisons 1983*, HMSO, 1984, para. 1.03.
11 *Penal Practice in a Changing Society: Aspects of Future Development (England and Wales)*, Home Office, HMSO, 1959, para. 56.
12 ibid., para. 66.
13 *People in Prison (England and Wales)*, Home Office, HMSO, 1969, para. 36.
14 ibid., para. 223.
15 *Report of HM Chief Inspector of Prisons for England and Wales 1981*, HMSO, 1982, p. iii.
16 *Justice in Prison*, Justice, 1983, para. 7.
17 *People in Prison*, op. cit., para. 72.
18 *Third Report from the Social Services Committee, Session 1985–6, Prison Medical Service*, HMSO, 1986, para. 72.
19 Raphael Samuel, *East End Underworld: Chapters in the Life of Arthur Harding*, Routledge & Kegan Paul, 1981, p. 74.
20 *Report on the Work of the Prison Department 1973*, HMSO, 1974, para. 132.
21 *Community Service Volunteers: Young Offenders Programme*, CSV, 1986, p. 1.
22 *Report on the Work of the Prison Department 1972*, HMSO, 1973, para. 128.
23 *Report on the Work of the Prison Department 1973*, op. cit., para. 131.

24 *Report on the Work of the Prison Department 1975*, HMSO, 1976, para. 130.
25 *Report on the Work of the Prison Department 1976*, HMSO, 1977, para. 115.
26 *Report on the Work of the Prison Department 1977*, HMSO, 1978, para. 95.
27 *Report on the Work of the Prison Department 1978*, HMSO, 1979, paras. 101–2.
28 I am grateful to Hugh Morley for this information.
29 *Report on the Work of the Prison Department 1975*, op. cit., para. 126.
30 *Report on the Work of the Prison Department 1980*, HMSO, 1981, para. 121.
31 *Report on the Work of the Prison Department 1983*, HMSO, 1984, para. 116.
32 'Regimes in Young Offender Institutions', *Circular Instruction 40/1988*, Home Office, 1988, para. 1.
33 *Private Sector Involvement in the Remand System*, HMSO, 1988, para. 98.
34 *Report of the Committee of Inquiry into the United Kingdom Prison Services*, HMSO, 1979, p. 278.
35 *Briefing*, August 1988, Home Office, p. 1.
36 *Minutes of Evidence taken before the Social Services Committee, Session 1985–6*, 20 November 1985, HMSO, 1985, Q. 1.
37 *Official Report*, House of Commons, 19 July 1984, col. 500.
38 David Riley, 'Demographic Changes and the Criminal Justice System', *Research Bulletin*, no. 20, 1986, Home Office Research and Planning Unit, 1986, p. 30.
39 Speech to Conservative Party Conference, 11 October 1983, p. 11.
40 *Forty-second Report from the Committee of Public Accounts 1987–8, Financial Control & Accountability of the Metropolitan Police: Court & Prison Building Programmes*, HMSO, 1988, para. 22.
41 *Report by the Comptroller and Auditor-General, Home Office and Property Services Agency: Programme for the Provision of Prison Places*, National Audit Office, HMSO, 1985, para. 2.
42 ibid., para. 9.
43 ibid., para. 11.
44 ibid., para. 25.
45 *Forty-second Report from the Committee of Public Accounts, 1987–8*, op. cit., para. 797.
46 *Minutes of Evidence taken before Committee of Public Accounts, Session 1985–6*, op. cit., Q. 1,257.
47 *Forty-second Report from the Committee of Public Accounts, 1987–8*, op. cit., para. 26.
48 *HM Prison Wandsworth Board of Visitors Annual Report 1985*, p. 9.
49 *HM Prison Wandsworth Board of Visitors Annual Report 1987*, p. 7.
50 *Penal Practice in a Changing Society*, op. cit., para. 91.
51 *Minutes of Evidence taken before Committee of Public Accounts, Session 1985–6*, op. cit., Q. 1,280.
52 *Programme for the Provision of Prison Places*, op. cit., para. 3.9.
53 *Crime: A Challenge to Us All*, Labour Party, 1964, p. 48.
54 *Observations on the Fifteenth Report from the Expenditure Committee, The Reduction of Pressure on the Prison System*, Home Office, HMSO, 1980, para. 5.
55 Letter to governors, Home Office, 23 August 1985.
56 *Report of HM Chief Inspector of Prisons 1987*, HMSO, 1988, para. 4.03.

57 *Fourth Report from the Home Affairs Committee, Session 1980–81, The Prison Service*, HMSO, 1981, p. xlvii.
58 Rod Morgan, 'How Resources are Used in the Prison System', *A Prison System for the Eighties and Beyond*, NACRO, 1983, p. 32.

10 A Structural Problem

1 *Consultative Working Paper, Working Party on Judicial Training and Information*, Home Office, August 1976, para. 9.
2 *Guardian*, 26 May 1986.
3 *Consultative Working Paper*, op. cit., para. 10.
4 ibid., para. 11.
5 ibid., para. 12.
6 *Judicial Studies and Information, Report of the Working Party*, HMSO, 1978, para. 1.6.
7 Andrew Ashworth, *Sentencing and Penal Policy*, Weidenfeld & Nicolson, 1983, p. 136.
8 Upton (1980) 71 CR App R 102 at p. 104, quoted in *Sentencing and Penal Policy*, op. cit., p. 133.
9 *The Times*, 22 February 1986.
10 *Sentencing and Penal Policy*, op. cit., p. 40.
11 ibid., p. 42.
12 ibid., p. 41.
13 Ken Pease, *Community Service Orders*, Howard League for Penal Reform, 1981, p. 56.
14 *The Sentence of the Court*, HMSO, 1986, para. 3.11.
15 *Review of Parole in England and Wales*, Home Office, HMSO, 1981, para. 58.
16 *Official Report*, House of Commons, 6 May 1986, cols. 58–9.
17 *Crime: A Challenge to Us All*, Labour Party, 1964, pp. 43–4.
18 Elizabeth Barnard, 'Parole Decision-Making in Britain', *International Journal of Criminology and Penology*, vol. 4, 1976, p. 147.
19 *Minutes of Evidence taken before the Expenditure Committee, Session 1977–8*, 20 February 1978, HMSO, 1978, Q. 804.
20 *Report of the Parole Board 1973*, Home Office, HMSO, 1974, para. 50.
21 *Report of the Parole Board 1975*, Home Office, HMSO, 1976, para. 20.
22 *Official Report*, House of Lords, 22 March 1979, cols. 1,381–2.
23 *Report of the Parole Board 1987*, Home Office, HMSO, 1988, para. 27.
24 *Review of Parole in England and Wales*, op. cit., paras. 39–40.
25 *Criminal Justice Act 1982*, HMSO, 1982, Section 32(I).
26 Quoted in *Criteria for Custody*, NACRO Briefing, 1988.
27 See Elizabeth Burney, 'All Things to All Men: Justifying Custody under the 1982 Act', *Criminal Law Review*, 1985, pp. 284–93 and Frances Reynolds, 'Magistrates' Justifications for Making Custodial Orders on Juvenile Offenders', *Criminal Law Review*, 1985, pp. 294–8.
28 *Fourth Report from the Home Affairs Committee, Session 1980–81, The Prison Service*, vol. II, HMSO, 1981, Q. 536.
29 ibid., Q. 1,013.
30 ibid., Q. 988.
31 ibid., Q. 988.
32 *Sentencing and Penal Policy*, op. cit., p. 96.

33 Home Secretary's speech to the Annual General Meeting of the Wessex Branch of the Magistrates Association, 11 April 1984, p. 12.

34 George Mair, *Bail & Probation Work: the ILPS Temporary Bail Action Project*, Research & Planning Unit Paper 46, Home Office, 1988, p. 17.

35 *Official Report*, House of Commons, 25 May 1988, col. 171.

36 *First Report from the Home Affairs Committee, Session 1983–4, Remands in Custody*, vol. 1, HMSO, 1984, para. 43.

37 *The Government Reply to the Fourth Report from the Home Affairs Committee, Session 1980–81, The Prison Service*, HMSO, 1981, p. 14.

38 *Minutes of Evidence taken before the Expenditure Committee, Session 1978–9*, 25 January 1979, HMSO, 1979, para. 430.

39 *Fourth Report from the Home Affairs Committee, Session 1980–81*, vol. I, op. cit., para. 52.

40 *Third Report from the Social Services Committee, Session 1985–6, Prison Medical Service*, HMSO, 1986, para. 62.

41 *Official Report*, House of Commons, 13 July 1988, col. 530.

42 *Fourth Report from the Home Affairs Committee, Session 1980–81*, vol. II, op. cit., Q. 1,025.

43 Parliamentary All-Party Penal Affairs Group, *Too Many Prisoners: An Examination of Ways of Reducing the Prison Population*, Chichester and London, 1980, p. 12.

44 *Fourth Report from the Home Affairs Committee, Session 1980–81*, vol. I, op. cit., para. 104.

45 *The Government Reply to the Fourth Report from the Home Affairs Committee, Session 1980–81, The Prison Service*, op. cit., p. 20.

46 Andrew Ashworth, 'Reducing the Prison Population in the 1980s: The Need for Sentencing Reform', *A Prison System for the Eighties and Beyond*, NACRO, 1983, p. 14.

47 *Fourth Report from the Home Affairs Committee, Session 1980–81*, vol. I, op. cit., para. 107.

48 ibid., para. 112.

49 ibid., para. 117.

50 *The Government Reply to the Fourth Report of the Home Affairs Committee, Session 1980–81*, op. cit., p. 21.

51 David Thomas, 'The Justice Model of Sentencing: Its Implications for the English Sentencing System', in *The Future of Sentencing*, 1982, University of Cambridge Institute of Criminology, Occasional Papers no. 8, p. 75.

52 Census of Custodial Sentencing Trends in Areas with LAC 83(3) Funded Alternative to Custody and Care Facilities, unpublished, NACRO, 1986.

11 One Bath a Week

1 Ian Dunbar, 'Purposes of Imprisonment', *A Prison System for the Eighties and Beyond*, NACRO, 1983, p. 54.

2 Section 17(I) and Schedule I Regulation 26.

3 *European Prison Rules*, Council of Europe, Strasbourg, 1987, Rule 17.

4 ibid., Rule 18.

5 ibid., Rule 65.

6 ibid., Rule 14 (i).

7 ibid., p. 5.

8 See Silvia Casale, *Minimum Standards for Prison Establishments*, NACRO, 1984, p. 42.
9 *Prison Standards*, Prison Governors Branch, Society of Civil and Public Servants, 1983, para. 2.
10 ibid., para. 1.
11 D. Faulkner, text of address to the South-West Region Board of Visitors, *Prison Service Journal*, July 1982, p. 18.
12 *Report of HM Chief Inspector of Prisons for England and Wales 1981*, HMSO, 1982, para. 1.07.
13 *Prison Standards*, op. cit., para. 17.
14 *Fifth Report from the Education, Science and Arts Committee, Session 1982–3, Prison Education*, HMSO, 1983, para. 51.
15 *The Prison Disciplinary System*, Prison Officers Association, 1984, para. 126.
16 *Minutes of Evidence taken before the Social Services Committee*, Session 1985–6, 27 November 1985, HMSO, 1985, Q. 154.
17 *TUC Statement on the Penal System*, May 1986, para. 9.
18 *Report on the Work of the Prison Department 1983*, HMSO, 1984, para. 7.
19 *Report on the Work of the Prison Department 1984–5*, HMSO 1985, pp. 137–8.
20 *Report by HM Chief Inspector of Prisons on HM Prison Rudgate*, Home Office, 1988, p. 95.
21 *Report by HM Chief Inspector of Prisons on HM Prison Pentonville*, Home Office, 1988, pp. 158–9.
22 *Report of the Committee of Inquiry into the United Kingdom Prison Services*, HMSO, 1979, para. 4.28.
23 *Fifth Report from the Education, Science and Arts Committee, Session 1982–3*, op. cit., para. 53.
24 ibid., para. 55.
25 *Briefing*, 14 November 1988, Home Office, 1988.
26 Quoted in *The Resettlement of Ex-Offenders: Towards a New Approach*, NACRO, 1983, para. 2.3.
27 *Report on the Work of the Prison Department 1983*, op. cit., para. 126.
28 *Report of HM Chief Inspector of Prisons for England and Wales 1981*, op. cit., para. 4.01.
29 *Report of HM Chief Inspector of Prisons 1984*, HMSO, 1985, para. 3.02.
30 Ian Dunbar, 'Long Lartin: The Development of a Concept', *Prison Service Journal*, July 1981, p. 7.
31 Roy King and Rod Morgan, *The Future of the Prison System*, Gower, 1980, p. 74.
32 *Report by HM Chief Inspector of Prisons on HM Prison Frankland*, Home Office, 1985, para. 7.05.
33 See *Managing the Long-term Prison System, The Report of the Control Review Committee*, HMSO, 1984, para. 20.
34 ibid., para. 16.
35 ibid., para. 17.
36 William Perrie, 'The Prison Dilemma', *Prison Service Journal*, October 1981, p. 11.
37 *Report of the Committee on the Prison Disciplinary System*, vol. I, HMSO, 1985, para. 2.22.
38 ibid., para. 2.23.
39 ibid., para. 2.26.

40 Tony Vinson, *Impressions of the Dutch Prison System*, Ministry of Justice, The Hague, 1985, p. 12.
41 *Report of the Inquiries by the Deputy Director-General of the Prison Service into Major Disturbances at HM Prison Haverigg on 5/6 June 1988 and HM Prison Lindholme on 15/16 July 1988*, Home Office, 1988, p. 23.
42 ibid., p. 24.
43 ibid., p. 25.
44 *New Directions in Prison Design: Report of a Home Office Working Party on American New Generation Prisons*, HMSO, 1985, p. 91.
45 Andrew Rutherford, 'The New Generation of Prisons', *New Society*, 20 September 1985, p. 408.
46 Vinson, op. cit., p. 7.
47 ibid., p. 6.
48 *Minutes of Evidence taken before the Education, Science and Arts Committee, Session 1985–6*, 4 March 1986, HMSO, 1986, Q. 51.
49 *Official Report*, House of Commons, 25 March 1986, col. 409.
50 *Report of HM Chief Inspector of Prisons*, HMSO, 1988, para. 4.12.
51 *Managing the Long-term Prison System*, op. cit., para. 95.
52 ibid., para. 96.
53 ibid., para. 90.

12 The Closed World

1 Una Padel and Prue Stevenson, *Insiders: Women's Experience of Prison*, Virago, 1988, p. 100.
2 *They Don't Give You a Clue*, NACRO, 1986, p. 3.
3 *People in Prison (England and Wales)*, Home Office, HMSO, 1969, para. 142.
4 *HM Prison Holloway Board of Visitors Annual Report 1985–6*, para. 4.10.
5 See Norman Bishop, 'Structural and Functional Requirements of a Present Day Prison System', Paper presented at the Centenary Celebrations of the Dutch Penal Code, 15–18 April 1986.
6 *Holloway Project Committee Report*, Home Office, 1985, para. 6.21.
7 *Minutes of Evidence taken before the Social Services Committee, Session 1985–6*, 27 November 1985, HMSO, p. 38.
8 See *The Government Reply to the Fourth Report from the Home Affairs Committee, Session 1980–81, The Prison Service*, HMSO, 1981, p. 11.
9 Roy King and Rod Morgan, *The Future of the Prison System*, Gower, 1980, p. 130.
10 *European Prison Rules*, Council of Europe, Strasbourg, 1987, p. 20.
11 Quoted in *The Resettlement of Ex-Offenders: Towards a New Approach*, NACRO, 1983, para. 2.3.
12 ibid., para. 2.13.
13 *They Don't Give You a Clue*, op. cit., pp. 1, 3, 4.
14 *Housing Aid in Prisons Project*, NACRO, January 1986.
15 *Women Prisoners Resource Centre*, Annual Report, NACRO, 1985.
16 *Circular Instruction 28/1981*, Home Office, 1981, para. 1.
17 *Report on the Work of the Prison Department 1984–5*, HMSO, 1985, para. 60.
18 Navnit Dholakia, *Race Relations in the Prison Service*, AMBOV quarterly, AMBOV, April 1985, p. 1.
19 *HM Prison Wandsworth Board of Visitors Annual Report 1987*, p. 23.

20 *Report of HM Chief Inspector of Prisons, 1984*, HMSO, 1985, para. 5.15.
21 Baroness Seear and Elaine Player, *Women in the Penal System*, Howard League for Penal Reform, January 1986, p. 10.
22 Mike Maguire and Jon Vagg, *The 'Watchdog' Role of Boards of Visitors*, Home Office, 1984, p. 26.
23 ibid., p. 207.
24 ibid., p. 141.
25 ibid., p. 158.
26 Graham Zellick, 'Justice and Accountability in Prisons', *A Prison System for the Eighties and Beyond*, NACRO, 1983, p. 65.
27 ibid., p. 66.

13 Conclusion

1 *The Government's Expenditure Plans 1988–9 to 1990–1*, vol. I, HMSO, 1988, p. 33.
2 *Address by the Home Secretary to the Governors' Conference: 14 November 1988*, p. 6.
3 See Sir Brian Cubbon, *Crime: Our Responsibility*, Home Office, 1985, p. 3.
4 See *Unemployment and the Prison Population*, NACRO Briefing, April 1981.
5 See Andrew Rutherford, *Prisons and the Process of Justice*, Oxford University Press, 1986, p. 46.
6 See Warren Young, 'Influences upon the Use of Imprisonment', *Howard Journal of Criminal Justice*, vol. 25, no. 2, May 1986, pp. 129–30.
7 Rutherford, op, cit., p. 6.
8 Thomas Mathieson, 'The Argument against Building More Prisons', *Scandinavian Criminal Policy and Criminology 1980–85*, Norman Bishop (ed.), Scandinavian Research Council for Criminology, 1985, p. 90.
9 See *Justice of the Peace*, 1 December 1979, vol. 143, no. 4, p. 683.
10 Ian Dunbar, 'Purposes of Imprisonment', *A Prison System for the Eighties and Beyond*, NACRO, 1983, p. 55.
11 Cubbon, op. cit., p. 5.
12 Speech by the Home Secretary, Rt Hon. Douglas Hurd CBE MP (Witney), to the 105th Conservative Party Conference in Brighton, 12 October 1988, p. 9.
13 Foreword to Adrian Speller's *Breaking Out: A Christian Critique of Criminal Justice*, Hodder & Stoughton, 1986, p. 8.
14 D. W. Wickham, 'Tinker, Tailor, Soldier, Sailor', *Prison Service Journal*, October 1981, p. 9.

Further Reading

ASHWORTH, ANDREW, *Sentencing and Penal Policy*, Weidenfeld & Nicolson, 1983.

BOYLE, JIMMY, *A Sense of Freedom*, Pan Books, 1977.

CAMPBELL, JAMES, *Gate Fever: Voices from a Prison*, Weidenfeld & Nicolson, 1986.

COMMITTEE OF PUBLIC ACCOUNTS, *The Prison Building Programme, Twenty-fifth Report*, HMSO, 1986.

COUNCIL OF EUROPE, *The European Prison Rules*, 1987.

HOME OFFICE, *Managing the Long-term Prison System, The Report of the Control Review Committee*, HMSO, 1984.

HOME OFFICE, *Punishment, Custody and the Community*, HMSO, 1988.

HOME OFFICE, *Report of Her Majesty's Chief Inspector of Prisons 1987*, HMSO, 1988.

KING, ROY, and ELLIOTT, KENNETH, *Albany: Birth of a Prison, End of an Era*, Routledge & Kegan Paul, 1977.

KING, ROY, and MORGAN, ROD, *The Future of the Prison System*, Gower, 1980.

MAGUIRE, MIKE, VAGG, JON, and MORGAN, ROD, *Accountability and Prisons: Opening up a Closed World*, Tavistock Publications, 1985.

MATTHEWS, JILL, *Forgotten Victims: How Prison Affects the Family*, NACRO, 1983.

NACRO, *Black People and the Criminal Justice System, Report of the NACRO Race Issues Advisory Committee*, NACRO, 1986.

PADEL, UNA and STEVENSON, PRUE, *Insiders, Women's Experience of Prison*, Virago, 1988.

PECKHAM, AUDREY, *A Woman in Custody*, Fontana, 1985.

RUTHERFORD, ANDREW, *Prisons and the Process of Justice*, Oxford University Press, 1986.

SHAW, STEPHEN, *Paying the Penalty: An Analysis of the Cost of Penal Sanctions*, NACRO, 1980.

Index